DIVINE CONTACT

DIVINE CONTACT

by
Losara

Copyright © 2009 by Losara.

Library of Congress Control Number: 2009905322
ISBN: Hardcover   978-1-4415-4194-9
               Softcover   978-1-4415-4193-2
               Ebook   978-1-4415-7670-5

All rights reserved. No part of this book may be reproduced or transmitted in any form or by any means, electronic or mechanical, including photocopying, recording, or by any information storage and retrieval system, without permission in writing from the copyright owner.

This book was printed in the United States of America.

To order additional copies of this book, contact:
Xlibris Corporation
1-888-795-4274
www.Xlibris.com
Orders@Xlibris.com
62760

*Dedicated to the Glory of God,
in memory of my brother, Rick,
and to my mother, who started it all*

For P.Y.

LIST OF CHAPTERS FOR DIVINE CONTACT

THE BEGINNING 11

    FIRST CONTACT—My story.. 13

COMMUNICATION WITH DEPARTED SOULS .. 21

1) COMMUNICATION WITH DEPARTED SOULS
   My first after-death contact:
   Joe's Father and Grandfather 23

2) RICHARD—Prediction of my brother's death
   and contact after his death 30

3) DANNY—Contact with a man
   who was schizophrenic before death 39

4) DEBRA LYNN—Spirit explains why a two-year-old
   had to die 48

5) ERNIE—An alcoholic makes contact after death to apologize to his
   family 52

6) ANN—A mother contacts her grieving daughter
   and gives predictions 56

7) BRANDON—Contact with a soul who died
   one day after birth 60

8) DAVID—A mother requests contact
   with a son who committed suicide 65

9) KIRK—Five contacts with a woman's deceased husband 70

10) WORKING WITH LAW ENFORCEMENT—
    My work on a twenty-year-old murder case:
    contacting the spirit of the victim 80

PAST LIVES 95

11) INTRODUCTION TO PAST LIVES—
    Why past-life reviews are beneficial
    and why we reincarnate 97

12) LAUREN—Deceased grandparents request a past-life review
    for their granddaughter 101

13) SHANNON—Why a man struggles
    with drug addiction in this lifetime 104

14) GEORGE—A wolf in sheep's clothing 109

15) HELEN—An eye for an eye:
    a story of negative karma repaid 112

16) PAST LIVES x 2: COUPLES—How a past-life review
    can help you see the true colors of others 119

17) TONY AND SHEILA—A rocky relationship that ends in
    suicide explained by past-life history 123

18) BRIAN AND AMANDA—A past-life review reveals a
    surprising reversal of nationality and true love 129

19) BRAD AND LAURIE—Spirit gives an unexpected past-life
    review and a lecture about attracting chaos 134

20) TYLER AND KIM—You can't hide things from a psychic Mom ... 142

21) MEDICAL IMPROVEMENT FROM PAST-LIFE REVIEW—
Spirit heals my shoulder 146

22) MEDICAL MIRACLE FROM PAST-LIFE REVIEW—
Hypnosis heals a woman's tumors..149

23) PAST-LIFE THERAPY—A STORY OF HEALING ANGER—
Spirit helps a five-year-old with a past life review...........................151

THE DARK SIDE 155

24) THE EXISTENCE OF EVIL—
My personal encounter with the Dark Side......................................157

25) A DANGEROUS ENCOUNTER—
A psychic friend's dangerous visit from an evil entity 160

26) CLEARING NEGATIVE ENTITIES—
Using Spirit to clear evil entities from people and haunted houses.163

27) DIRECTIONS FOR CLEARING NEGATIVE ENERGIES—
How to clear yourself and your home of negative spirits................168

28) A WORD ABOUT HELL—
Mother Mary takes me to "Hell" 171

SPIRITUAL ADVICE 175

29) INTRODUCTION TO SPIRITUAL ADVICE—
Be careful what you ask for: the humorous, touching,
practical, and profound words of Spirit...177

30) THE DEFINITION OF INNER HARMONY—
A dissertation from a spiritual Master about personal chaos...........179

31) TRYING NOT TO THROW UP ON AN AIRPLANE—
Spirit diverts my attention from sickness by telling a story.............181

32) THE LESSON OF BETRAYAL—Why we must
   all suffer from betrayals in our lives 183

33) DEALING WITH BULLIES IN THE WORKPLACE—
   Spiritual advice regarding an employer
   whose tactics were hard to endure..188

34) PURPOSE AND FREE WILL: THE GIFT OF
   SELF-DETERMINATION—Spirit answers a client's
   questions about the "unfairness" of life..191

35) THE CAUSE OF PHYSICAL PROBLEMS—Clients ask
   Spirit about ailments that their doctors cannot cure 195

36) TEENAGERS: SUICIDE, GANGS, AND DRUG USE—
   What is wrong with our society's children? 201

37) DAN GETS A LECTURE FROM SPIRIT—
   A college student asks Spirit how to "get rich quick"......................206

38) GOD THE TYRANT OR GOD THE PHILANTHROPIST?—
   Why doesn't God fix your life?..211

39) STUCK ON THIS SIDE OF HEAVEN—
   Night terrors in a neighborhood of children 216

40) THE CREATION EQUATION: MANIFESTING DESIRES—
   How to attract good things into your life
   by using the Tools of Manifestation 222

41) THE EMOTION WAVE: THE STAMP OF GOD—
   A being of Light takes me into a human cell
   and reveals a grand secret..233

THE GOAL..**241**

42) HOW DOES SHE DO THAT?—
   What happens when I contact Spirit...243

THE BEGINNING

FIRST CONTACT

My story

"You can do this, you know," the old woman said to me.

"Do what?" I asked, puzzled.

"This! Psychic work! You have the ability to do this," she explained. "I have never taught anyone how to do this method of card reading, but I will teach you."

I was sitting across from an older woman who was telling my fortune, using an ordinary deck of playing cards. She was the grandmother of a friend of mine, and she was in town visiting her relatives for a few weeks. Over the next week, the woman showed me how to lay out the deck, taught me the rhymes that helped her remember which cards meant what, and how to finish the original reading with a closing mini-forecast for the client. I never saw her again. She was right, however; I had a natural aptitude for card reading, and had an intuitive sense about what the cards meant to the person who was sitting with me. I was sixteen years old, and this was my first experience with psychic phenomena.

My friends were delighted with my new talent, and were amazed at the accuracy of the readings. "You could make money doing this!" they said to me. I knew immediately that this was not the path for me: becoming a "professional" card reader and accepting money. Instinctively, I knew that these "gifts" came not from me, but from Someone Else, and that this Someone Else was not for sale. Friends thought I was crazy, but I felt deeply that if I charged money for this trade, it would not be wise. Many years later, I could articulate my reasons for not charging for any of the psychic/medium work that I do: what I receive comes from the Holy Spirit, which is freely given by God, and I give it freely to others. Some psychics are uncomfortable with my no-charge stance, but I feel that to truly serve people through the Spirit, you must do so with no thought except to *be of service*. When your entire reason for providing the "medium" for contact with deceased loved ones or contact with the Holy Spirit is only for the benefit of others, your channel is pure, clear, and unlimited. Spirit has told me a million times, "INTENT IS ALL" and that pertains to the *reason* that you do any of the things you do. It is the mark of where you are in personal spiritual growth.

I stopped doing card readings when I was eighteen years old. Back then, my mother and I were wondering one day if I could do a card reading for someone who wasn't present in the house with us. I decided to try, and learned a very valuable lesson: this wasn't a game. I was dealing with spiritual powers that transcended time and space. We did a card reading for a friend of hers, and the cards were ominously warning of this woman's death. I saw the doctors, the hospital, the illness, and her passing all in the layout of cards before me. This shook us up, but when it actually happened I was horrified. I knew I hadn't caused her death, but the fact that it was so easily predicted with the use of a deck of playing cards left me very confused and frightened.

My ability as a spiritual channeler did not surface until I was thirty-four years old. I had kept up with the metaphysical world through the reading of great spiritual books, but nothing out of the ordinary had ever happened to me. I was a wife and mother, and was fully occupied with running a family. And I was also very depressed. The reasons are not important to this book, but as anyone knows who has suffered a very deep depression, it was painful and all-consuming. No one on the outside knew of my depression, even my husband. I kept a smiling countenance to the world, and my tears to myself. One night, as I was sitting on my bathroom floor and crying my eyes out, I prayed deeply for God to kill me. I was too scared to commit suicide, but I figured that if I prayed hard enough the Almighty might just come and get me, right there in my bathroom.

As I pleaded with God to end my pain and take me from this world, my spirit flew out of my body and toward an incredible LIGHT. It was so bright that it should have hurt my eyes, but it didn't. It was *everywhere*! I was totally immersed inside an expanse of light, and I could hear many voices, joyously shouting, "Welcome home! Welcome home!" I could not see anyone else, but I could feel them, and the love they sent was so intense that it took my breath away (not that I was breathing). I had only the sensations of weightlessness and joy, and something even better than joy: *PEACE!* Wonder-struck, I looked around, and began to hear the Voice of what could only be The Holy Spirit. It sounded like there were many people speaking the same words to me, and it felt like a "they," not an "it." Since then I have always referred to the Holy Spirit as "them." They began to ask me questions, which I later understood were to help me realize who and what I am, and to define what I really wanted in this lifetime.

"Why do you want to die?" they asked me. Every time I answered one of their questions, they asked me the question, "Why?" so that eventually I was face-to-face with the TRUTH of where I was in my life and what really mattered. The voices that had greeted me were all around, surrounding me in a healing, all-accepting love. I was given the choice of staying there or returning to my bathroom floor. I realized that if I stayed I would be welcomed with great warmth and joy, but it dawned on me that if I did stay I would have brought nothing to this Light. We bring all of our experiences with us when we die, and these are added to the whole. Sure, I had been a nice person, but I had done nothing of great value to bring to this heavenly place.

The Holy Spirit asked me, "Why does it matter that you bring something of value with you when you die?" I replied that I wanted to enhance this Light, and that I had not done anything in my life that would add to the brilliance I was experiencing there. Spirit asked me again, "Why does it matter that you should bring anything to the Light?" And suddenly, there it was, the awakening to the fact that I was ONE with all of the beings in this brilliant place. They were all me, and I was all of them. There was no separation between us, and I loved them. That meant that *I LOVED ME*. The feeling was overwhelming! The grandest love imaginable washed over me, and I zoomed back into my body on the bathroom floor, changed forever.

The Beginning

I had an immediate and powerful drive to meditate every night, and within two weeks, I was hearing voices during these sessions. I began writing down the incredible words of wisdom the Holy Spirit was sharing with me, and before long, I was having visions to go with the words. Spiritual teachers came to me every night, and we discussed many topics. I thought I was crackers. I had read of this kind of "channeling" being done by people, but this was happening to ME! I was afraid to tell anyone, so I kept it a secret, hiding my pile of notebooks of the dictation I received from Spirit in a desk. I finally took my mother into my confidence. She has been a rock of support for me in all of this, and is the reason I launched into "trance channeling" or what I like to call talking to Spirit.

I had been secretly doing dictation readings for myself and for my mother, and while she was visiting one day she asked if we could try to do a dictation from Spirit while she was there. She would ask questions of the Holy Spirit, and I would write down the answers I heard while she was present, instead of me writing a question and sitting in meditation for the answer to be given later. As I was preparing, through prayer, to enter a deep meditative state, I began to feel strange. I opened my eyes to look glassy-eyed at my mother, and said, "Mom? Someone's here, and they want to talk to you." Immediately, my eyes shut, my body sat straighter, and *a Voice came out of my mouth.*

"Greetings! We are Holy Spirit," the Voice said through me.

My mother, bless her, kept her wits about her and grabbed the pen and paper from my lap and began writing down everything the Holy Spirit said. She even asked them questions. I was far, far away . . . Eventually, I heard her calling my name, over and over, and then the concern in her voice reached me and I opened my eyes. I was dazed.

"What was that?" I asked my mom.

"It sure wasn't you!" she exclaimed. "They were so graceful!" That remark referred to the graceful movements that the Holy Spirit made with my arms and hands while they were present in me. I had been "out" for at least an hour, and was exhausted. The first encounters with this kind of energy were depleting, but eventually the sessions were energizing, as I learned to adapt to the higher frequencies. The only thing that kept me from becoming convinced that I was losing my marbles was that the wisdom coming through this channel was beautiful, practical, and true. My spiritual teachers took me to incredible places through consciousness travel, gave practical advice to me for a variety of everyday problems, and helped me overcome human habits that hindered my soul growth. I have plenty of habits to go, but progress has been made.

The deep gratitude I have and the great sense of humility I feel for the privilege of learning from the wise Masters who have come to me cannot be fully expressed in language. People often express wonder at the "gift" that God has given me. I have learned that it is not a gift. The Holy Spirit told me that clairvoyance, and the related abilities that go with it, is a *talent*, not a gift. These talents were honed over many lifetimes. Saying that God has given me a gift would denote that God has favorites, and He does not. He loves us all the same way: completely and eternally. Just as the scientist who now has the ability to understand complex mathematical concepts has practiced these skills over many lifetimes, so a person who is a psychic in this lifetime became so because of previous lifetimes studying and practicing metaphysics. It is what you DO with these talents that matters. INTENT IS ALL.

Coming out of the closet with this ability was very hard for me, and my avoidance in doing so only added to the things that led to my divorce from my first husband. (Just because one is psychic does not mean one is wise in all choices. The "school of hard knocks" accepts all students on Earth.) This divorce had been predicted for me by Spirit, and I was told that I would meet my "mate of souls" and have another child. Impossible, I thought at the time, but as usual, Spirit was correct. They even gave me a detailed dream about Joe and our future life together five weeks before I first laid eyes on him. When I met Joseph, Spirit was shouting to me, "Old friend! Old friend!" My husband has been the catalyst for many, many wonderful sessions of Spirit's wisdom.

Over the years, my clients would ask me when I was going to write a book. I had absolutely no desire to do so, and would tell them that when I died my grandchildren could sort through the mountain of notebooks and hundreds of cassette tapes and do something with it all. Spirit had other ideas! One morning at 1:30 a.m., I was awakened with a sense of urgency by Spirit. Wondering what the heck this was about, I centered my mind

The Beginning

and immediately saw a vision of a bench sitting in the middle of a beautiful forest of pine trees. I knew this was an invitation by Spirit to pay attention to something, and I walked over to the bench and sat upon it, only then seeing there was a book lying on the seat next to me. I reached over to pick it up, and saw that MY name was on the cover of this book, as author. "Oh no," I whispered to myself. Suddenly a glorious vision of the aspect of Divine Mother appeared in front of me. She was smiling and nodding, and told me that She wanted me to write a book.

"You've got to be kidding!" I protested. "Do you know how chaotic my life is now?"

(Silly question, of course She knew.) Divine Mother gently insisted that this is what I was to do. I pointed out to Her three major things that would need to change in my life for me to be able to write a book. My family was going through immense financial difficulty, and I didn't even have enough money to buy the new glasses I needed so desperately. My husband had been out of work (his profession in the engineering and electronics industry was dying in Colorado) and I had a small daughter to care for. We couldn't afford preschool or a sitter to watch her while I sat to type. (During this hard time those who criticized me for not accepting money for spiritual work had a field day.) Divine Mother simply smiled and nodded Her assurances, and vanished. I was awake for a long time, overwhelmed by the entire visitation. There were YEARS of material to go through. It would take forever just to sort it all out!

The very next morning, Divine Mother took care of my first excuse not to write a book. My mom called me and said, "Now, I am your mother, and I want no arguments—I am paying for an exam and a new pair of glasses for you. Make the appointment now!" She couldn't get the thought out of her head last night, she told me, and wanted to make sure I got right to it. In my heart I was on my knees to my Divine Mother. How appropriate that She would influence my Earth mother to get me going. I was convinced I had to get busy on the project. Over the next six months, with a lot of effort in learning to use the Law of Attraction, my husband got a new job, we moved, and our daughter went off to preschool. Time to fulfill my part of the bargain.

Where to start? There were volumes and volumes of notes, readings, and dictations to re-read and put into categories, and eighteen years' worth of tape-recorded channelings! When I remembered to seek out the advice of the Holy Spirit, things went much smoother. They apparently had an agenda for the book already. I was surprised to learn that they wanted to start out with what my kids call "the cool stories" about Spirit. My husband agreed.

"Don't you see, Losara? The stories are the proof that all of this Spirit stuff is real, that all of this is true," he explained.

"Yeah, Mom, do the cool stories! You can do the Teachings later," my teenaged son advised.

When I listened to Spirit's ideas, all went smoothly, and I would find myself waking up in the night with whole chapters in my head, and material for each section would be presented as I ate, performed household duties, or took a shower. This is how Spirit communicates with me, anywhere and all of the time. My personal wish is that each person who reads this book will see that GOD IS REAL, and that *He is right here, with you, all the time.* God cares about you and everything you are doing, and He set up the world so that you can learn how to create a good life intentionally. The writings in this book are completely true, and happened to real people. In most cases, their real names have been used, with their permission. I was overjoyed to see how many clients that I contacted were thrilled to be a part of the book. All of them have the same hope that I do; that reading these experiences will make a difference in the lives of the people who read them.

Enjoy the cool stories!

Given with great love,

Losara

July 2009

COMMUNICATION WITH DEPARTED SOULS

Chapter 1

COMMUNICATION WITH DEPARTED SOULS

My first after-death contact: Joe's Father and Grandfather

About sixteen years ago, the Holy Spirit gave me a series of predictions about my life. They seemed fantastic to me, and totally out of line with where I thought my life was leading. Spirit told me that I would begin to do spiritual readings with people. I was skeptical, but it happened. They told me that I would do channelings for groups, and showed me a crowded room full of people. It will never happen, I thought. But it did. I was told that I would remarry and have another child. I scoffed, but several years later I met my mate of soul, and we eventually had a sweet baby girl. Spirit showed me information about the Earth Changes, and important events leading up to, and after, the cataclysms. Time will tell about those predictions. Then they told me I would be speaking with the dead.

"WHAT?" I asked, in shock. (This was way before it became popular on TV.) "What would I want to do that for? I don't do séances."

"There will be a great need for this service, and it will ease suffering," Spirit assured me.

"I am going to be talking to dead people?"

Chapter 1

"Yes."

"HA! Fat chance!" I laughed. I wasn't believing any of these predictions.

And, of course, it happened.

My first full-blown contact with a soul who had crossed over happened right after my husband and I had returned from a few days in the mountain town of Winter Park, Colorado. We were driving down to the valley when I complained to Joe about hearing the same song in my head for three days. It was driving me crazy. He asked me what the song was, and I replied, "'Yellow Bird'. It's an old song that you have probably never heard of."

He began to sing it: "Yellow bird, up high in banana tree . . ."

I joined in and then said, "Yeah, that's it!" He told me that his dad used to sing it on stage during his musical comedy act in the 1950's. Joe's father had been in show business with some of the great talents of the 40's, 50's, and 60's. He had even been on *The Ed Sullivan Show* on television. He had died in the 1980's, and I had never met him or seen a picture of him. Late that night in bed, I groaned and sat up, and woke up Joe.

"What? What is it?" he asked, sleepily.

"I can't get that song to go away!" I complained.

"It's midnight, Losara!"

"Tell that to whomever is singing to me!" I grouched back.

"Hey, wait a minute. Why don't you just let it play; don't fight it, and see what happens," he suggested.

"Well, I haven't tried that. Maybe it will stop." I agreed to give it a try and, hearing the song for the fiftieth time, I sighed and allowed it to flow through my mind.

Chapter 1

In my inner vision, I began to see pictures of a man on stage in Hawaii. He was wearing a tropical print shirt, was thin, and had an incredible head of dark hair. He was standing behind a strange little table that had a stringed instrument on top of it. And next to him was (oh please, I thought) a guy with an accordion. I described all of this to Joe.

"THAT'S MY DAD!" he said, incredulous. "Losara, that is my dad! He used to play gigs in Hawaii, and that table held his steel guitar! And he always used an accordion player in his band. What else do you see?"

Concentrating on the scene before me, I continued to describe the pictures that flowed effortlessly to me. "There's something unique about his hair. He really has a thing for his hair. And he LOVES Hawaii, like a second home."

"Dad used his hair in a comedy sketch," Joe told me. "He would pretend to have a problem with the electrical cords, and then after bending down to 'fix' them, he'd pop up with his hair combed straight up, as if he'd been electrocuted." Joe laughed at the memory. "He told me once that he thought he had lived in Hawaii in another life. He was very drawn to the islands, and the Hawaiians accepted him as one of them. They even taught him to speak Hawaiian and to play their music. It was a great honor."

I began to see some visions that were not so nice. "Um—your dad says that he had affairs with women in Hawaii. Boy, he's pretty honest to admit that. He is now showing me some other places." I could see a terrible place in what I thought was New York. It was filthy, smoky, and felt very heavy. I was seeing Joe's dad as a small boy, dressed in knickers, a sweater, and a cap. He was standing in the alley of several tall brick buildings, and I could hear people yelling at each other. No one was speaking English. It felt absolutely dismal.

"That's Jersey's 'Hell's Kitchen,' where my dad grew up," Joe explained. "He rarely talked about it, but said that he had no idea how he survived his childhood. He had to work at a shoe factory as a child to help support the family, and had to quit school at age ten. He was Sicilian, and lived in the tenement housing where there were lots of immigrants. He saved a few dollars of his wages to take music lessons, and eventually surpassed his teacher

Chapter 1

in the art of playing the steel guitar. He could read, write, and score music. Then he played in the Mafia clubs of New York at age fourteen."

Joe's dad continued to show me pictures from his life. These images were very unique. He showed me scenes from strange angles, as if he were the director of a film, using the "camera" to enhance the images from different viewpoints. In my vision, I saw him step out of a Cadillac into the desert, from the view of underneath the car! I saw two cowboy boots, with the pant legs tucked inside, walk away from the car out into a desert area. He loved the desert, I told Joe.

"That's right! He did! He said it was clean out there. After living in the filth of Hell's Kitchen, he loved the outdoors, and especially the desert. And I hated the way he wore his pants tucked in his boots. Wow! Losara, this is incredible!" Joe said.

This is where I edited what I was seeing, believing that this vision could not possibly be correct. I did not tell him that the Cadillac his dad was driving was pink: Pepto-Bismol pink! I had seen another slanted camera angle of his dad, dressed in a white T-shirt, driving the car with his arm out the rolled-down window of a pink Cadillac from the 1950's. It wasn't until the next day that I admitted I had seen what I thought was an error in perception. Joe was incredulous. "When I was three my dad let me pick out his new Cadillac. He asked me, 'What color do you want, Joey?' And I said, 'Pink!'" Joe's dad continued on that night to show me scenes that were frustrations in his life, and odds and ends that meant nothing to me, but I reported them to Joe, who verified each one. Then, suddenly, I saw an image that was truly frightening, and I nearly lost my contact with his father.

"What is it? What's the matter?" he asked, concerned.

I had apparently yelled out in fear. "OH! I saw something horrible!" I said, shaken. "Your dad was surrounded in darkness, and he was waving his arms at me and screaming, but his arms were gone!" It was a truly frightening picture.

"Oh, Losara! My dad had diabetes, and he eventually had to have his arms and legs amputated. It was terrible! The diabetes eventually killed him. I am so sorry you had to see that."

Chapter 1

I calmed down, and returned to the visions. Joe's father began to send me feelings of great love. "He was so proud of you! He says, 'My Joey' and sends so much love to you." It brought tears to my eyes. "I think he is leaving now. He is getting fainter." Joe was very excited about the whole thing, but we apparently weren't done yet. Spirit was going to break me in to this new ability to communicate with the deceased with a double-header. As Joe's dad left, I felt someone else with me.

I was seeing a man in his sixties, with glasses and a fedora hat that would have been worn in the 1940's. He was standing in the yard of a small home that had many trees surrounding it, and from each tree hung Spanish moss. There was a one-lane dirt road that led to the property, deep with ruts from many years of use, that went to the left of the house. Suddenly, the man was joined by a circus of dogs, big hounds with tails that would leave a welt if they smacked into your leg. They were wonderful, stupid dogs, and the man was crazy about them.

"That's my grandfather!" Joe exclaimed. "He had three hounds that he thought the world of. I used to go into their pen as a child and create such a stir among them! They were nuts! And you described my grandfather's place in Florida perfectly. What else do you see?"

The visions continued very clearly. I was inside the small house, and saw one light bulb suspended from the ceiling as the only source of illumination. There was a stove in the corner, an old wood stove, which was the only source of heat. Joe confirmed these facts with great excitement. The scene changed then, and his grandfather was showing me another property beside a body of water. It was not a lake, nor a pond, and I could hear, smell, and feel the outdoor setting with great clarity. It was night, and the heat of the day had not diminished with the setting of the sun. Humid and dark, the night was filled with the sound of frogs croaking by the water. Tall grasses, cattails, and trees heavy with moss surrounded the water's edge. Across the body of water, in the distance, I saw a large house, its lights glowing a soft yellow in the night. There was music and laughter coming from it, drifting over the water to blend with the sound of insects and frogs. I described all of this to Joe, who whispered, "Go on." Standing in a small clearing in the foliage, I saw a band of men, dressed in white shirts, sleeves rolled up to their elbows, pants held with belts or suspenders, and every one of them with a hat on.

Chapter 1

It appeared to be in the early 1930's, judging by the style of dress and the type of truck parked beside the men. Each man had a rifle.

"Go on," Joe said quietly, as if he knew what this was.

"They are all scared! Their hearts are pounding, and they are all sweating buckets," I related. "This has something to do with that house across the water, and your grandfather is the ring leader. This is dangerous! I don't know what they are doing." The vision ended right there, with no other explanation or clues. Waves of love came for Joe as his grandfather departed.

"Holy cow, Losara! I know exactly what that was! When I was little, my mother told me the story of my grandfather confronting a famous gangster. It was during the prohibition days, when the drinking and manufacturing of liquor was outlawed by the government. My grandfather and some of his friends made moonshine to support their families. He had the best whiskey in the south. His secret was to store the whiskey in a certain kind of keg, solid oak. He was arrested once by the Feds for breaking the law, but he went back to it. The body of water you saw was a bay, and across the bay was a speakeasy run by a gangster from Chicago who was also selling liquor in the area. This cut into my grandfather's business, and he and other moonshiners were really hit hard by the competition. One night he got a group of men together and went to the speakeasy. They were armed with rifles. When they got there, he knocked on the front door and asked to speak to Mr. Capone."

I was incredulous. "Al Capone?"

"Yes," he answered. "My grandfather told him that his sale of liquor was hurting the business of the men there, and they were trying to feed their families from the sale of their moonshine. He asked him to stop selling booze in Florida."

"What happened?" I asked.

"Mr. Capone said he understood about men trying to keep their families going, and agreed to not sell liquor off the property! He kept the speakeasy open, but never once went back on his word."

Chapter 1

Needless to say, we were astonished at the events of the night, and didn't go to sleep for quite awhile after the visions. I had no idea at the time that this particular talent to tune into the souls of the spirit world would eventually lead me to a service that I cherish today: communicating with the departed loved ones of people who are grieving and who need comfort with the assurance that the "dead" are still alive in spirit, and are doing very well.

Chapter 2

RICHARD

Prediction of my brother's death and contact after his death

I have always had a deep sympathy for anyone who has lost a loved one, and it has increased even more so because my family lost our oldest sibling in 2005. This story is unique because the Holy Spirit told me that my brother would die before anyone else knew about it. I have had foreknowledge of several people's deaths, and I believe that this was given for several reasons: to prepare me for a trauma, to test my maturity of soul, and to emphasize that we come with a complete plan when we incarnate here; complete with the cause and time of death. There truly are very few "accidents" in our lives. I have had people tell me after the death of a loved one that, in retrospect, they may have had a warning about it. These warnings can come in a dream, or a feeling, or even in words from the departed one that something bad was going to happen. I received much more than that.

One afternoon in meditation, the Holy Spirit said to me, "Your brother is dying."

"What?" I asked, breaking my silence in great surprise. I had four brothers. Spirit showed me an image of my brother, Rick. I struggled to regain my composure and attune again in peace.

"You do not understand," Holy Spirit continued. "Your brother is dying NOW. He has brain cancer and lung cancer."

Chapter 2

In great anxiety, I came out of my room and went downstairs, meditation over for the day. My husband noticed my worried look, and asked what was wrong. I told him what Spirit had just said to me, and he expressed concern, saying perhaps I should call him in California that night. Two hours later the phone rang. It was my brother, Rick.

"I want you to sit down. I have something I need to tell you." He paused. "But you know already, don't you?"

Through tears, I confessed that I did know what he was going to say, but I wanted to hear him say it. He told me that he had brain cancer, lung cancer, and melanoma, and that the doctors had given him two months to live. I almost fell on the floor. Joe, watching my face, whispered, "What's wrong?" On a sheet of paper I wrote : Cancer—two months to live—and pushed it over the counter for him to read. The nightmare had begun.

My brother was a loner. He kept to himself, was extremely self-reliant (once sewing up a deep cut he had by himself), and didn't fuss over anything. He also didn't go to the doctor, always taking care of things his own way. That is why his condition was so advanced by the time he did seek professional care, at the insistence of his close friends. As he told me of the opinion of the specialists, I could tell that he was in denial of the true nature of his illness, and how serious it was. I didn't blame him. That was a lot for one person, even this Mountain Man of independence, to handle alone. When he finally did relent to the idea that perhaps the doctors were correct about his prognosis, we had an incredible talk about what happens to a person when they die.

I feel so very thankful that I had two hours to talk to him about the soul, the Astral World (heaven), and Spirit that day. He was already very well versed in the metaphysical side of life, having studied most of his adulthood on topics of the supernatural, spiritual, and unexplained aspects of life. I had the added advantage of having had actual conversations with the spirits of people who had crossed over and many teachings given by advanced spiritual Masters from the other side. We covered a lot of ground. I look on that day as a gift from Holy Spirit, for his ability to reason and his word recognition centers went downhill afterward.

Chapter 2

Another gift from Spirit was how my brother's death reunited him with our father, whom he had not seen in seventeen years. I had talked to him about making amends before he died, so he would not have the added karma of an unresolved problem to take with him. He agreed, and asked me to call Dad. Rick was very stubborn, very brave, and refused all painkillers, all medications, wanting to be as clear as he could be. He only lived six weeks after our first phone call, and our family managed to make it there to see him, some of us just hours before he passed. Interestingly, when my mother called the hotel the next morning to tell me my brother had died in his sleep during the night, my first thought was, "He MADE it!" Rick died on my sister's forty-fifth birthday. She felt honored.

As all people know who have had to handle the estate of anyone who has crossed over, it is an immense task. My brother, God bless him, was a slob of the first order, so his "estate" was an absolute mess (he won't mind that I called him a slob). Handing out rakes and shovels—just teasing, Rick—we got started. As I was scrubbing away in his home office by myself, the room lit up with a glow, and I beheld my spiritual Master in front of me. "Labor of love?" he asked, smiling. Through tears, I nodded yes. He let me know that my brother was doing well, but was tired, and that he had greeted Rick when he crossed over, as I had prayed for him to do. I was elated, and ran to tell my mother who was cleaning in another area of his apartment.

My brother's ashes were spread where he had requested, in the mountains near Visalia, California, where he used to pan for gold. My father said it was the most beautiful place on earth. We all went back to our lives with a hole in them, but it didn't take my brother long to make his presence known! One week later, during my nightly meditation, I saw my brother for the first time since he had died. He was standing under a tree and looked thirty years younger. My spiritual teacher was with him, and was using his Divine energy to help my brother appear to me, since Rick hadn't been on the other side long enough to generate enough energy himself. What a joy and relief to see him, and how well he looked! Within three weeks of this visitation, I saw him appear right before a reading I was going to do for a client, and he had achieved what I call "radiance." He was beautifully fit, glowing with a light that made him radiant to behold. Healthy, energetic, and beaming with a grand smile, he was as far from the wasted shell of himself at death as he could possibly be.

Chapter 2

It was right after my brother had achieved his radiance that my family experienced some wonderful physical manifestations by Rick. One late afternoon at home, I was sitting with a friend and dealing with the general chaos of my children, when the toddler required help with the bathroom. My three-year-old daughter and I climbed the stairs to do the deed, leaving my friend sitting on the couch in the living room. Five minutes later, I descended the stairs with my daughter and my twelve-year-old son. He stopped in the middle of the stairway.

"Very funny, Mom!" he commented, looking at the wall.

"What's funny?" I asked. I had stopped on the last step of the stairs.

"Where did you finally find them?" he asked, nodding at the wall of the stairwell.

"Find what?" I was totally confused. I then looked where he was looking. There, on the tiny box that houses the doorbell mechanism, were two Fisher-Price Little People, perfectly balanced on a sliver of plastic that slanted toward the floor. We had lost these characters six months prior, and had looked everywhere for them. I couldn't believe it.

"That's cute! Where did you find them?" I asked my son, not getting it.

"I didn't put them there. I just came down the steps with you."

"Well I just came up and down in the last five minutes, and they weren't there!"

I turned to my friend, who said, "Don't look at me."

Then we all got those goose-bumps that tell you something really strange just happened. "Okay, if you didn't do it, and I didn't do it, then who else is here?" My daughter was too short to reach it, and she had been with me. It was obvious that my brother had been there, showing off, trying to let us know he was doing just great on the other side.

Just two days later, he did another physical manifestation in the home of my sister in Michigan. She had set up a small table with his picture and

Chapter 2

some of his belongings as a place honoring his memory in her dining room. She often talked to him during the day, and prayed nightly for his soul to be happy and strong. There was a family conflict going on about a piece of jewelry that Rick had not had time to designate to anyone in his will, although most of us knew that he had wanted it to go to my sister. This debate of ownership greatly upset her, and she wished she could talk with my brother to work it out the way he would have wanted. As she prepared to go to work, she walked through the living room and stopped to pick up an object on the floor. It was the business card of a local psychic.

"Hey, Lennie?" she called. "Where did you find this card? I thought I put it in the cupboard last year."

"What card?" he yelled back from the kitchen.

"The business card with the psychic's name on it. What's it doing here?"

"Wasn't me, April. Maybe you dropped it," he yelled again.

"I just vacuumed this floor. It wasn't there," she insisted. She, too, then decided that Rick had done this to get her attention. Perhaps she was supposed to see this person. She called and made an appointment, and at the reading, the woman said, "Your brother is trying to get your attention. He is showing me a gold ring with diamonds on it. He says it belongs to you now." That night I called my sister to tell her that Rick had come to me in my evening mediation to tell her that the diamond ring he owned was supposed to go to her. She told me the story of the business card and what the psychic had said that afternoon. She was very excited that our brother had come to see her!

In the last two years, I have seen my brother twenty-three times. He has appeared when we needed help or reassurance, to give messages for others in my family, and to just say he is doing well. He came one evening dressed in a white karate uniform, which I thought was unusual. I called one of my sisters to tell her about his visit, and she said, "I have his karate uniform, and just unpacked it and put it into my dresser today!" I had not known that he owned one. Another time Rick came to me to pass on a warning to his son, who lived in Missouri, about being careful with the power tools that he had left to him when he died. I had not been in contact with my nephew in

Chapter 2

years, and didn't have his phone number. Two days later, my nephew called me. When I relayed the message from Rick, my nephew said that he had almost cut his thumb off with a power saw a few days earlier! He was lucky that his wife had been home to get him to the hospital.

One of the most unusual messages from my brother came initially as a repeating theme. I had done a meditation where I found myself walking up a very beautiful mountain trail. In the distance near the mountain top, I could hear a wondrous and familiar piece of music. It was a hymn being sung by a men's chorus, and I knew it from my childhood singing in the church choir, but I couldn't identify it. I had this vision many times during my nightly meditations, but could never go far enough up the mountain to hear the words. I was stopped by some invisible force or was led away to experience something else. Eventually, I began hearing this piece of music in my head every day, and it was driving me crazy. I called my mother and hummed the melody to her.

"I know that song," she said. "It has something to do with water." Well, that didn't really help me. I prayed to Spirit to solve this mystery, as I was tired of hearing this hymn day and night.

The next day it was my turn to choose a movie to rent at our local video store, and as I was cruising the aisles of films, I asked Spirit to inspire me as to what movie we would enjoy. (In our family, if you pick a stinker of a movie to rent you are fired, never to have that privilege again.) I walked down several rows of DVDs and then was directed by Spirit to look WAY underneath a stand of shelves; the movie "Crimson Tide" was hiding there, and I took it home for that night's viewing. Five minutes after Joe and I began watching it, I yelled, "Stop the film!"

"What is wrong with you?" he asked, freezing the movie frame with the remote.

"THAT'S THE SONG!" I yelled excitedly.

"What song?"

"The song that's been playing in my head for weeks! The song from the mountain top! Go back and play it again!"

Chapter 2

He did so, and turned it up. A magnificent men's choir sang the song, but we still couldn't make out the words. They played the hymn two more times during the movie, and afterward we watched the credits for the title, but it wasn't there. I couldn't believe it! So close and yet so far. Later, in the middle of the night, I sat up in bed, elated.

"JOE!" I called to my husband, sound asleep next to me.

"What? What is it? Is the baby okay?"

"Closed-captioning!" I said, triumphantly.

"WHAT? What are you talking about?" Poor man; I do this to him a lot.

"I know how to find out the title and the words to that song! Just play the movie with the closed-captioning for the deaf. It will be in the words on the screen. It has to be!" I was very pleased that the answer had come to me.

"Okay, Losara, good. We'll do it in the morning." He rolled over, instantly asleep.

The next morning, before breakfast, we set up the DVD player, and forwarded to the place in the movie where the submarine was diving into the ocean. The music began, and the screen lit up with the words to the Navy hymn "For Those in Peril on the Sea." I ran to my bookcase to get my old hymnal and found it there, with all four stanzas. It had been written by John B. Dykes in 1861. I still didn't know why I had been hearing it for so long. I called my mom and played the song from the DVD for her over the phone, and she got teary-eyed. "I know that song! I used to sing it when your brother was out to sea while he was in the Navy. It's a song of protection." It was identified now, and it had something to do with Rick, but the real explanation came that night during a meditation. He had apparently set this whole thing up to show me something wonderful.

As I deepened my concentration for meditation, I found myself back on the mountain path I had seen many times. My brother was there, smiling and waiting for me. Rick took my arm and we began walking up the pathway.

Chapter 2

I could see beautiful people coming down the path from the mountain, all very healthy, fresh looking, and happy. They were simply dressed, and were all ages and seemed evenly numbered as to male or female. Their JOY was apparent and unusual. I had seen these smiling people before, but never understood what was going on. They had never stopped to talk to me. As we walked toward the demarcation spot I had never been allowed to go beyond, I was astonished to find that, with my brother, we walked easily through the invisible barrier and up toward the mountain top where I had longed to go. I then realized that I was not able to go up before because I was not dead. I was being given a glimpse into a place that the living cannot see, and I could only go now because my brother was with me.

I could hear the Navy hymn plainly now, sung with beautifully rich male voices, full of deep passion and cause. Then I saw them, hundreds of men in their spirit bodies, being conducted by a man at a podium. The music was, for lack of a better word, heavenly, and it brought tears to my eyes.

> Eternal Father, strong to save,
> Whose arm hath bound the restless wave,
> Who bidd'st the mighty ocean deep
> Its own appointed limits keep;
> Oh hear us when we cry to thee
> For those in peril on the sea.

My brother explained that the souls that I saw walking down from the mountain were spirits who were reincarnating, and that this chorus from heaven was singing *to* them as they made their way back into the world, " . . . the mighty ocean deep." It was a song to honor them for their bravery and a prayer for their protection

There were many perils, indeed, upon the ocean of life on Earth. He said he had been privileged to sing in this choir several times since he had died, and that it was a great honor. This is not the only song that they sing, of course, but he knew it was one I would remember and would eventually tie to him so we could have this conversation. I think he enjoyed watching me solve this puzzle very much.

Another memorable visit from my brother was on the first anniversary of his death. As I mentioned earlier, Rick passed away on my sister's birthday.

Chapter 2

That night I was giving a reading for a client, and before Holy Spirit came in for the channeling, Rick appeared to tell me that he wanted us not to mourn for him, but to think of this day as his birthday, too: his re-birth into Spirit! He truly was so very happy, and was obviously doing very well. Although I miss being able to pick up the phone and call him (sometimes I forget he is gone and have the receiver in my hand to do so), I know with certainty that he is alive—more alive than on Earth—and is aware of my family and all of our lives and what is going on in the world. I thank God for this talent to contact the so-called "dead," which shows God's compassion for our grief and sorrow over those who are not with us physically anymore. They are RIGHT HERE, as is God!

Chapter 3

DANNY

Contact with a man who was schizophrenic before death

In the many hundreds of readings I have done through Spirit, there are those that have touched my heart deeply. The reading for contact with Danny changed my life and my perceptions of life, and for that I am eternally grateful. His is a soul that is pure with joy, something you would not believe possible, given the life that he had on Earth most recently. It is a great privilege to tell the story of this remarkable man.

I met his mother, Mary, at an open house for a jewelry show. The artist who designed the pieces on display was recovering from cancer, and my husband and I had been asked to attend in support of her. We had never met the artist, but we wanted to show her that people cared about her struggle in life. She was an inspiration; upbeat, strong, and determined to beat the disease that had befallen her. And her jewelry was beautiful. A friend of ours came over to me during the open house and asked if I would be willing to speak with a woman attending the jewelry show whom she knew had lost a son. My friend had told her I was a psychic medium, and the woman was very interested to meet me. I consented, and asked her to send Mary over my way. Mary was an attractive woman in her middle years, and had wonderful, expressive eyes. I liked her immediately.

"My name is Mary," she started, introducing herself. "I was told that you are a medium, and that you might be able to contact my son." I never like to talk about these private matters in public, so I suggested we go outside on the patio. It was a warm autumn day, and we found ourselves alone near the flower garden. "My son has been gone for a couple of years, and my friends say that I should be over his death by now, but I am having such a hard time with this."

"You'll never be over it," I said. My bluntness surprised her. "How can anyone 'get over' the death of their child? What you can attain is peace about where he is now. People who tell you that you are mourning too long are unfeeling, and haven't lost a child." She told me about going to a spiritualist church and trying to get a popular medium there to contact the spirit of her son. He told her that her son's spirit was too busy in the Astral World to be able to talk with her, and that she should leave him alone. This really angered me! "That tells me that he did not have the ability to contact your son, and was trying to get out of your request! Holy Spirit can do anything! Your loved ones are accessible, and they are often very near to you. Yes, souls continue to learn, live, and study in the Astral World, but they do not stop loving you, and God, in His compassion, knows how much you miss him! That's why He allows people like me to use the Holy Spirit to contact souls who have crossed over to the other side."

She told me she was a painter, and that she had works in galleries all across the United States. She began to say something about her son, and I quickly stopped her. "I understand that you want to tell me all about him, but I cannot be given anything before the reading; that way you will know I really have found him, and am not repeating what you have told me. I need a 'clean slate' to work with, to avoid thinking and misinterpreting anything I see. Just give me his name and birthday, and I will contact Spirit to see what we have. Then I will call you and verify what has been given to me, and if I have your son, we can set up a time for a longer reading in your presence."

I always pray deeply for the departed soul and for the person who made the request before doing a reading. These are people's lives, and it is imperative to me that only the truth come forward for them. Mary had given me her son's full name, as I requested, so I began by asking Spirit to find Daniel. He came through loud and clear, and had great energy, one of the very best "senders" I have ever encountered. He began by playing some

Chapter 3

music. I heard a song called "Spirit in the Sky," a song popular in 1969, written by Norman Greenbaum. (My husband looked it up after I hummed it to him later.) I thought the lyrics were very appropriate:

> When I die and they lay me to rest,
> Gonna go to the place that's the best.
> When I lay me down to die,
> Goin' up to the spirit in the sky.

I felt an absolute JOY from him, and a very keen sense of humor. This guy was really funny! The music continued for awhile, then I saw the images of the NASA rocket launches of the 1960's and 70's, complete with audible countdown. These things meant nothing to me, but I recorded them faithfully in my notebook, having learned it is usually the smallest of details that can be the mother lode of proof to the family that this was, indeed, their relative or loved one. The rocket launch was followed by TV pictures from the old news casts of the splashdowns of the Mercury and Gemini space capsules in the ocean, their red and white parachutes wide open for a successful reentry. He followed this sequence of images with scenes that showed him and his brother in tiny Speedo swimsuits at a large pool, and I had the impression that he had competed in swimming meets. The image of him showed a young man with BIG hair, the style of the times, and he made a real fuss over it, making sure I didn't miss this piece of information. He then gave the name Tim or Timmy.

He continued by showing me a man with dark, wavy hair, of average height and weight, wearing glasses and sporting a beard. Surrounding him were books, and I saw this man walking on a college campus. He was very intelligent, and Daniel had a great fondness for him. The man felt like a teacher. I then heard the name Heather, followed by an image that showed me that Daniel had been in Cub Scouts. These "identifiers" are priceless, for there is no way I can know of these small details in a person's life whom I have never met nor heard of. These identifying facts are a joy to their relatives left behind on Earth, for these are shared and precious memories. They make the contact real. These images, sounds, and impressions come without a linear time-line and are often just stuck together at random. I sort them out and record them separately, leaving room on the page for notes of the client's verification or rejection of the information I see and hear.

Chapter 3

The seemingly random images and words continued: I saw the Grand Canyon, which signified the state of Arizona. I heard the word "brain" several times. Then he told me not to call him Daniel anymore, that he preferred Danny, and he played the tune "Oh Danny Boy" for me. The next scene took my breath away. We were in the cosmos, the vast reaches of space, viewing galaxies, stars, and colored gasses of nebulae. It was like being inside the Hubble Space Telescope! Danny accompanied our journey with the music from the movie "2001: A Space Odyssey." What a dramatic flair he had! Then, showing that great sense of humor, he gave me the fanfare of "Up We Go into the Wild Blue Yonder," the official song of the United States Air Force. With that great finish, his energy grew faint, and he left. I was quite puzzled over the fact that Danny had not shown me his adult years. He focused solely on his youth, excluding any images of career, wife, or children. That was very unusual, but I had more than enough information to call Mary with the following day to see if this soul was her son.

Mary was quite excited to hear the reading for Danny, and was amazed at all of the correct "hits" I had received from her son. She laughed when I told her that I picked up on his great sense of humor. "That's Danny," she said. "We called him the jokester. He was always happy and so thoughtful. He loved music, too. I will have to ask his brother Tim about the song you mentioned ("Spirit in the Sky"); I don't remember how it goes. He participated in swimming competitions, and yes, he had the big hair! I have a picture of the boys with their '70's hair. And he was in Cub Scouts, too. Heather is Tim's girlfriend, but Danny never met her!"

"Don't forget, he can see all of you now, so he does know about Heather," I explained.

"The man you saw with the wavy hair and the beard is my brother," she continued with excitement. "He is a college professor, back East. Danny loved him. And our whole family followed the NASA space program back then. He knows I love the images of the stars and planets our scientists have taken photos of. We moved to Arizona from the East Coast when the boys were in their teens, and Danny lived there for over twenty years. We always called him Danny, and his grandfather used to sing 'Oh Danny Boy' to him." She paused. "And there is a reason he said 'brain' to you."

Chapter 3

I asked her not to divulge anything else, as we were going to schedule a longer reading now, in her home. We set up a date in November, which happened to be the day he died, two years prior. When I went to Mary's home, I met her fiancé, Bill, and we sat down in her lovely living room, glowing with the warmth of many lit candles. Before we began, I gave Mary a copy of a magazine that Danny had asked me to take to her. On the cover was a beautiful image of the cosmos, taken by the Hubble Space Telescope. He wanted her to know where he was, and he said, "Give this to Mom." She loved it. There was no trouble at all in contacting Danny, as he was so energetic and eager to give messages to his mother. Souls on the other side give me pictures, words, music, and feelings to relay to their loved ones while I am in deep meditation. I pass these on as precisely as I can, and always tape these sessions for the clients. Oftentimes a certain message or image cannot be explained right away, but will make sense to the friend or relative later, so the tapes are invaluable as a record of what was given.

Danny began the session by giving the name "Christine."

"Oh!" Mary cried out happily. "That was his girlfriend. At least, that was the girl who wanted to be his girlfriend." We were off to a good start.

He then showed me a very clear picture of an old school bus, painted purple and black. He said that they traveled to Arizona in it, and made references to "The Partridge Family" with great humor. "It was the best of times," Danny said.

"Amazing!" Mary said tearfully, reaching for the tissue box. "One summer we bought an old school bus that was painted purple and black, and, turning it into a camper, we moved from New York State to Arizona in it. We made jokes all the way about the Partridge Family. Yes, it was the best of times."

"He's showing me a dog, a yellow lab, on the trip with you," I told her. "And he said you have seen the movie 'Ghost' several times."

"Yes! We did have a yellow lab, and I do watch that movie and think of him," she acknowledged.

I then saw a drawing of a glass building, a tall structure made of glass. This meant nothing to Mary—yet. He gave the names Mark and Mike,

43

Chapter 3

whom Mary said were his cousin and another brother. He asked me to tell his mom that he wanted her to see the movie "Contact" (with the actress Jodie Foster), and that this would show her where he was. He showed again the vastness of space, and the glorious spectacle of galaxies and planets and stars. Danny then showed me little pencil and watercolor sketches, very simple and clean, of flowers and landscapes and things.

I heard the song "Spirit in the Sky" again, and the guitar piece "Classical Gas" with a message to have his brother, Tim, listen to them. Suddenly the visions were of a small lake or pond, where I saw Mary, Bill, and a few others standing by the water on a chilly day. Mary told me that they had traveled up to Bear Lake in the Colorado mountains to spread Danny's ashes at the pond the previous month. Danny, of course, had been there with them.

"He is telling me that he lived in a city with a name that starts with the letter *M*," I began to tell them, when suddenly, everything changed. I saw a hospital and started to feel very sick, quite nauseous, and drugged. It was very difficult to get through the real physical feelings Danny was giving me. He was a fantastic sender! I told Mary and Bill what I was feeling, and said that wherever this place was, he did not like it.

"Oh yes," Mary said, quietly. "The drugs that they gave him in the hospital made him very ill."

"Now I am seeing another hospital—no, not a hospital—Danny is correcting me. He says he lived at this other place, that I am seeing now, with very good people, very good friends. He says everyone liked him and that he was very popular. He is saying the word 'brain' again."

Then Mary told me when Danny was just out of his teens he suddenly began to change, and that he was diagnosed with schizophrenia at the age of twenty. Now I understood why he had only shown me images of the first years and last years of his life, no home, no occupation, no wife or children. He had ended up on the streets of Phoenix, and had been addicted to drugs and alcohol. He refused to live with any of his family, though they tried to get him to stay with them.

"He was a VERY generous person," I said. "He was extremely kind, caring, and funny. Danny didn't cause trouble. He is telling me, 'I was here

Chapter 3

to share.' He is also telling me that he was very handsome, and he had a beard at one time."

"Yes, that's true!" his mother laughed. "Danny was the most giving person in the world. Sometimes I could get him to come home with me, and he'd eat, and I'd give him new clothes and shoes to wear, and the next time I saw him, the bum next to him on the street was wearing his clothes. I'd say to him, 'Danny, where is your new shirt?' And he would answer me, 'But Mom, he needed them!' If he had a quarter in his pocket he'd give it away, cheerfully. He told you correctly, everyone loved him at the halfway house. He was so funny and caring, and he had his own little fan club of workers and tenants there. He was only there for two years, but he was happy, and I didn't have to worry about him anymore. He was living in the streets, on and off, for almost twenty years, and he died at the age of forty-two."

Danny then showed me a telephone, saying he called his Mom often, which she verified. He gave a message to Bill about his health problem, and said to me, "Tell my mom, 'Happy Birthday!'" Apparently, Mary's birthday was a few days prior to this reading.

Mary began to cry, saying, "He never forgot my birthday, even when he was on the street!"

Danny also wanted me to tell his mother he had lived a good life, and that it was a success. The feelings that went along with that message were incredibly joyous and sincere; he really meant it. Whatever he had come to Earth to do he had accomplished. As Danny was leaving, he yelled, "Francis! Francis Goodman!" His mother had no idea who that was, and it took a month to figure it out.

After the reading was finished, Mary brought something out from her study and handed it to me. It was a file filled with simple sketches in pencil and watercolor, scenes of the outdoors, flowers, and other things. These were the drawings Danny had done for his mom while he was in the halfway house, the ones he had just shown me during my contact with him. They brought tears to my eyes. It was quite a wonderful thing to see the physical proof of something a spirit had shown to me. Mary then showed me old pictures of Danny—there he was with the "big hair," and all of his brothers had it, too. I picked him out of the photos easily, for I had seen him clearly.

Chapter 3

I saw pictures of him with the staff and some of the other members of the home he had lived in his last years of life, and it was very apparent that there was a great fondness between them all.

Mary and Bill played the DVD of Danny's life celebration collage that his brother and his girlfriend, Heather, had put together for the funeral. We all cried. I finally asked her how he had died. Usually, a soul will hint at or tell me outright how they had crossed over, but Danny had not. It was a sad story. Two years prior, he had been eagerly anticipating a Thanksgiving visit by Mary and Bill. He was so excited about their arrival that he had not slept in several days. Knowing they were coming the next day and that he needed to rest, he had gone into the bedroom of another resident and taken some of their sleeping pills. He, not being of sound mind, took too many, and he was gone the next morning.

Before I left, late that night, Mary handed me a package. "What's this?" I asked.

"It's for you," she said, kissing my cheek.

Under the wrapping was a painting Mary had done as a gift for me. It was beautiful, and is one of my prized possessions. Two days later, Mary called me excitedly from her home. "I know what the glass building is!" she exclaimed. "I had called my son, Tim, to tell him about the reading, and he said to me, 'Mom, don't you remember the glass building? It was in Phoenix. Danny used to get into the glass elevator on the outside and ride in it over and over.' I had forgotten about that!" I was thrilled at the report, and reminded her to rent the movie "Contact." My husband and I owned the video of the movie, and hadn't seen it in a long time, so we watched it one evening. To our surprise, in the middle of the movie the song "Spirit in the Sky" was played!

About a month later, I was in the shower, thinking about the night I heard Danny yell, "Francis Goodman! Francis Goodman!" Then I reeled in surprise. That message wasn't for Mary and Bill, it was for ME! When I was a little girl, growing up in Michigan, my brothers and sisters and I had attended a Vacation Bible School during the summers. It was run by a wonderful minister of God named Reverend Goodman—Francis Goodman! Oh, the sweet memories his name brought back! Reverend Goodman was a

Chapter 3

saint. He was the most loving, caring, unselfish, joyous man I have ever met. Mr. Goodman picked us up each morning in an old school bus, singing at the top of his lungs. We loved him dearly. He obviously had crossed over and had used Danny to get a message of acknowledgment to me. I called Mary excitedly, and explained what the message meant. True to form, sharing being his nature, Danny had given me a gift as he left on that night of contact.

Chapter 4

DEBRA LYNN

Spirit explains why a two-year-old had to die

In a world where there is so much suffering and pain involved in losing children, it was a great comfort to hear the reason for one such death; to make sense out of the senseless. I include this story to try to explain that there is a reason why these things happen; not that every death of a child will be for the same purpose, but it does help to know that there was a plan behind it. This particular plan was, as are all life plans, designed in-between lives, and is extraordinary for its courage and selflessness. The only way to know about the purpose behind this two-year-old's death was to contact the Holy Spirit.

A former client of mine called one afternoon to see if I could do a reading on a child who had passed away. I agreed immediately, but when she gave me the circumstances of why she wanted to do this, I was hesitant. The reading was to be for her husband, who had been very angry at God over the death of his two-year-old daughter from his first marriage. Debra Lynn had died over forty years ago. That is a long time to be angry. I was hesitant because I knew intuitively that he might not be able to handle the outcome of the reading, the reason his little girl died. Any explanation could be a threat to someone who had invested forty years of negative energy into a certain perspective about God. But it absolutely would be healing if he let it be so.

(I will call this couple Jim and Dorothy.) Jim had said to me one time that I might look into his daughter's death for him, so I felt I had permission.

Chapter 4

His wife wanted to surprise him with the reading. I told Dorothy I would see what Spirit had to say about it, and then she could use her judgment as to whether it was appropriate to give the reading to him. I took down the full name and birthday of Debra Lynn, and began to pray for her. In a very short time, the Holy Spirit came through with the identifiers I check for verification that I have the correct soul. Then Spirit told me why the little girl had died; not only the clinical reason, but the soul's reason. It was so moving that I cried. I called Dorothy the next day with the reading.

"The first information I received about Debra Lynn were the words 'New York,'" I told her.

"Yes, that's where it happened. Jim and his wife lived in New York. I had gone to school with Jim there, but we didn't get together until years after their divorce," she explained.

"Then Spirit said that Debra Lynn had suffered with a very high fever and a high level of toxins in her body. It weakened her terribly," I went on.

"That is correct. The fever is what ultimately caused her death. She only lasted a few weeks after that," Dorothy responded.

"I also heard the name Eleanor," I said.

"Eleanor!" Dorothy exclaimed. "She was a classmate of ours! She died three years ago."

"I believe she was present to say hello to you and to give you a sense of truth about this reading," I said. "Spirit also wanted to tell you the reason behind Debra Lynn's death, so that Jim could have some peace with this after all of these years. I will read it to you:

* * *

HOLY SPIRIT:

"This was a short life to experience joy after a life of sorrow previously [before becoming Debra Lynn], and to know that joy CAN be experienced here on Earth. A lesson/experience for the parents to enhance their

Chapter 4

compassion was granted, and they made an agreement to give brief love to one who could not stay long. The GRANDEST form of love is self-sacrifice, and they volunteered to sacrifice the privilege of raising her for a lifetime, and instead honored her need for a brief life here. A true 'accidental' death is rare, and Debra Lynn's was planned by her before incarnating. This was known on a soul level to her parents. Debra has reincarnated on Earth, and is now twenty-five years old. She lives on the East Coast of the United States and is in medical school."

* * *

I explained further what this meant. "Debra Lynn had been traumatized in the previous lifetime on Earth, and I have an intuition that she was a victim of the concentration camps run by the Nazis or the Japanese during World War II. There are a lot of these souls here on Earth now, and they are having real problems, because they don't want to be here. They associate Earth now with horror and have no desire to return. Since this is the place where the damage occurred, this is the place where they must heal. These issues are intense, and it can take more than one lifetime to heal them.

"There are beautiful souls who volunteer to help these ones who have been traumatized on Earth. They see them on the other side and say, 'I can help! I'll help you!' These parents take on the task of raising a soul who has been damaged psychologically. They serve as examples of what is good in life, and they become the example of what these souls need to realign to. In the case of your husband and his first wife, they agreed to love Debra Lynn with all their hearts for two short years so that she would not be afraid to come back to a life on Earth. She needed this example so she could trust her own decision to try again. Jim and his wife gave her the most unselfish gift that anyone can give: PURE LOVE for the short amount of time she had here. They knew before she was born (on a higher soul level) that she would not be with them long. They did their job well, and she was able to come back in the 1980's to pursue a life of unselfishness and service."

I was crying. So was Dorothy.

I know of many parents who have volunteered to help souls who have been traumatized by their past lives. If they knew this was their role, they would have an understanding that they have not done anything wrong to

Chapter 4

warrant having a child who dies early, or is born with physical problems, or becomes a problem teenager or irresponsible young adult. We forget the soul agreements that we make in-between lives, and I feel that in our compassionate zeal we also forget how hard it is down here on Earth. I like to say that there is a special pew up in heaven for the parents who have had difficulties with a child, and especially for those who have lost a child.

As Spirit said, this kind of service is the most self-sacrificing of all, and is done from a level of compassion that is close to the Mercy of God. To put an end to the question, "What did I do to deserve this?" takes away an enormous source of pain and unrest in a person's heart. This man needs to be proud of his gift to his daughter, and to realize that Creator allowed him to choose, to volunteer, to serve Love in this very special way. Some peace may be reached within when this realization is gained, and perhaps the sweet memories will be washed of the taint of anger, and a truce will be struck with God. Our Creator will be glad to have Jim talking with Him again, after all of these years.

Chapter 5

ERNIE

An alcoholic makes contact after death to apologize to his family

Sometimes a person lives a life that is full of very difficult lessons, lessons that they seem to fail. We cannot judge the lives of others, for we are not privy to what they signed up for—what lessons and experiences they agreed upon before entering their lives here on Earth. Just facing these difficult lessons, choices, and experiences should earn them our admiration at worst, and our support at best. Being human, we tend to judge harshly those who seem to fall off the edge of the fine line to success, but these ones, when seen through Divine Eyes are applauded for having the courage to try to overcome habitual circumstances set into motion from previous existences. Sometimes souls who have passed on want their loved ones to know that they appreciated how hard it was to live with them and watch them as they struggled with these issues in life. Ernie was determined to get this message through.

A lifetime struggle with alcoholism and making poor choices took its toll on him. By all accounts he was pleasant, if shy, and had a dry sense of humor, but he had trouble dealing with the temptation of taking the easy way out of life's circumstances. Doctors said he would only live for six months, but he proved them wrong. By the time he crossed over to the other side, dying of complications of cirrhosis of the liver, he had outlived their diagnosis by ten years. Ten very hard years. I had a dream about Ernie two months before he passed on. At that time he lived many states away, and I had not seen him in years, nor had I any contact with him. In the dream,

Chapter 5

I saw him at the end of a dirt road, standing in a white, three-piece suit, looking frightened. Spirit told me that he was going to die soon.

I have received information of people's deaths ahead of time in several cases, and each time I have had to decide what to do with that knowledge. In most cases I do not pass it on to anyone, unless instructed to do so. This time I called a family member to see how Ernie was doing. The report was not good, and the person I called immediately wanted to know why I had asked. I told her of the dream and the warning. Two months later, I received the news that he had passed away, and that in terms of human suffering, it was a blessing. I prayed for his soul, knowing that he was in very good hands now, and felt relieved for him.

Three days after he passed, as I was in meditation, I was astonished to see Ernie! The quickest appearance by a soul that I had seen after death was one week, and that was the spirit of my brother, Rick. Ernie was wearing the same white three-piece suit (very unusual attire for him) and was accompanied by two eight-foot-tall angels, one on either side of him. The angels were holding him by each arm and generating the energy he needed to come through to me. His determination to get his wishes and words across was immense, and Divine Grace was given to help him accomplish this. Ernie was a big man, and the angels dwarfed his size. It was quite a sight.

I was thrilled to see him, knowing that his family would be so excited by the news that he was alive on the other side. He had been very ill, and I knew from experience with this type of communication that sometimes it takes awhile for the soul to realize that they are indeed well. To appear in only three days after dying from such an illness was just incredible. He told me to say hi to Linda Lou, which I found out later was a nickname for his ex-wife, Linda. It was apparent that the driving force behind his rapid appearance after crossing over was to apologize to several people for behavior that he felt badly about. I am sure that being able to do so lifted his heart and energy greatly. I wrote down all of his messages, and he left very quickly, only staying with me for about fifteen minutes. It was enough to bring joy to those he left behind. I felt I should call his ex-wife immediately, and excitedly blurted out that I had seen Ernie, and he had messages for her and for his mother. As "luck" would have it, she was on the other phone line with his mother in Minnesota! We exchanged messages and phone lines in a type of relay to one another, and the tears of gratitude and joy flowed freely.

Chapter 5

Ernie wanted his mother to know he loved her dearly, and that he was sorry he had been "so much trouble." He said to tell her that "Patrick is here with me, and he is as big as I am." Linda passed this message on, to the astonishment of his mother, and explained to me that Ernie's brother Patrick had died at the age of three. This was evidence again that children do mature on the other side. He told me he wanted his ashes spread at a lake, and showed me an enormous body of water; I couldn't see the end of it. This did not make sense to me at the time, however, because the whole thing was shallow. How could that be?

"Oh my God! I know where that is!" Linda exclaimed. "Ernie's family lives on an Indian Reservation on Red Lake in Minnesota. The lake is so big you can see it from space, and the entire lake is shallow—you can walk across it! And you won't believe this: that is where his brother, Patrick, drowned when he was three, and where his father's ashes were spread when he died." Ernie's stunned mother received this news on the other phone line with joy.

I went on with the messages concerning a few names of people who were identified as a sister-in-law and a few cousins, and then Ernie gave a name that turned out to be a friend he had played darts with for years. Ernie said that his favorite times with Linda were fishing, and showed a picture of a place called Vern's. Linda agreed that those quiet times of fishing were the best, and told me that he loved to eat breakfast and the infamous cinnamon rolls at the little café called Vern's, just outside of Buckhorn Canyon in Colorado. These messages did so much to alleviate some of the grief at Ernie's passing, especially for Linda, who had not been able to make it to the hospital in Minnesota when he died.

Later, my mother volunteered to write a letter to Ernie's mother, explaining how I receive messages from the deceased (as best as we can understand it) and detailed what Ernie had said to me. I found out that this letter had a great impact on his family, and that his sister had taken the letter to her church, where it was received with great enthusiasm. It had sparked a new interest in some of their American Indian beliefs about the afterlife. One year later, Ernie's memorial was held at Red Lake in a beautiful American Indian Ceremony, where Linda was asked to take a boat out into the water and spread his ashes. She said it was the hardest thing she has ever had to do, for it truly meant goodbye. Knowing that this was what he

Chapter 5

wanted helped her tremendously. She said his family had prepared a special funeral book about Ernie, and that the letter with his messages after death was included. There was also an eagle feather his nephew had found on the beach where his ceremony was held. The eagles had been soaring over this spot for days, and they represent the Spirit to the tribe. His family prepared a dinner for the guests after the ceremony. It was their tradition to set a plate for the one who has passed. On the table was his mother's favorite picture of Ernie, dressed in a white, three-piece suit.

A few months later, Linda had a dream about Ernie. She called me the next day and said that she had dreamed of him lying in a hospital bed, and he gave her a huge smile. She said Ernie was showing her that he now had beautiful teeth. This was very interesting to me, because my brother, Rick, had shown me he now had "new teeth" after he died, and he was very happy about it. (Rick had to have dentures, which he hated.) Ernie told Linda he understood why she had not been able to come to the hospital a year earlier. This dream was a great comfort to her, and was a real gift from the Holy Spirit. Ernie's gift to us all was his determination to get through the veil of death and give messages of love to his family, apologies for past problems, and to show all people that your soul does indeed survive after the body dies.

I'd say that was a grand way to end his lessons here.

Chapter 6

ANN

A mother contacts her grieving daughter and gives predictions

The loss of one's mother is especially difficult, for it cuts the cord forever. Or so it seems. My sister called me one afternoon to ask if I would do a reading for a woman she worked with whose mother had passed over only two months prior. Kathy was grief-stricken, and all of her co-workers were concerned over her plunge into despair. I talked with Kathy by phone later, and she gave me her mother's name and birth date, her spirits lifting a little at the prospect that there was a possibility that contact could be made through the Holy Spirit. For the next two nights I prayed for her mother, Ann, and received not only clear pictures of her, but some information from my spiritual teacher on why she had died. I called Kathy on her cell phone, and found out she was in her car, driving home. I offered to call her back later, but Kathy couldn't wait.

"I saw a woman with short, layered brown hair," I began. "She was wearing a blouse, pants, and a sweater, and she was very thin."

On the other end of the line, Kathy began to cry, "That's my Mom! That's my Mom! She had that exact hair style, and she always wore layered clothes and a sweater because she was cold all the time! And she was thin."

Chapter 6

"A spiritual teacher of mine appeared during this reading and told me some things about your mother," I went on. "First, he wanted you to know that she is well. He said that the physical problems she had were a result of suppressed anger and resentment over a very bad marriage. These emotions were turned inward instead of outward, and caused blockages to vital areas of the body. He said that anger could not be cut out by a surgeon's knife, as the fields of energy simply continue to move and infest another area when inner healing of these emotions is not accomplished. Then your Mom showed me ambulances in the night, over and over, with their lights flashing and sirens wailing."

Kathy was incredulous. "Oh my God! My mother had brain tumors, and the doctors tried many times to cut them out, but more always came. Her marriage to my father was awful, with abuse and alcoholism. She suffered from lots of seizures, and was taken by ambulance at night down through the canyon to the hospital many times."

"She gave me the name Kenny, and said October, 1952," I told her.

"Kenny was her favorite cousin back east!" she cried. "I have no idea what the date means, though. You are remarkable!!"

I laughed. "Holy Spirit is remarkable, I just know how to listen. I think it is safe to say we have made contact with your mother. Let's set up a time to do a longer reading." We made plans to get together at her home the next week and said good-bye. Then I gave great thanks to God for this blessing. I received a phone call the next day from my sister. She told me that one of Kathy's co-workers had thanked her for getting Kathy to contact me, saying her transformation from grief to joy was astonishing. Now she knew that her mother was okay, and was really alive on the other side.

I drove to Kathy's house the following week on a cloudy, wet autumn day. I had been hearing Christmas carols from Spirit all the way there, as I prayed for Ann and her daughter. Kathy opened the door into a spacious, split-level home, made cheery with drawings from her five-year-old son everywhere. Kathy was a doll; you couldn't help but like her open and friendly personality. As she led me upstairs to the living room, I was drawn to one corner of the room by a bookcase. "You mother is right here," I told her.

Chapter 6

Kathy smiled. "Yes, she is." She pointed to a pretty, wooden box on a shelf. "She IS right here—these are her ashes." I was surprised. That had never happened to me before, and I marveled once again at Spirit. Ann's presence was very strong, and I was eager to get started with the reading. Kathy got me a glass of water, and I reminded her to get a box of tissues handy. (My mom's advice to me before every reading I do: "Don't forget the Kleenex!")

Ann's energy was amazing, a fact that Kathy said had been true in life, too. The images, sounds, and names she gave were all right on the money, and Kathy verified these facts with joy. I kept hearing the Christmas carols, and found out that they were Ann's favorite music. I saw a vision of a piano organ, which her daughter said she had played very well. There were references to the abusive husband, but most of the information Ann gave was all about special times with her children. Ann told me she had three children, which was correct.

"Your mom keeps saying, 'I can SEE!'" I told Kathy. "She says to tell you she loves this house."

"My mother was blinded from the tumors, and she never got to see this house, for we moved shortly after the funeral. I knew she would like it!" Kathy said.

"She likes this green wall," I said, pointing to the wall behind the bookshelf.

"I painted that last week!"

Ann went on to give the name Margaret, and then said someone in her family was a nurse. She then showed me lots of pine cones.

"Margaret is the mother of a friend of mine, who died two years ago! And my mom's sister is a nurse. She is visiting us now. I can't wait to tell her about this! The pine cones are really special; every year mom and I would collect pine cones for making Christmas wreaths. We had done that since I was very little, and she would sell them. I wasn't going to make any wreaths this year, but I will now!" Kathy reached for the Kleenex box. "This is amazing!"

Chapter 6

Then Ann told me some information about Kathy's future. "She says that you are getting married, and that you will be pregnant shortly afterward." That made Kathy laugh. "She's also showing me that you are getting a dog and a cat soon."

"My fiancé and I plan on surprising my son with a dog for Christmas, and I will be cat sitting for a friend for several months soon. We plan to be married next year. Wow, a baby!" she cried. (More Kleenex.)

Just as Ann's energy was fading and getting ready to leave, she yelled, "Tell Kathy CHRISTMAS IS REAL! CHRISTMAS IS REAL!" She was trying to convey that the story of Jesus' birth and life was true.

I have had other souls yell with joy, "GOD IS REAL!" It is as if they remember very vividly how people on Earth question their religions, and want to tell them to have faith because they now KNOW that there is a Divine Presence that cares for us very much. When I see the kind of elation that I saw on Kathy's face during the contact with her mother, I know there is a God who cares for us deeply, and that there is a need and a purpose for what I do through His Holy Spirit. This also shows that our loved ones look in on us while they are on the other side, for Ann knew all about what was going on in Kathy's life and what was coming up for her.

And yes, Kathy got married and became pregnant right after the wedding.

Chapter 7

BRANDON

Contact with a soul who died one day after birth

When a family loses a baby it is beyond devastating. It is the death of dreams. You love your children before they are born, anticipating with great excitement the joy of the day you will see the face of the person who has been in your dreams at night, kicking you all day long, and causing morning sickness for months. To have that joy taken away so suddenly is a shock that some never recover from. This is the story of Brandon and his family, and how God, through the Holy Spirit, allowed them to be a complete family nineteen years after Brandon's death as an infant.

One spring day, as I was preparing to leave the gym, I was approached by a man who had been working out with a friend of mine.

"I heard about what you can do," he said, towering over me. The man was a mountain, but he had the face of a kid, with freckles, and warm brown eyes. Not wanting anyone to hear our conversation, I motioned him over to the side away from the front desk. "Can you help my wife?" he asked. "We lost a son."

My heart went out to him immediately. "Don't tell me anything more. Have your wife call me and I will talk to her," I answered, giving him my phone number. His wife, Denise, called me the next day, and I got her son's birthday and full name. I told her I would do a short reading to verify that the Holy Spirit could have him speak to me, and I would call her back. That night, after deep prayer, Spirit came through with some facts about

Chapter 7

Brandon. I called Denise the next day to have her stop in for tea and to tell her what I had learned.

Denise was a very warm and friendly person; you would never have guessed the heartache she carried. I started off with the small list of facts that I had received from Spirit. "Your son lived only one day," I said.

Across the table from me, Denise became very still, her eyes growing large.

"You miscarried him when you were six months pregnant," I went on, carefully.

Her eyes filled with tears.

"He was just too small. His organs were underdeveloped, and he passed that day."

The tears spilled over now, and she reached for a tissue. "Yes," she whispered.

"He is buried in a town that starts with the letter *G*," I added. This, too, was correct.

She told me that she had been carrying around a teddy bear that matched the one they had placed in his little coffin, and that she had taken it everywhere she had gone for nineteen years. Her husband had seen what he believed to be Brandon's spirit in their house, and sometimes doors would open and close by themselves. He would always look up and say, "Hi, Brandon." We set a date to do a long reading a week later, where I would contact him in her presence, and tape the session as information came to me. I began to pray every night for Brandon to come to me, and I was surprised and concerned when he did not do so. A woman kept showing up instead. She had short, permed hair, and glasses, and appeared to be in her fifties. Each night that I saw her, I would acknowledge her presence and politely ask her to leave, as I was looking for Brandon. On the last night I saw her she actually turned to the side so that I could see her profile! A very tenacious lady! On the day I was to do the reading I was really worried, for I had not

61

Chapter 7

seen Brandon yet. I prayed mightily, and a gigantic angel filled the room, saying, "Just let God do it." That was good enough for me.

As I entered Dave and Denise's house that afternoon she led me into the kitchen for a glass of water. There, on the door of their refrigerator was a picture of the lady who had been bugging me for five days!

"Who IS that woman?" I asked Denise. "She has been appearing to me all week!"

"Oh, that's my mom," she told me. "She died ten years ago."

I knew then that all would go well. Sure enough, as I entered a deep state of meditation, there was Donna, Denise's mother, and Brandon. The two of them were right in front of me, arm in arm. Donna was a powerhouse, full of energy. There were six or seven souls behind them, but Donna was not about to give them any room to come through. She was running the show, thank you, and that was that!

Denise laughed. "Yes, that's my Mom! She was always the boss."

Donna kept saying, "He's mine, he's mine." I asked Denise if her mother had ever had any miscarriages. She told me that she had experienced several. Spirit said that Brandon had tried to be born through Donna years ago, but he did not make it, nor did he through Denise. He was now nineteen years old. All "baby" spirits are mature in the Astral World, and will choose a look and an age that they prefer. The grandmother kept saying to Denise, "He looks like you." Then, to prove that he was around Dave and Denise, Brandon played some island music, and said he couldn't wait to go with them on a trip.

"Oh my God! We're going to Hawaii on vacation!" she exclaimed, delighted.

Donna then told me she would be walking with Denise this weekend, and suggested she bake a cake. Denise verified that she would be going on a March of Dimes Walk that weekend. The March of Dimes organization had helped them out years ago after Brandon had been born. All of this time, an older gentleman kept peeking out between Donna and Brandon,

Chapter 7

and smiling at me. I finally acknowledged him, and told Denise that he was insistent on saying hi to Abigail or Abby.

Denise was astonished. "That's my grandma, Abby! She is here in Colorado, visiting this week!" I identified this man as her grandfather in a photo she showed me after the reading. Brandon told me that his dad was a real practical joker, which Denise said was certainly true. He also commented that he liked "the cars," referring to, it turned out, his dad's hobby as a race car driver. Donna, the grandmother, told me that she had been the one who took care of Brandon's grave when she was alive, as she lived in the town where he had been buried. That was also correct. Other facts were given to Denise by Donna and Brandon to show that they were alive and well on the other side, and great love was sent to her before they departed.

After the reading, Denise brought out a very special book she had kept about Brandon all these years, with pictures of every birthday party they had celebrated for him. I felt like I was holding a holy Bible, and it made me cry. As I leafed through the album, I saw a picture of a young woman sitting in a chair. She looked exactly like Brandon.

"If you want to see what your son looks like now, take a look at this. He looks just like her," I said to Denise, pointing to the woman in the album.

"That's me!" she exclaimed. "I was nineteen when that picture was taken." Denise, now a blonde, was a dark brunette in the photo, and was the spitting image of Brandon now, just like her mother, Donna, had said during the reading. We had spent almost two hours together before I left their house that day. A few days later, her husband, Dave, called to thank me for the reading about Brandon.

"You have no idea what you have done for my wife," he said. "It has taken a very heavy load off of her heart. She had been trying for years to get on John Edward's TV show (the famous medium), but could never get tickets. She is so happy." I ran into Dave occasionally at the gym after that, and he asked if the whole family could have a life reading sometime. I promised that when it was right, I would call him. Months later, as I was preparing to enter into a meditation one night, I saw Donna and Brandon, arm in arm in front of me. They asked me to call Denise the next day and

Chapter 7

say hello for them. When I got her on the phone to tell her their message, she laughed with joy, and said, "Today is my birthday!"

Spirit finally gave me the "go ahead" sign to do the family reading for them several months later, and I called to make an appointment with Denise. Spirit had chosen a specific day in March. It is not often that Spirit chooses a particular day to do a reading, so this was unusual. When I called her to find out if the twenty-third was available for me to come over she was quiet for a second, and then said, "Sure, that will be fine." I arrived at 7:00 p.m. and we set up the tape recorder. During a life reading by the Holy Spirit I have to go into a deeper "trance," or meditation, and Spirit animates my body, turning my head, moving my arms, and speaking through my throat. My eyes are always closed. When Holy Spirit came into my body that night, they smiled hugely and said, "Well! Who's birthday is it?" All four family members gasped, and the women began to cry. It was Brandon's birthday! (I had completely forgotten his date of birth after his first contact, as I do many readings a month.)

The rest of the night was full of great fun, with information on each one's most relevant past life (there was great laughter over Dave being a warrior in old Scotland, as he had a mighty temper in this life, too), answering questions, and hearing stories from Spirit. When we were through, the amazed family told me that they had decided on a secret test for me, to see if I would know it was Brandon's birthday. They showed me a vase full of beautiful flowers that they were going to place on his grave the next day. Well, I didn't know it was Brandon's birthday, but the Holy Spirit did. It also explained why I had been hearing Spirit in the car on the way to their house saying, "Happy birthday!" over and over. I had no idea what in the world that was about, and was hoping I could ask Spirit later.

This family has become a part of my family, and they are very dear to me. Their minds are intelligent, their hearts are deeply caring, their characters are full of integrity, and Dave can lift a washing machine over his head by himself! (The whole family helped us move.) I thank them for allowing me to print this very personal story of their loss, which is now a story of great healing. I have no doubt that their story will help others who have suffered from this kind of grief. And I have no doubt that Donna and Brandon will show up again to me in meditation, their arms around each other with big, silly grins on their faces.

Chapter 8

DAVID

A mother requests contact with a son who committed suicide

One wintry evening, my sister called to ask me to contact a departed soul for a mother who had lost her son. My sister, Linda, is a Rescuer of the first order and is always attracting people who are in need. She told me the military had sent word to this woman that her son had committed suicide, and she was understandably distraught. At the time, I was very ill with a severe head cold and could not meditate well, so I had to turn her request down. I told her I would get to him as soon as I was able to. That night in bed, I awoke to see the spirit of David, the son who had passed, at my bedside. He was accompanied by an enormous angel, who was helping him send his energy to me. He was quite young, around twenty years old, had blonde hair and friendly eyes. I acknowledged their presence and apologized for not having the energy to speak to him for a longer period of time.

It was quite awhile before I felt it was the right time to try to contact David. By the time I called his mother to set up a reading, six months had passed from the day he had died. This was the first case of suicide I had asked Spirit to help me with, and I was very eager to meet his mother, Ardie. I already knew one thing—he was not burning in a pit of brimstone! He looked quite well, and was eager for the contact with his mother. I arrived with my mother at Ardie's house on a rainy night, and as we entered I noticed the hallway lined with family portraits. "There he is!" I said, pointing to a photo on the wall.

Chapter 8

"Yes! That's right," Ardie answered. I could feel him everywhere in her house. My mom, bless her, had been in touch with Ardie for moral support, and had talked with her at length on the phone. I never allowed her to tell me anything about their discussions, as I must be totally blank on any details so I may listen to Spirit with no preconceived ideas. Ardie told me that David was nineteen years old when he passed. It was clear that she was suffering terribly from grief, and I was grateful to Holy Spirit that we were there that night to help. We set up the tape recorder in the living room, and in a few minutes I was deep into meditation to contact David. He was there instantly. The first thing he showed me was a living room with a Christmas tree and a baby's crib.

Ardie was incredulous. "No one knows about that!" she exclaimed. "He had gotten a girl pregnant, and the baby was just born at Christmastime."

Next, I saw David in a room full of fishing gear, floor to ceiling.

"Oh my God! He loved fishing more than anything!" his mother cried.

Moments later, in this same scene, an ugly, shaggy, black dog the size of a small horse bounded over to David and knocked him down. David was laughing.

"That's Buster! He died two months ago," Ardie explained. "This is amazing!"

David continued to show things from his childhood that I related to Ardie, and although the delivery was slow, it was very accurate. One thing that he did stumped her as to what it meant. He would reach into his pocket and pull out a ring of keys and shake them: "ka-chink, ka-chink, ka-chink." He did this three times during the contact. It wasn't until after the reading that she suddenly remembered what he was referring to. Ardie told me that when the kids were little and were not paying attention to her when it was time to get into the car to leave, she would reach into her pocket, grab her keys and shake them in her hand—a gesture of impatience.

"I had forgotten about that!" she said, smiling at the memory and reaching for a tissue.

Chapter 8

David did not give the reason for his death, although he alluded to being mistreated in the military. I have found that there is no way to ask questions of the departed during the reading, and I believe that this has to do with the level and amount of energy the soul has to work with. A great deal of energy is required to get through, and most have to have the aid of a Divine Being or another soul who is very high in energy. They do progress on the other side, however, and some can attain a level of energy to make themselves felt by their loved ones after a period of time. David did give a message to his mother. He wagged his finger and asked me to tell his mom to stop smoking . . . and he didn't mean cigarettes.

This really surprised her. She had been trying to deal with the stress and grief by using marijuana, and he had called her out on it.

For the next forty-five minutes, the Holy Spirit took over as I entered a deeper trance state, answering the many questions that Ardie had about life and metaphysics. It was a wonderful conversation, and the room was full of joy. This night had a profound effect on David's mother. Her heart, not being so heavy, was ready to embrace life again, and she began to read about Spirit, reincarnation, Eastern philosophy, and astral travel. Ardie was eventually able to experience an actual out-of-body event, and continues to study and learn about metaphysics.

The unfortunate and untrue teaching by the church that souls who commit suicide go to "Hell" causes much undue anguish and suffering by those loved ones who grieve for them. Remember that the definition of a "sin" in the days of old meant "mistake," or missing the mark—as in an archery competition. These ones who perform suicide do commit a mistake because they are mentally unable to see their way out of a very painful condition. They simply want to stop the pain, as it is unbearable. Free will dictates that they have the right to do this, and most would not do so, if they truly could think clearly and see the pain it causes others.

My spiritual teacher says that just as a father could not put his own son into a furnace and burn him alive for a transgression, neither could our Creator Father do so to any of His children. We all learn from our mistakes, or sins, and will have a chance to right these wrongs in a future incarnation. The young man I saw by my bedside and in his mother's home was doing just fine, thank you. And now, so is Ardie.

Chapter 8

Personal note: The Holy Spirit really pushed me to get started on David's story one weekend, and I argued that I wasn't ready to begin the chapter on suicide yet. I couldn't find my notes. Spirit INSISTED I should start writing this story anyway, and that they would help me with it. I bowed to their wisdom, knowing I wouldn't win the argument, and after aligning with Divine Energy to begin writing, it all came back to me, without notes. I was having trouble finishing up the story, and asked Holy Spirit to write the last two paragraphs for me. Spirit had no problem with that, and I liked their commentary very much. The night I finished the chapter, a new client from Baltimore called to request an appointment for a reading. Her father and a friend of hers had committed suicide, and she was still carrying a lot of emotional pain from these events. In fact, she was studying to become a grief counselor. I read the last two paragraphs of David's story to her, and it helped her very much. We talked at length about my readings with souls that had performed suicide. The next morning, a client from Colorado emailed me, wanting to know if I knew anything about the repercussions of suicide, as her grandfather and her uncle had crossed over this way. I sent her the last two paragraphs of this chapter, and typed at length on the subject, telling her what I had experienced in contacting these souls.

That evening, another new client, from Virginia, called and wanted me to contact her brother, who had committed suicide twenty years ago. I read her the entire chapter about David, and we had a great talk about God and metaphysics and the soul. She thanked me with great sincerity, and said how she wished her mother could have heard our conversation. A week later, I did a contact reading for her with her brother. Interestingly, at first she did not recognize the spirit of the soul who came in.

"No, that's not my brother," she told me.

"Just wait and see what happens," I said. I went on giving the identifiers for the young man who was before me in spirit. I was seeing a high school student in a red football jersey. He was very good in sports and was popular in school. He had curly hair.

"Oh!" she exclaimed. "That's my cousin!"

As soon as she acknowledged her deceased cousin, her brother appeared right behind him, and the rest of the reading was about Michael. He gave many personal pieces of information to show that he was alive in the spirit world. He had come in piggy-back with his cousin because he did not have the higher spiritual energy to come through on his own. I have seen this before, and especially with suicides. Usually an angel will accompany them. His life had been very sad, and frankly, it was difficult for me to experience his pain. I was happy he came through to alleviate some of the grief that his sister had gone through. And here it was, twenty years later!

I include this note because it shows how the Holy Spirit knows what is going on in our lives, even before we do. Two days later, a very dear friend of mine from Texas called to tell me that her ex-husband, whom I had known, committed suicide. Even though I had known this woman for many years, I had just told her that I was a psychic medium six months earlier. I was more prepared to talk with all of these people about their personal experiences with suicide because Spirit insisted that I begin this chapter *immediately*. God IS right here, all the time!

Chapter 9

KIRK

Five contacts with a woman's deceased husband

Kirk and Gloria Benish are two of the most incredible people I have never met. That was not a typo; I have not met them physically in this lifetime. I became acquainted with Gloria by phone, and I met her husband, Kirk, after he died. I have saved this story for last in this section because it is so extraordinary. Gloria Benish is a very talented spiritual healer from Montana. She is what we used to call "the real McCoy," and her incredible stories of healing with the Christ energy can be found in the books she has written. I will begin by writing about Gloria, who healed our daughter on Aug. 8, 2004.

Our daughter was born with scoliosis of the spine. This put pressure on the brain stem, and as she grew she suffered from numerous seizures every day. The heartache and worry we went through are indescribable, and we feel deeply for any parents who go through life with a child who has special needs. My husband and I opted out of the "normal" medical trial and error procedures, and focused on chiropractic care to straighten her spine. Our chiropractor in Parker, Colorado, Dr. L. S., is a saint, and he learned from one of the best in the world. He saw our daughter every month for three years for free, and these treatments helped her immensely. Her spine straightened out very nicely, and the seizures diminished somewhat, but did not stop. She was delayed developmentally as well, and she did not speak until she was three. One day my mother stopped by with a book that someone had given to her. She did not have time to read it, she told me, but perhaps I would find it interesting. The book was called *Go Within or Go Without,* by

Chapter 9

Gloria Benish. I almost read it straight through in one night, and I KNEW this woman could heal our daughter.

I wrote Gloria a six-page letter about our daughter's problems and about what I do. She is a real kindred spirit, literally, and like me, she has never charged for her services. She called me the following week and we had a wonderful conversation. She told me she would pray for our little girl, saying, "Don't panic if the healing takes three days. I don't know why, but sometimes it does." Three days to the hour later, our daughter stopped having seizures forever! She began to blossom immediately, catching up hand over fist in all of the areas she was behind in. My gratitude to God and to His servant, Gloria, are forever in my heart, and I used to pray that someday I would be able to repay Gloria for her wondrous, unselfish gift to my family. I did not know that my opportunity to help her would be only a few years away.

Gloria and I had become occasional phone pals, and we had wonderful talks about our spiritual work. She understands me like no one else. Gloria and Kirk were true soul mates, and their personal story is one of deep love and friendship. One day she called to ask me to do a reading for her, and mentioned that Kirk was bugging her to get a job—one that pays—and she couldn't understand why. They were not having financial trouble, and he would dodge the question when she put it to him. That night, a contact with the Holy Spirit revealed that Kirk thought he was going to die soon, and that was why he wanted Gloria to find employment. When she confronted him with this information, he acknowledged that it was true. He had not been feeling well, but had no reason to suspect that he was going to cross over. It was a premonition that proved to be true a year later.

While out in the hills of Montana panning for gold, Kirk had a nasty fall that broke his hip and shattered his femur. He had surgery, and was resting at home with Gloria in loving attendance for several weeks. He had a dream, he told her, of his grandmother waiting for him in a farmhouse with his father. They had died years before. His grandmother called to him, and motioned for him to step up on the porch. "Time for you to be here with me," she told him. Gloria felt unsettled by his dream, but she changed the subject after he told her about it. Although not happy about being bed-ridden, Kirk seemed to be doing well, when suddenly he could not breathe. Alarmed, Gloria called the paramedics, who were just minutes

Chapter 9

away. He only had time to give her a last few words of love, and he was gone. Apparently, he had died when a blood clot from the surgery in his hip dislodged and went up into his lungs. Her shock and devastation were immense, and the trauma took a toll on her health as well.

My husband and I were greatly saddened by Gloria's loss, and we cried for them for days, knowing how we would feel had it been one of us who had passed. I prayed deeply that Kirk would come and see me so I could give a message to Gloria from him, and in some way repay this saint of a healer who has helped so many around the world. Not only did he come to me, he turned out to be the very best sender I have ever worked with.

One night in meditation, almost one month after Kirk's passing, I saw him standing before me. I had never met him, but I knew it was him. I saw a very handsome man, who was quite tall and broad shouldered, with silver hair and a beard. He was wearing jeans, cowboy boots, a belt with a large buckle, and a cream colored long-sleeved shirt. He had very big hands and long arms, and I got the impression that he never wore short-sleeved shirts. His shirt was not a dress shirt, but one that was soft and made of cotton. I grabbed a pen and paper to write down his words. He had only been in the spirit world a few weeks, yet I could receive him plainly, and he did not need any help from an angel or other high frequency being to get through.

"Gloria!" he said. "Gloria! Rose!"

Kirk began to show me things that I call "identifiers," things that help prove to those here on Earth that he was indeed alive and well, and that this was really him speaking to them from beyond. Because I had never met Kirk or known anything about him, these identifiers were quite spectacular. I began to see carriages, big spoke-wheeled antique carriages. He focused on the wheels especially, and he gave the impression that he had been involved in metal working and woodworking. I then saw dogs, and a scene of camping: a trailer with an awning, chairs around a campfire, and a beautiful piece of property with trees and water nearby. It was a heavenly picture, and he loved this area. He said something about a special song being played at his funeral. I heard the name Taylor, and then he was gone.

I called Gloria immediately and left a message on her voice recorder. "Gloria! Kirk came to see me!" It wasn't long before she called me back,

Chapter 9

giving me an A+ for the messages from Kirk, explaining that they were all correct and definitely from him.

"Rose is my special spiritual symbol and means that I am to pay attention," she said. "Kirk was a master craftsman of antique carriages, and his specialty was making the big wooden spoke wheels. He could build them without measuring them, and they were always perfect. He did the metal welding and woodworking with his brother in their shop." She continued to sort out the messages. "Kirk loved camping, and we have a piece of property that is just beautiful. The dogs and grandkids and friends would join us there for some really great, relaxing times. I'd cook for days before we left. Taylor is our four-year-old granddaughter. And you described Kirk's favorite outfit! He never wore anything but long sleeves, and he had enormous hands." She grew quiet, remembering. "There was a special song that we did at his funeral. I had written it years ago as a surprise for him." We talked for awhile before hanging up, grateful for his contact.

Kirk wasn't done, however. He continued to show up for three weeks, every Friday night, and then again six months later. Each time he was very strong and clear, and his great sense of humor began to show through. The following week, as I was in meditation one evening, I found myself standing before a beautiful meditation pond. It was surrounded by a three-foot-high wall of white stone, and the water inside of it was clear as glass with lily pads and water lilies floating peacefully on the smooth surface. I sat there to meditate, and after a short while I saw Kirk standing on the other side of the pond, dressed as I had seen him before. He immediately began to show me images and speak to me by way of mental telepathy. I picked up a pen and paper, and wrote down the long list of images, names, and scenes he gave to me for Gloria. It was late when I finished with Kirk, but I knew she would want to know he had come again, so I dialed her home number and asked her to verify the information he had sent to me. She was thrilled that he had visited so soon after the first contact.

I went down the list. "First, he showed me the picture of a young woman who was very tiny, with dark hair, and was wearing a military uniform. He said the name Danielle."

"That is my daughter. She is very small, like me, and she is in the Air Force," Gloria said.

Chapter 9

"Next, he sent images of model airplanes. Not the ones that sit on a shelf, but the kind you fly, really expensive ones with radio controls," I went on.

"Kirk and my son used to fly those! And they are quite expensive. They enjoyed that so much."

"I heard several names: Phil or Bill. This person was associated with a huge workshop, where he said they built the carriages. It was really tall and open, and smelled like wood. And he also said 'Colton,' if I got that name right," I told her, going down the list.

"Phil is an old friend of his, but Bill is his brother, who does work in the carriage shop. The shop is a big barn, and so it does have a tall roof. It is full of woodworking and metalworking tools and supplies," she explained. "And Colton is our grandson, Taylor's brother."

I told her of seeing boxes and boxes of books, many stacks of them, and hearing the name Bob associated with them. It turned out that Bob was a family friend who had volunteered to help send boxes of Gloria's books to the prisons she donated them to. She was overwhelmed with the paperwork, legalities, and sorting that one has to do after the death of a spouse, not to mention wading through the awful grief, so Bob had come to the rescue to do all the shipping for her. This was Kirk's way of acknowledging Bob's timely and unselfish act for his wife.

"Next I saw a series of images," I said. "I heard the word *Houston*, then saw a woman, whom I believe is a daughter, with a new baby. Then Kirk showed me the insignia for NASA, and a rocket launching. He played these scenes over and over for me. The launch was amazing, as the view was right up close, with flames and smoke clouds billowing with a tremendous roaring sound!"

Gloria was really excited over this. "That's our daughter who lives in Houston! She does have a new baby, and she works in mission control at NASA! They just had a launch Saturday, and she is the voice you hear over the intercom that speaks to the astronauts! She will be so happy to know that her Dad saw the launch! We were supposed to be in Florida to watch it."

Chapter 9

"You tell her that he was there!" I said. "He then gave me a name that I wrote down incorrectly, so he said it again: 'D.W.' And then there was a picture of a motorcycle."

"Our son's name is D.W. and he just bought a motorcycle! I'm not thrilled with the idea," she said.

"Kirk told me that 'Daddy' is ill, and then told me to tell you 'No smoking!'" I went on. "But, Gloria, you told me you had quit smoking awhile ago."

"Well . . . the stress, you know," she hedged. "I started up again after he died. And my dad is very ill." Gloria ended up losing her father just half a year later, and she was also present when he crossed.

"Okay, Gloria, here's where it gets weird. Many times people play music for me from the other side, but this one takes the cake. If this means anything I will be amazed," I paused, not really wanting to go on, but I have learned that no matter how bizarre, I have to report everything. "He played the theme song from the old TV show *Bonanza* for me three times." I waited.

Gloria burst out laughing with joy. "He loved that music! That was one of his favorite TV shows, and he grew up in a town called Bonanza Land!"

"You're kidding!!" I exclaimed. I couldn't believe it.

"Swear to God, it's true," she replied, laughing. "Not only that, but our daughter is thinking of buying a house in Bonanza Land, too."

"Well, that beats all!" I was dumbfounded. "Wow! Okay, the last thing he said before he left was, 'Thanks for all the cooking.'" Gloria is a champion cook and used to cook for days for the hunting and camping expeditions Kirk went on. It was a labor of love, and he appreciated it. I was impressed by his courtesy in thanking her for something usually taken for granted, as well as by how accurate all of the information was that he gave. His energy was amazing. I was very happy that I had been able to receive Kirk twice in such a short time. He continued to surprise me with his tenacity for getting through for Gloria, as he showed up again the next Friday. I had gone into a special place in meditation, the place where I worship the Divine Mother

Chapter 9

aspect of God. It is an outdoor shrine of sorts, with a clearing in a forest, surrounded by pine trees. I was sitting on a bench there when I saw Kirk.

"Hey, I know you!" I called to him, smiling. Dressed in his favorite outfit, and looking wonderful, he got right to it and presented names, images, and sounds. I had trouble getting the first name—Hillary or Haley, or something—and then he went on to show me a very strange piece of equipment. I had never seen whatever this was, so all I could do when I called Gloria later was describe what it looked like.

"It looked like a small cement mixer, but he said you don't use it for cement, you put rocks in it. And water. It wasn't a polisher, though; he said it was used for gold panning," I explained to her.

"Yes!" she exclaimed. "That's called a trommel, and that is exactly what it looks like. You use it to sift the rocks and gravel when you are panning for gold. He had one of those."

Kirk had played the *Bonanza* theme song for me again, to my delight, and then showed himself getting into a black pick-up truck with a black topper. It was full of tools in the back. He told me he used to help the local folks with repairs. Gloria laughed and told me that he was very proud of his truck, which he had named the "Black Beauty," and that he was always helping neighbors as a handyman. Kirk went on to tell me he used to go deer hunting with a friend from Arizona.

"He did! He went deer hunting with his friend Phil, who is from Arizona, and his brother, Bill," Gloria acknowledged.

"Kirk gave me images of a trip that you and he made to Arizona, too," I said. "He told me that he had been in lots of pain, and that 'Gloria was at her best.'"

"That was last year," Gloria said. "I don't know if I was at my best, but it's nice that he thinks so! He had been having severe headaches, and when the doctors here couldn't help us, I loaded him up in the car, and I drove to the Mayo Clinic in Arizona, no appointment, no nothing. The woman at the front desk said that we were welcome to wait, but that it could be days or even weeks before anything opened up. I sat down to fill out the

Chapter 9

mountains of paperwork, and about thirty minutes later she motioned for me to come up to the desk. Her expression was one of astonishment. 'Gloria, you're not going to believe this. I just had a cancellation. We can see him in half an hour!' That kind of thing happened all week long for Kirk. One opening after another came our way. They finally diagnosed him with high blood pressure, and the small amount of medication he needed changed everything. He was feeling well and was his old, happy self again." Miracles are a way of life for Gloria. I believe it is because she is so connected to Spirit and is so giving of her time and healing talents to others.

Kirk had then sent so much love to Gloria through that evening's contact that it almost choked me, and the tears had poured down my face. He thanked me for being his messenger, and then his energy had faded. I had repeatedly asked Kirk to tell me where he had put his will, as Gloria had instructed, but he was unable to give me an answer. I have not had any luck in getting the departed ones to answer questions. I believe that the energy needed for this kind of question-and-answer communication is not present in a contact with departed souls as it is in the channeling sessions I do with the Holy Spirit and entities of great advancement. People have an agenda, it seems, when coming to give messages for their loved ones, and they concentrate on getting these things across to me. I had noticed this trend for years, and discovered that the departed souls will "replay" their messages in exactly the same way if I do another contact reading the following day for them. Sometimes I will double-check the reading, if I feel unsure of the quality of the energy present, and it is always the same, right down to the music that they send to me. It is a good confirmation for me to receive a rerun of the images and messages that the soul presented the first time I contacted them.

It is amazing that Kirk had such powerful energy shortly after crossing over, being able to come to me in three successive weeks and give messages that were one hundred percent accurate.

His next message for Gloria came five months after the first three visitations. It was a short appearance, but was very important to him, so I called her right away with my notations. He told me someone was having a birthday soon. This was correct, as his daughter, Danielle was soon to be a year older. He said to say thank you to "James," but did not say why. Gloria laughed at this, telling me that James was his nickname for their daughter,

Chapter 9

Jamie. He also wanted Gloria to know he could hear her and that he loved her, and then he showed me an outdoor scene. I saw a coastal area with white sandy beaches and seagulls flying overhead. I could not tell which coast it was, but he gave the impression that Gloria was to go there.

"It's the west coast of Oregon," Gloria acknowledged. "It was one of our favorite spots in the world, and I am going to spread his ashes into the sea there."

Kirk had then tried earnestly to show me something that I could not make sense of. He kept showing me his hands, turning them over and over. His hands were enormous, a fact Gloria had validated before, and he was pointing at something. I finally realized that he was pointing to his wedding ring, but I could not determine what he meant. Gloria understood instantly, however, and said just three days prior, she had taken his wedding band out of the jewelry box and put it on a chain to wear around her neck. I didn't hear from him again until the following Easter Sunday, two months later. He appeared to me while I was preparing to do a past-life reading, so I did not have time to listen to him. I happily acknowledged his presence, and asked if he would come back later. He did, appearing each of the next two nights, but again, I had clients I had promised readings for. Finally, on the fourth night, I was able to devote my attention to him.

His trademark now, the theme song from *Bonanza*, announced his arrival. (I will never hear that music again without thinking of Kirk Benish!) By the process of mental telepathy, he shouted, "Gloria! Gloria!" He then showed me an image of her in a house with a dog. I found out later that she had been at her parents' home during Easter, and that they did own a dog. He told me Gloria was now giving his things away, and that he approved of this. He said he wanted D.W. to have his hunting rifles, and then showed me a big watch for his grandson, Colton. Kirk's brother, Bill, was to have his tools, and he wanted Gloria to wear his favorite shirt, the one he was always dressed in when I saw him. I wrote down everything he said to me and called Gloria.

She verified that she was giving some of Kirk's belongings to the people she thought he would want to have given things to, and was delighted to hear that they agreed on some of the special items, like his pocket watch to their grandson. Kirk had shown me Gloria dressed in a blue uniform with a

Chapter 9

Delta Airlines insignia. Gloria confirmed she had been hired by the airline. (She later turned down the position.) He told me he had been making his presence known to her, both mentally and physically.

"Yes! That's true!" Gloria exclaimed. "Not only have I sensed him around me, he has also been opening the door and creating footsteps at night when I am in bed, and I often hear knocking on the walls. He also manifested a birthday card for me on my dresser." I told her of how my brother had manifested or moved physical objects for my family after he died, too.

Kirk had given me a strong impression of Gloria going to Arizona, and said something about his mother. Gloria confirmed she had just returned from a visit to Phoenix where she had stayed with her mother-in-law. He said the name Carol, whom Gloria identified as his sister, and then he gave the names Jamie, Heather, and Danielle, who are their daughters. Gloria was so happy to have absolute knowing that Kirk is doing well and can still watch her in her everyday life. She already believed this, but it was a comfort to have word from him that he approved of how she was handling things, and that yes, he really did appreciate all of that cooking for all those years!

This brings an end to the question of whether the "dead" are *really* okay. Our loved ones who have crossed over to the Astral World still have the ability to observe what we are doing, still love us dearly, and strive to send us thoughts of support and love. These types of communications prove that there is a continuation of the soul, the personality, after the bodily shell has been discarded. It shows that there IS a "heaven," a place where you exist when you die, and encourages us to think about that for a minute or two. What will you take with you when you are done with this life? You will only take two things: all of your experiences, and all of your opinions about your experiences. Your character is what survives, the true essence of YOU. And it is what you will take with you into your next life. These readings show that love truly is "the tie that binds," for it was Kirk's tremendous love for Gloria that fueled his ability to get through to me for her, time after time.

It has been a great honor to serve as Kirk's personal secretary over the last year, and I look forward to hearing from him again in the future.

Chapter 10

WORKING WITH LAW ENFORCEMENT

My work on a twenty-year-old murder case: contacting the spirit of the victim

This case was truly one of the strangest things Spirit has ever asked me to do. After many years of listening to the Holy Spirit and my Guides, I have learned not to ignore even the most unusual request. About sixteen years ago, I did refuse a request by Spirit. I was in a meditation one evening, when the spirit of a woman came to me, asking that I contact her son and tell him that she was okay. She had died recently and was concerned about his depression over her departure. I was aghast. This man was my eye doctor and I did not know him at all, except as his patient. He would think I was crazy and I would have to get another optometrist. I decided that I couldn't do it. The next morning I woke up with one of the worst eye infections I have ever had! "Okay, okay!" I said. "I'll do it!" That day, during my exam with my eye doctor, I was very nervous. I hadn't come out of the closet, so to speak, about my abilities, and feared rejection and ridicule. As my optometrist was writing my prescription, I took a deep breath and began.

"Can I talk to you?" I asked.

He didn't look up from writing on his prescription pad, but said, "Sure."

Chapter 10

"Well, I am a psychic medium, and your mother came to see me last night and she wants you to know she is okay. Her name is Millie, and she died so suddenly that you didn't have a chance to say goodbye. And she wants you to read this book." I handed him a copy of the book, *Witness from Beyond*, by R.M. Taylor, that she had requested for him.

Dr. S. turned slowly around to look at me, tears in his eyes. "I have been praying that I would know, somehow, that she was okay." He took the book and thanked me. A new friendship was born that day. And I learned to trust Spirit. Not only did they want to help the doctor who was grieving, but he turned out to be the one who introduced me to my future husband, Joe.

Sixteen years later, my husband and I moved to another state, leaving our beautiful Colorado behind. We had only been in our new home for two days when Holy Spirit made a request of me to get busy right away, saying, "No downtime for you." The moving van had not even been unloaded yet, so I was surprised that I would be doing a reading for someone in a city where I didn't know anyone. We headed off to breakfast at a restaurant in town across from the inn where Joe had stayed while he interviewed for his new job. As we finished eating and exited the small restaurant, I saw a poster on the window that drew my attention. It was a "wanted" poster, and had a photograph of a man who had been murdered twenty-three years ago. The state police were looking for information to help solve this crime, now that new methods in forensics had been developed. I immediately had an enormous spiritual reaction to this man's picture. Joe was loading our toddler into the car, and I got into the passenger seat in a daze. I started crying.

"What's wrong?" Joe asked, concerned.

"I have to help that man." I answered.

"What man?"

"The man in the poster." I said.

"What poster?" Poor Joe. I often think people can see what I see, and leave out important details. He says I do this a lot, and it's exasperating.

Chapter 10

"The poster on the restaurant window. Let's go back."

We got out of the car and as I showed my husband the poster, I began to take notes of the victim's name and date of death and the phone number for the state police hotline.

"Oh, no. You have got to be kidding me!" he exclaimed. "They will think you had something to do with this because you'll know all about the murder!"

"Joe, I can prove that I was in Colorado twenty-three years ago. Spirit really wants me to do this, so I must do it. There is so much grief over his death! I can feel it," I explained.

I did a personal reading with my Spirit teacher to verify that this was what I was being directed to do, and got the green light. My next evening's meditation and prayers were not quite finished when in came the spirit of Johnny, the man who had been killed so long ago. Each time I contact a soul on the other side it is a different experience, and this was no exception. Johnny played tunes from the 50's and 60's throughout our entire time together! It turned out to be an important verification for the police. So, to the strains of "Beyond the Blue Horizon" (so appropriate, I thought) and many other songs, Johnny gave me his story. I began by hearing the name "Jean" and felt great love surrounding this name. He loved her very, very much, but I felt it was not returned, that he was too shy to let her know of his feelings for her. I saw red, perfect roses and smelled them in my room. A rendition of the song "Bonnie Jean" played in the background, to be followed by the song "Johnny Angel."

I first saw Johnny in a state police uniform. That explained why they were trying everything and anything to get this case solved: he was one of their own. He then appeared in a ribbed knit tank top and a pair of sweat pants or workout pants, and was barefoot. He had a can of soda or beer in his left hand and was approaching an interior door, which was hinged on the left side. The doorbell had rung and he opened the door. Then the visions changed and leaped around to show some of his interests: motorcycles, dogs, and of course, more 50's music. He mentioned several names: Ryan, Maggie or Margaret, and Donald. The vision forwarded to his funeral. It was an autumn day, but there were still leaves on the trees. There were many people

Chapter 10

at his funeral, and many uniformed policeman. I saw a color guard and an American flag, then had an amazing feeling of someone at the funeral who was very anxious and fearful. *It was the man who killed him.* He was at the funeral, and he had known Johnny. Johnny repeated this exact scenario for me over the next three nights, so I knew that the information was what he wanted me to present. The first contact with a deceased person is usually short for me. This way I can call the person who requested the reading, and make sure we have the right soul, following it up with a personal sitting and a longer reading later.

Meanwhile, my husband, still paranoid since the request did not come from the state police, was resistant to the idea of me calling the hot line with the information I had received. "Use a pay phone!" he insisted. We finally decided on a much better alternative: I would write a letter. In that way, the facts could not be distorted or misunderstood, and they could not trace me. "Okay," he relented. "But type it! And wear gloves!" I typed up the information Johnny had given me, and included a letter of introduction, without using my name, to tell them who I was and what I do and why I was doing this. I felt this was very important, not wanting the state police to think this was a hoax or someone playing a joke on them.

It was a tremendous relief to send the letter. I was done, or so I thought. Several days after I had sent the information I had a vision of Divine Mother. She was standing before me with two angels, one on either side of her. The angel on her left had my letter to the state police in her hands. She tore open the envelope, which told me that the detectives had received it and were reading it. Two nights later, I had another vision of Divine Mother. She had two angels with her, one on either side of her, and the angel on her left was looking at the letter I had sent to the police with a magnifying glass. That told me they were considering my letter and its information very carefully.

I went on with my days, unpacking the moving boxes, getting our daughter settled in a preschool, and doing readings for people from around the country on a variety of topics. The days were busy and full, and my husband was getting adjusted to his new workplace, so we were trying to get our lives back to normal. Then I had another vision. I saw Divine Mother standing in front of me with two angels, one on either side of her. The one on her left side had my letter to the state police in her hands and had an empty chair in front of

Chapter 10

her. I knew this meant that the detectives wanted to interview me and I was to contact them. I went up to the angel and sat in the chair to see how it felt. I had Divine Mother to my right and an angel at my back; what could be better than that? I decided to call the hotline.

Joe had a fit. He only wanted to protect me, I knew, but I explained to him that this was a task given to me by God, so no harm could possibly come to me and I must follow through with it. I agreed to call from a pay phone, in case it did not go well. I placed the call the following morning.

A man answered the phone. "This is detective Jones of the _____ State Police, thank you for calling the information hotline."

"Hi. I'm the psychic medium who sent you a letter two weeks ago about Johnny's murder. I thought you might want to talk to me," I said, nervously.

"Yes ma'am! We sure would! Thank you for calling me," he answered excitedly.

"I wanted to explain, as I did in the letter, why I sent the information anonymously. And I wanted to receive verification of the messages Johnny sent to me, as it helps me with my work. Were you able to contact his family members to see if they would like to sit with me?" I asked.

"I was not able to reach his family, but we would really like to meet with you. The information that we could verify was very accurate. Can we arrange a meeting?" he inquired. "How much do you charge?" I explained, as I had in the letter, that I have never charged for my services. The Holy Spirit gives me this information freely, and I give it freely to others. It is all about service and relieving suffering in people's lives, showing them that God is REAL and that He cares about everyone.

"So, you are a religious person?" he asked me.

"Not so much religious as spiritual." I answered.

We made arrangements to meet in a few days in the state police department in my city. The morning of our meeting, I aligned with Holy

Chapter 10

Spirit and asked for guidance in the interview. I saw a vision of a man and was told that he was a Christian, with a capital *C*. This was a surprise to me, as I had anticipated that I would be grilled by an intellectual cop who would ask for references (which I had prepared) and "just the facts, ma'am." Sometimes Christians were antagonistic, depending on which denomination they represented. There are some religions that believe spirit communication is "of the devil," regardless of the depth of belief in God the medium has. At the appointed time, I made my way to the address I was given by Detective Jones. I entered a business complex that had one-story brick buildings along several short streets. I could not find the address I had been given, and stopped into one of the businesses that had the number that should have been adjacent to the state police office. There were many people working busily at their desks when I entered, and I spoke to the person closest to the door, asking if she knew where the state police department was. She looked at me like I was crazy. The manager of the facility came up to inquire what I was looking for, and he, too, looked very puzzled at my question, saying he had no idea. A woman in the back of the room, who had heard me asking for directions came forward, saying, "Wait a minute. I thought I saw several men in police uniforms across the street one day. Try over there."

I drove over to the line of brick offices across the street and found the address, but there was no sign, no emblem, no clue whatsoever as to what kind of business this building housed. There were no state police patrol cars out front. Thinking this was certainly odd, I went into the door that was marked with the address number I had been given, and was greeted by a middle-aged receptionist in a small lobby. I gave her my name and told her that I was there to see Detective Jones.

She nodded her head, saying, "He's in a meeting right now, but they should be finished soon."

I had a seat and looked at a stack of magazines on an end table, and saw that they were all about insurance. This was really strange, I thought. This place had no identification anywhere that could lead a person to believe it was a state police department. I figured out later that this must be where they brought informants, and they made it look like an insurance company to protect the people who came for meetings with the detectives. A short time later, the meeting broke up and about ten men in suits and shoulder holsters filed out of the conference room. Each one gave me a strange look

Chapter 10

as they went by, with one or two stopping to say hello. The look, I decided later, was the "oh, that's-the-psychic" look, as I found out that they knew why I was there.

A man who matched the vision I had been given that morning came around the corner, and I offered my hand and said, "Hello, Dave."

He looked surprised as he shook my hand, knowing he had never met me before. He thanked me for coming and spoke to a man who had walked out with him, saying, "Are you coming in for the interview?" The other detective said that he could not attend, but that Detective Smith would be there. I had not known that anyone else would be present, and this is how I surmised that all of the men who had left the meeting knew who I was and why I was there. It turned out that detective Smith was the one who had the authority to say whether or not I would continue to do work with them.

As Jones led me down a hallway to the conference room, I saw a uniformed state trooper talking to another well-dressed detective. He was saying, "Thanks a lot for having me up here." They shook hands and the trooper went out a back doorway. *No uniforms up front*, I thought. I was ushered into a meeting room cluttered with coffee cups, papers, napkins, three boxes of doughnuts, and a coffee maker. Pictures of suspects and maps lined the walls, all in disarray.

Detective Smith entered the room in a suit, tie, and shoulder holster. He was humming under his breath, and had an air of being rushed and tense. After thanking me for coming, he directed my attention to a poster on the wall.

"This is the original poster we had put up on the streets after Johnny was murdered twenty-three years ago." he said.

I looked at it and saw Johnny's picture, and below this, three small photos of evidence found at the crime scene: a pair of sunglasses, a hard helmet, and a wig.

"No," I said, immediately. "This is misdirection. These items had nothing to do with the person who killed Johnny. They were planted there on purpose." I could only assume that Spirit knew this, as I had no idea where that came from.

Chapter 10

The two officers looked at each other and asked me to sit down. Detective Smith opened the interview with a direct hit: he asked me what my religion was. I found his questions and attitude to be unprofessional and arrogant, and the constant humming of hymns was irritating. I was thankful that Spirit had warned me about him. I told him that I had been raised in the Episcopal Church and that I had looked into many, many churches and religions other than Christianity. I told him that I didn't attend any church, finding them to be intolerant, political, and usually quite judgmental of what I do. He asked me what I thought of Jesus Christ.

"He is the finest soul in the universe," I answered. Hoping to turn the conversation to the reason I was there, I gave them my references and began to explain to him why I had come.

"I am not sure if the information I have will be of any benefit to your police investigation, but I must share with you what has become known to me for Johnny's sake. I am a psychic medium and my particular expertise is in communication with the spirit world. I had chosen not to contact your phone hotline originally because I thought a letter would be more accurately understood, and my husband wanted to protect me. There are some people who cannot accept the kind of work I do, and they do not see the value and truth involved in mediumship. I had only lived in this state a few days when I saw the poster of Johnny on the restaurant window, and I had an immediate psychic reaction to it. I was told by the Holy Spirit to contact Johnny and to reveal his messages to you."

Smith interrupted here, saying loudly, "And the angel of the Lord appeared to Joseph in the night and gave him a message to get out of Egypt!"

I had no idea what that had to do with anything. I looked at Jones, who was being very quiet. I continued to tell my story. I explained to him that I had been doing this kind of work for sixteen years, and that I did not charge for these services and why. Each time I mentioned the words "Holy Spirit" Reverend Smith, as I was now beginning to call him in my mind, would interrupt with a Bible verse. I kept on task and ignored what he said at these times, and proceeded to explain how I achieve this communication with deceased souls through the Holy Spirit. I could see that he most definitely

Chapter 10

did believe that God could speak to people through the Holy Spirit, and that helped immensely. As I began to describe in detail how I work, using only the name and birth date or date of death for contact, I explained how I would receive images, sounds, words, and names from the deceased.

"I see how these game show psychic people work on TV," Smith sneered. "They give a lot of meaningless names of people and everyone in the audience cries and is real entertained." His obvious attempt to claim that mediumship was only a cheap parlor trick or that the unsuspecting public would buy into anything riled me a bit, but I kept my composure.

"Excuse me, but giving out names of friends, relatives, and personal interests that these people had when they were alive on Earth are very important clues to the personal history of the soul that has been contacted. I call them 'identifiers.' I have to know that I have reached the right spirit. There are so many spirits out there who want to be heard! You have to be sure that you have someone's Aunt Martha, or Grandpa Ed, or their son Carl. And as far as people taking this as entertainment, what a shame! They should be wondering how this is possible, asking what really does happen when we die, and thanking God that He cares so much about our grief that He allows people like me to find your loved ones to ease the shock and suffering caused by someone's death." I paused. "I have a question for you."

"YOU don't ask us any questions," he said in his best authoritative voice. "WE ask the questions."

"I don't want any information from you," I said in an equally firm voice. "I cannot know anything more than a person's name and date of birth, for that interferes with the reception. I need a clear screen." I turned to Jones. "What I need to know is, did the identifiers check out? Do I have Johnny?"

Jones nodded his head, "Yes ma'am, you sure do."

Smith took over the conversation. "I haven't read your letter. What information did you get?"

Chapter 10

I went over the details of the images, sounds, and words that Johnny had given to me. Jones took more notes. They were very interested in the messages and asked questions from several different angles. I suspect this was training on their part, to see if I would change my story:

"What happened when Johnny opened the door?"

"I did not see him open the door."

"You said that Johnny was holding a can of something when he opened the door. What kind of drink was it?"

"I did not see him open the door, and I have no idea what he was drinking."

I could tell what information they did not have already by their questions and keen interest in certain points of the images Johnny had given to me. It was clear that they had very little to go on originally, and they were very interested about the feeling I had that Johnny had known his killer, and that the murderer had been present at the funeral. I offered to do another reading on Johnny and to pass along any information I received. Smith reminded me that anything I gave to them could not be used in court.

"I know that," I said. "I am only doing what Holy Spirit asked me to do. And I'll tell you something else: I know that someone has really been praying about this case." They shot a glance at one another and Jones nodded. "You see, God answers sincere prayer, and look at all that He had to do to get me involved in this. I didn't live here two weeks ago, and what are the odds of my husband staying at the Inn across from the restaurant where you put up your poster? Keep up the prayers." They thanked me for coming, and I left the building with a sigh of relief. Then I got into my car and blasted Spirit.

"What was THAT? What have you gotten me into now? That guy was a total arrogant jerk! I'm only doing this because YOU asked me to!" I vented to the heavens all the way home. I was very upset over the treatment I had received, but my husband laughed.

Chapter 10

"Losara, don't you know 'good cop, bad cop' when you see it? They were testing you! How would they know you weren't some kook? Sounds like you did pretty good because they want you to continue."

It took me a few days to get to the next step in a longer reading for the State Police about Johnny. Usually, I have the advantage of having a family member present for the second contact, and I have found that the love present from the family is a huge boost to communication with deceased persons. I did not have this available, so I prayed a lot for Johnny, and asked my husband to "stand in" for the missing relatives. I taped the second contact, as it is so much easier than having to write down what is being given, and I can concentrate fully on the spiritual screen that I see when I close my eyes and look through the third eye, the point between the eyebrows. In readings for souls who have crossed over, I tell the family or friends of the deceased that they cannot ask questions. It just doesn't work that way. I believe these persons do not have the higher frequency it takes to achieve this level of communication. I can attain this level when dealing in direct contact with the Holy Spirit, certain saints that have come to me, and angelic beings. In the case with Johnny, I had to tune into him through the Holy Spirit and accept whatever he gave me, hoping it would be something the troopers could use to track down his killer.

After prayer and aligning with Spirit, Johnny came in with his usual 1950's music. He showed me images of himself on a motorcycle wearing a black leather jacket. I could not see the model or make of the motorcycle, as he showed it to me from the rear. I also saw a dog, a white mutt with black markings, possibly named Willie, and felt his love for his pet. I wasn't sure if this was his dog as a child, or if he owned it as an adult. Here is where patience on my part plays a role; no matter how much I want to receive more about a given image, I must relax and let the soul present what they want, for if I interfere I can interpret images incorrectly or color what I receive. It's "just the facts, ma'am" when doing spiritual mediumship work. I heard the names Ryan and Maggie, and he showed me "movies" of his childhood at his home with his parents. They were having a barbecue out in the back yard, and everyone was dressed in 1970's clothing.

The reading continued slowly, with long pauses between images. I heard the number 396. This number was repeated three times during the session, but no clue was given as to what it referred to. Johnny told me he

Chapter 10

had been an athletic person, and that he played basketball in high school. Here was something that could be verified through school records. He gave me the month of April, which was either a birthday or an anniversary of an important event in his life. He told me he had thought of a military career, but after watching the Vietnam War he decided not to go into the service. Images of the war on television were sent to me. I saw him at a firing range, shooting a pistol. He then said when he was a state trooper there was a joke going around between the officers about being a ranger from the Yogi Bear cartoon; this referred to the kind of hats they wore, because they matched the one the "Mr. Ranger" character wore. He then said the name "Ranger Rick."

I saw scenes in a tavern or a bar, which he liked to frequent. He would ride his motorcycle there, even though it was not far from his apartment. Johnny liked the image of himself on his bike. It gave him confidence, and he needed this, for he was shy with women, he said. I do not know, but I wonder if his beloved Jean worked there. I saw the bar clearly, as it was back then, and there was a juke box on the far wall, behind a pool table. The bar went halfway down the wall to the right as you entered the door, and he liked to sit on a barstool near the door. He told me that one of his favorite TV shows was *Happy Days*.

I suddenly began to experience tremendous, sharp pain in my back, the upper left side, and below this on the left as well. This was Johnny projecting to me where he was stabbed the day he was attacked. He had forwarded to this very important event, and it took me by surprise. His surprise at the attack was enormous, as if he had never expected to be harmed by the person in the room with him. He did indeed know who killed him. He was stabbed from behind, initially, and said that he could not breathe and that there was fluid in his throat. I could not swallow, and my lungs felt full, so I am pretty sure he died from drowning in his own fluids. The shock of the attack was immense, and he knew he was dying. He said the name "Ranger Rick" twice.

I experienced his death from his perspective and did not see the face of his attacker. I felt physical relief as he pulled away from the scene. This is where this work can be very frustrating, as I so wanted him to turn around and look at the man who murdered him. Why he did not give me more is not known, except that he just did not have the energy to do so. I saw, again,

Chapter 10

a brief glimpse of his funeral, and it was the same as before. I felt it was very important to find out who "Ranger Rick" was. Johnny then talked about (gave impressions to me of) his life as a state trooper, and how he loved his job. He told me that State Police are *different* (his emphasis), implying a superiority over other police departments. He said troopers have a high code of personal honor. Johnny disliked the part of his job that had to deal with traffic fatalities, and he implied that some of his work had to do with apprehending drug dealers. This marked the end of our communication.

The next day, as I was typing up the notes to fax to Detective Jones, I sat for a moment to connect with Holy Spirit and to ask that if I had made any errors that they be corrected now. I immediately saw a vision of Divine Mother with two angels, one on either side of her. The angel to her left was holding a three-ring binder which was opened to a page with Johnny's picture on it. I had the impression the binder was a file of unsolved crimes. She looked up at me and said two words: Richard Whitaker. (Not a real name for this book.) I was stunned. In all the years that I had been doing this work, I had only received the full name of a person three times. Obviously, this may be the real name of "Ranger Rick." The detective was very excited to receive the report, and especially the full name from Spirit. As of this writing, I have not heard whether the contact with Johnny has helped the detectives solve their case. I spoke with detective Jones sometime later, and he said that the information had been helpful. He was quite closed-mouthed about it all, and I knew that they would most likely not reveal anything more to me. He wanted to know if I had seen Johnny since that last reading. In fact, I had. Johnny had come to me a week after the last contact, dressed in his State Police uniform, to say thank you. That may have also been his good-bye. All I know is that whenever I hear the tune "Johnny Angel" I think of him.

Personal note: Just a few weeks before getting this book to the publisher for the final formatting procedure, I received a call from a good friend and psychic, Bill, in Colorado. Our conversation turned to the chapters of this book, and as I was reading the titles of the various stories to Bill he began to comment on them, psychically picking up bits of information on each. As soon as I read the title on Johnny's chapter, he said, "You won't hear from the police on that case again. They don't want you to know about it."

"Yes, that's what I felt, too," I replied.

Chapter 10

"He was stabbed from behind," Bill said, "It was someone he rode motorcycles with."

This was validation for me, for Bill knew absolutely nothing about this case, nor what I had written about it. It drives my husband crazy not knowing how all of this turned out, but I am confident that Johnny got the information he wanted to present to the detectives. He would still be singing old 50's tunes to me if he hadn't.

PAST LIVES

Chapter 11

INTRODUCTION TO PAST LIVES

Why past-life reviews are beneficial and why we reincarnate

"What am I doing here?" This question can be answered, in part, by seeing one's previous lives upon this world and other worlds. Past-life reviews can give us clues as to who we were before, what lessons we have to work upon, and can show us that there is something beyond this present existence. I have heard of people who remember a past life so clearly there has been enough information given to find actual proof of that person's existence in written records of the past. Why these facts do not make the evening news on television or the front page of the world's newspapers is a sad commentary on the backward and controlled media that stifle the incredible news that reincarnation is fact, not fiction.

I have been astonished by the past-life readings the Holy Spirit has channeled through me. In all cases, it is very evident that we have a tendency to repeat life themes with the same people, and that we are working on countless lessons for our progression of soul. It is also very apparent to me that we are a culmination of all of the experiences that we have ever had—thousands of lifetimes' worth of opinions, experiences, dislikes, beliefs, dreams, loves, and hates. *Clearly, there is an agenda for each soul: the progression into spiritual maturity and mastery of one's Self.* Thank God we do not have only one shot at it! Perfection takes a very long time indeed.

Chapter 11

When I contact the Holy Spirit for the purpose of looking at a person's past life, I always ask for the previous lifetime to be shown that is the *most relevant* to their present one, for there are definite reasons you are living the life plan you are currently involved in. It is fascinating to see how one's personality continues on through the centuries of living, dying, and reincarnating. Hopefully, a new perspective can be gained in this lifetime, one that propels the soul to a higher understanding. That is why each person plans their new life before being born with lessons, goals, and events of importance. Free will is the Law, and you use your free will to make these decisions before you are born. It then becomes your destiny. (Your destination.) You still have the free will to negate your choice of destiny, however, and that is why there are some souls who need "Plan B" in the wings. As Spirit has told me countless times, "The Plan is perfect, because it is flexible!"

I have yet, in all the readings I have done, to come across anyone who was someone famous in a previous life. Most of us are just plain folks, trying to make a living and to make sense out of life. But the lives are fascinating just the same, because they tie in so remarkably with the present life of the person I am reading for. Historical facts, when given, are astonishingly accurate; this is especially amazing because I am not a scholar of history or geography. I usually have to look up the facts provided by Spirit. I have only been given the full past-life names of two clients during a reading, and have not heard if they ever attempted to "find" themselves in records of the past, though it would have been very exciting to look for clues of their previous existence. *What is important is for people to take a look at who they are in relation to who they were,* and what lessons in life they still struggle with. What can they improve upon and how does this knowledge affect their perception of life and the universe?

Occasionally, I will receive a past-life vision of someone that is very negative, and it is not fun to report to a person that they were not of the best moral character a hundred or a thousand years ago. (Don't kill the messenger!) When viewing a negative past life, (which ALL souls have had) be sure to remember that Spirit does not view these experiences as "good" or "bad," but as WISE or UNWISE choices in response to life situations. A mature soul, one who has made progress in personal growth, will make more wise than unwise choices. The key word here is CHOICE! No one is bound eternally to make the same mistakes over and over. *Chances are given, through reincarnation, to correct the beliefs that create unwise choices,*

Chapter 11

and a person can change his life by making the decision to do so. Bad habits and errant thoughts can be hard to break, but are not impossible.

I will give details of some very interesting past-life readings from the Holy Spirit in this section, but first, an explanation of how this incredible vision takes place. Since I have already set up the agreement with the Holy Spirit that those who need to receive my services will find me, I know that anyone who hears of me "through the grapevine" is supposed to have a reading. I take the person's request, only allowing them to give me their name and birth date, and also that of any other person they wish to know their relationship to in a past-life setting. As stated, I pray for the most relevant past life to be shown. There are several ways in which I am shown, or introduced to, someone's past life. I can see the surrounding city or countryside where they have lived, and I will see them as they appeared in that lifetime. Sometimes music will play of the era in which they lived. It is very much like stepping into a movie, only I can feel every person there, knowing their thoughts and their soul's progression. I can see, hear, smell, and even feel temperature in these visions, and all with great clarity. The scenes tend to jump forward to important times (emotionally) in the person's life, and astonishing details of history and geography are sometimes given.

The person's feelings are very apparent, and their motives for their actions in that life are given. All the "players" in the story are perceived down to their character, ideals, motivations, and expectations. In short, the true picture of each person, "warts and all," is presented. It is presented because it is the truth, and Spirit only deals in truth. Sometimes the theme of the life reviewed is obvious, and sometimes a follow-up reading by Holy Spirit is given to explain what the lesson was to be. I have yet to see a past life that was not a mirror to the person who requested it, and it is a real wake-up call for those who see the merits of knowing what you did before this lifetime. It can be a release, knowing the "why" of things unexplained. Contemplation, wonder, and deep introspection—that is what I hope each client takes away from their experience of having a past-life reading.

In the past-life readings I have chosen to present, I will also give a synopsis of how they correlate to the client's present lifetime. This was always the most fascinating part for me, because I usually know nothing about the people I read for. I love how Spirit will choose, out of thousands of lives, the perfect and relevant previous life that shows that the person has lived

Chapter 11

before and is doing the same thing again, with a few variations. It appears that way because the soul is determined to get a certain error of belief out of the way, and will repeat circumstances that highlight it for examination and redress. The goal is change! That is another invaluable asset of past-life review, to be able to decide to change an obvious error in thinking that causes pain or stagnation in soul progress.

If you think it is cruel that we have to reincarnate and relive past errors with people that you didn't get along with the first time, think about how it would be if we were not given that chance to change. One evening, in mediation, I asked the Divine Being who came to me to give God my apologies for not meditating for several nights.

"That is alright. He has no expectation of you," he said.

"What?" I asked.

"Yes. He has no hope for you, either," he replied calmly.

"*WHAT*? What do you mean he has no hope for me?" I was incredulous.

"No hope for you or for anyone," he went on.

"Well, if God has no expectation or hope for us, then what does He have?" I asked, really upset.

The being smiled. "Knowing."

"What?" I asked, still not getting it.

"He *KNOWS* that you, and all other souls, will eventually come to him, so he has no expectation or hope. He knows!"

And that is why we are given chance after chance, lifetime after lifetime.

Chapter 12

LAUREN

Deceased grandparents request a past-life review for their granddaughter

Many clients request information on their past lives, and it is always very insightful and helpful material. This past-life request did not come from the person it was intended for, and instead came in a very unusual way. I had just completed a contact with a client's deceased parents who had been dead for many years. Although Cathy's parents had been divorced on Earth, they came through from the other side together, and gave facts about their lives that their daughter was able to verify: things like what branch of the military her father had been in, that her uncle had been a boxer early in life, and that her father had kept horses. He also gave the nickname he had called her mother for years—"Pete." The contact had gone well, and I was ready to go on to the next reading on my list, but Cathy's parents had other ideas.

Two nights later, while eating spaghetti at the dinner table, I heard a spirit shout, "Cathy, Cathy, Cathy!" I immediately tuned into whomever was there and got the strong impression that Cathy's parents were back and wanted to tell her something very important. My husband, Joe, saw that look on my face, and asked what was going on. I told him that I'd have to eat later because someone was being really insistent on the other side, and I had better see what was up. My kids were used to this, so they didn't even bat an eye as their Mom went upstairs to talk to the dead people.

Chapter 12

As I aligned myself in meditation with the spirit world, I saw Cathy's parents sitting together on a bench with smiling faces. They were so very happy that their daughter now knew that they were alive and well on the other side. They had several messages for me to relay, all of which pertained to their granddaughter, Lauren. They wanted her to know they were very proud of her, and that they watched over her. They wanted her to know that Grandma Phyllis sits on her bed while she sleeps and loves her very, very much. And they wanted her to know they knew she was being lazy at school and could do much better in her studies. With this admonishment, they showed me a picture of Lauren in a beautiful prom dress with her hair up—an event that was to take place several months from then. Lauren's grandparents then asked me to give her a review of a past life. It was very important to them that I do this immediately, and they had already chosen which past life of Lauren's I was to see.

I began to see a vision of two men. They were dressed in period clothing of the 1600's in Europe. Lauren, a man in that past life, was dressed in a beautiful coat with long bell sleeves and a ruffled shirt, riding breeches, and boots. His hair was black, very long and flowing, and quite wavy. He sported a thin moustache and a goatee. He was engaged in a fencing duel with another young man, whom spirit told me was the current stepsister of Lauren. As the overall personality of Lauren washed over me, I could feel that he was from an aristocratic and wealthy family, and had dined with kings, queens, and all manner of high society. His wealth was immense and he owned property all over the coast of Europe. The sea was his passion and his life, as he carried on the family business of shipping in France, Spain, Portugal, England, Wales, Ireland, and Scotland.

Lauren was a Frenchman, and had a very keen and intelligent mind. He was incredibly athletic in all areas, and was an expert in fencing, horsemanship, and archery. His competitiveness was legendary, which was what I had been seeing when the first vision came in. Lauren was fencing with a young man who would become a stepsister in the twentieth century. They were extremely competitive with one another, great rivals in all areas, and there was a strong dislike for Lauren from the other man. I suspected it had to do with the fact that, although he was superb in the arts of the day, Lauren was superior in every category. Lauren did not harbor any ill will toward the other man and had been his childhood opponent in many friendly battles that honed their skills over the years.

The vision ended abruptly, and Lauren's grandparents came back to leave another message for her. They wanted to tell her she had the ability to

Chapter 12

do anything she wanted to do in life, and that she would make an excellent doctor. This did not mean she was to pursue medicine in particular, but that she could succeed in it, if she chose to. They stressed again that Lauren needed to get busy studying, and sent great love to her before they departed. I went downstairs to finish my supper and called Cathy soon after. She was very surprised to hear from me, and even more surprised that her parents had come back for a second time. Cathy was very intrigued that her folks had wanted Lauren to hear about a past life, and when I relayed what I had seen and felt in the vision, she was astonished.

"You have described Lauren to a tee!" she exclaimed. "She has extraordinary hand-eye coordination and is a nationally recognized athlete. She is good in everything she does and is very intelligent. She has always been interested in medicine. Lauren used to watch medical shows on TV when she was very young, actual surgeries! And when she had to have surgery on her foot she somehow persuaded the doctor to let her watch—at eight years old!"

She went on to tell me of Lauren's love for the water and for all sports, and about the rivalry between her and her stepsister. "Lauren worshiped her older sister, but it was not returned. Her sister is also a top athlete, but Lauren is better. How strange that they should end up in the same family after hundreds of years! And my mom and dad are correct, she has been letting her grades slip. She is usually at the top of her class, and I don't know what is going on with her not doing as well as she can."

Cathy decided to tell Lauren about her grandparents' visit to me and what they had to say about her. I received a very excited call from Cathy the next night, and it was another eye-opener as to how the Holy Spirit is always listening and keeping an eye on us. When she had gone into Lauren's room that night to explain about the past-life review and the messages from her grandparents, Lauren was stunned. She told her mother that just two nights previously she had been praying and wondering about who she might have been before this lifetime. Her grandparents' messages had made an impact on her, I found out several months later. Lauren had brought her grades up and had received a full scholarship at a major university, through women's softball, to study nursing. (She later changed her major to pre-law.) Her grandparents' love was so strong that it crossed the seeming barrier of the other side to encourage Lauren to work hard and succeed at whatever she chose. No slacking off while grandpa and grandma are watching!

Chapter 13

SHANNON

Why a man struggles with drug addiction in this lifetime

When parents have a child who has had a hard time in life, there is a grief that stays with them like a low-grade fever. It is always there. They ask themselves, "What did we do wrong?" Trying to figure out where they slipped up in Johnny's upbringing to account for the lack of success, the deep-seated depression, the uncaring attitude toward personal responsibility, and the tendency to drift toward alcohol and drugs leaves parents with a shame and sense of failure that does not belong to them. Most every family I know has a child or relative who fits this description. These are wonderful families with parents who are exceptional examples of "normal" life. Why did they have a child who falls short of prospering in all areas?

I was approached by a former client with these questions. She asked me if a past-life reading might shed some light on why her thirty-something son was still such a mess, unable to get it together even after all of these years. The reading from the Holy Spirit was very enlightening, and did help the client, for now she knew the reason why Shannon turned out the way he had. The thing that helped Shannon's mother the most was my explanation of why he reincarnated into her family. I could put this explanation on a handbill and give it out by the thousands to people on the street. Many parents are in the same boat, it seems, and there IS a reason why.

Chapter 13

During the history of our old Earth, there have been times when human beings have committed great atrocities upon one another, and whether it was for religion, a nation, greed, or power does not matter. What do you suppose happens to the souls who endured these tremendous sins? Since we, as souls, are the sum total of all of our opinions and experiences, we carry the memories of these horrendous actions with us lifetime after lifetime. I think of the millions who suffered in World War II, and how most of them have, by now, reincarnated back on Earth. They carry with them the unconscious memories of horror, torture, and grief. God, in His Mercy, tries to help those souls. God works through people—you and me.

Stronger and more mature souls in the Astral World, eager to be God's instruments of Grace, volunteer to help these unfortunate, damaged souls. We rush up and say, "I'll help! I'll help you!" We forget how hard it is on Earth, I think, and we sign up to help those souls who need guidance. We are the examples of how to be more mature, more successful. Here is where it gets sticky: that suffering soul, who came into your family as a wonderful baby, has free will. He can take your example and emulate it, or he can reject it. It isn't up to you. Your job is done when they reach the age of accountability, which Spirit says is thirteen years old. Now the real hard part begins: watching the soul, whom you volunteered to help and love, try and fail, try and fail, and stop trying altogether.

Repairing this type of damage will often take more than one lifetime, but the repair has to start somewhere, and it may have started with YOU. Seeing your children or grandchildren as SOULS will help your anguish. Knowing that they are many thousands of years old, and knowing they will get another chance at healing will help, too. Knowing that God approved of you to be His example here for this child will help. Past-life readings help, too, for they are specific; they identify the attitudes and beliefs that the person brought forward with them into this incarnation. If the child is old enough and open enough to hear the information, it can lead to powerful breakthroughs in understanding. I knew nothing about the son of my client except for his birthday and his name. Here is what Holy Spirit showed me about this young man:

As in a movie, Spirit showed me an image of Shannon as a young man in the early 1900's. His name in that life was Jimmy. He was aboard a steamer ship coming into the harbor of New York, looking at the Statue of Liberty

Chapter 13

with thousands of other wildly cheering immigrants. He was from Ireland, about seventeen years old, dressed in a tattered suit and a wool cap. The ship was very crowded, but he had made it up on deck to view the harbor, and was among the first to disembark and stand in a very long line at Ellis Island to enter the United States of America. He had one knapsack and five dollars in his pocket when he entered the country. Jimmy made his way to the Bronx, New York, where he had an uncle and an aunt who were willing to put him up while he looked for work and a place of his own. Jimmy's mother and seven siblings were waiting for him back in Ireland. He was young and free and determined to make it on his own.

His uncle was a fireman for the city and his aunt took in washing and ironing to help supplement their income. They had no children, and welcomed Jimmy with open arms. He quickly adapted to life in America and embraced their national pastime, baseball. Jimmy loved baseball, and went to any Brooklyn Dodgers game that he could. He had gotten work at a bar in a rough neighborhood, cleaning up the floor and washing dishes. Eventually he graduated to running "errands" for the owner—passing money for organized crime. His aunt and uncle had no idea that he was doing anything illegal. Soon he became involved in gambling and won a great deal of money. He sent money home to his mother, who thought that he had legitimate work, to help out with their large family. Jimmy invested in the stock market, and found he had an aptitude for picking rising stocks, which led to investing for others as well. This included important men in the world of organized crime.

He was wealthy by his early twenties and began to drink and gamble to excess. He had loose women, new cars, and a luxury apartment in New York City. Jimmy was involved in many illegal pursuits, and had many hard-core criminals as friends. He eventually bought an estate in New York and moved his entire family from Ireland to the United States. During these years, he married and divorced twice, and had children by each wife. Although Jimmy was Catholic, he was continually unfaithful, and stayed out late at the clubs in the city. Jimmy was heavily involved with the sale of alcohol, but continued to invest large sums in the stock market, where he had made his original fortune. He became rich enough to buy politicians, judges, and police to help his customers and employees whenever they had a brush with the law. His lifestyle was extravagant and included the best cars, clothes, and European vacations that money could buy. The stock market crash of 1929 wiped him out completely financially, as well as many of his clients. Unable to face this enormous failure and personal ruin, Jimmy killed himself with a revolver in his high-rise office a few days later.

After showing me this past life, Spirit offered a further insightful reading to help explain how this short life affects Shannon's current one:

* * *

HOLY SPIRIT:

"This was a true 'rags to riches' story that ended in suicide. Shannon has deep-seated beliefs that money is evil because of this life, and he unconsciously avoids the accumulation of money. His past life was very superficial and frivolous and, as a result, he has trouble with holding onto relationships with women in this incarnation, feeling he doesn't deserve to have a lasting relationship. He also falls prey to the excesses of women and alcohol or drugs from that lifetime. This is a case of self-inflicted karma for past deeds of selfishness, dishonesty, and excess in the lower material greed of the Earth plane.

"A love for family, especially his mother, is present also from that lifetime, and a taste for the expensive. It would be wise for him to see outside of the self and volunteer to help others in this lifetime. It would be wise to curb the desire for excess and to live in gratitude of simplicity. LOVE AND FORGIVENESS OF SELF is crucial for this one to experience. The volunteer work will get his attention off of himself. He will feel good about helping others and see how all souls here are struggling with the result of past choices. Curbing desires that are unwise or destructive is a matter of mental discipline, again a CHOICE. Conquering addictions, *which is a choice to be made every minute*, requires determination to view one's own thoughts, as if taking a step back from one's self and correcting the direction, like the captain of a ship when he must correct his course.

"Suicide can be a temptation for those who have done so in another life, and a test to see if one can avoid the easy way out of life's great difficulties is planned before the next incarnation. Seeing that there IS a way out of an unsatisfactory life other than ending it yourself is a major test. Studying the Law of Attraction is very valuable in each soul's life, especially for those

Chapter 13

who have thought of suicide, so that they can see HOW to change the merry-go-round of disappointment. Love and forgiveness of self is also difficult, given this society's low tolerance for mistakes and poor choices and penchant for guilt. Past-life reviews help one see that everyone is working on something, and how strong influences from earlier lives create the opinions, feelings, and beliefs that carry one to certain ways of expressing. To realize that the influence comes from another life can be very liberating and can help a person decide not to continue in that unwise course in life. You do not want to have to do the test again, you say, and use it as an incentive when self-discipline waivers. There is still time to make wise choices!"

* * *

Shannon's mother was truly grateful for the insightful reading by the Holy Spirit about her son. She said it explained so much about why he had the problems he has had in this life: the addiction trouble with drugs, the suicidal tendencies, and his inability to hang onto money. He is an intelligent man, but he couldn't seem to get it together. He went from woman to woman, never having a stable relationship, and was always broke. Shannon also had expensive tastes in this life that he had no means to support, and was a big fan of baseball, just like before. All of these tendencies were carried over from the previous lifetime. His mother's decision to share this past-life reading with him will hopefully help him to see that he has had these problems before, and that there is always a chance to turn things around. The key is DECIDING to do so.

Chapter 14

GEORGE

A wolf in sheep's clothing

At the beginning of my career as a psychic medium, I was quite naïve, and lucky for me, Spirit was always watching over me. I had not learned how to read people yet, and always thought the best of everyone. My husband tells me I have a "Pollyanna" outlook on life, and for the most part it serves me well. This particular day it did not. I had met "George" at a new age potluck dinner, where I was the guest speaker and channeler of the evening. He was a French Canadian, very charming and very interested in what I did. He had attended another channeling session that I had done, and at this dinner he asked if I would do a life reading for him sometime. I said yes and took down his phone number and address. We agreed upon a time and I arranged to meet him at his apartment later in the week. That was my second mistake. The first was in not checking with Holy Spirit about him.

Later that week, I walked up the flight of stairs to meet him at his apartment, which was lovely and open, and had many windows to let light in. We had some tea, and talked, and I eventually set up my tape recorder to record the session. Holy Spirit usually speaks to those who ask for a life reading, and I am somewhere else in a trance state—a place I have yet to identify. Sometimes different spirits come into my inner vision and we go off to visit, and at other times my consciousness will be at the "sidelines," watching and listening as Spirit gabs away with the client. This reading was very different from the start. After aligning with Divine Energy and exiting my body, Holy Spirit did not come in. One of my spirit guides showed

Chapter 14

up instead to talk with George. This had never happened, and although I thought it odd, wherever I was, I did not perceive any danger.

The reading began with George asking to know if he and I had ever had any past lives together. This, too, was different, as clients usually don't care about me at all; they want to know about themselves and their problems in life, or their relationships with family, spouses, or love interests. My guide answered that yes, we had been together before in a life long, long ago, thousands of years prior. He told George that in that life he had wanted to marry me, and that he could not, because I was betrothed to another. I usually can see all the pictures and images that Spirit is talking about, but I could not see anything. That, too, was suspect. Suddenly, in only the first five minutes of our session, my guide called an end to the reading, saying this was "an inappropriate time for Losara," and that she (I) needed to return at once. I was quite literally plunked down into my body without any preparation and was quite confused as to what had happened.

I apologized to George. "I have no idea what that was about, but for some reason, we will have to reschedule this," I said to him, feeling embarrassed. Then I heard Spirit shout to me, "GET OUT! GET OUT!" I began to feel alarmed, and making polite excuses, headed for the door. George blocked the door with his body and embraced me.

"I am in love with you," he said, trying to kiss me. His arms were around me and he was literally in my face. "I knew we had been together before. I lie awake at night, wishing you were in bed with me. I have imagined what it would be like to make love to you. Let's go into the bedroom."

Maneuvering myself out of his hold was not easy, and I said to him, "George, I am a married woman, and I have no intention of going to bed with you. Your feelings obviously stem from a long time ago, but you have to put this into perspective and realize that this is impossible. I have to go NOW." I opened the door, ran down the steps, and never called him back for another appointment. I was shaking as I drove home, and was so grateful to Spirit for protecting me. I believe Spirit allowed me to experience this to teach me a lesson in discernment. I now do readings in my own house, or if more than one person will be present, I will go to the client's home. I always check in beforehand with the Holy Spirit, as I pray for my clients prior to their readings, to see if everything is a "go" for them.

Chapter 14

Being aligned with Spirit is important for everyone, everyday. You are then in the "flow" of energy that allows for wonderful "coincidences" to happen to you, helps your day go smoothly, and protects you in difficult or dangerous circumstances. As a rule, you should make sure you begin your day aligning with Spirit and with prayers of gratitude. There is no faster way to God than through gratitude. It opens your heart wide and places you in His Grace. You are then able to receive Divine Energy well, and your state of mind is of a higher frequency, allowing for higher energies to reach you. This aborted reading taught me that when it comes to Spirit, you "don't leave home without it."

Chapter 15

HELEN

An eye for an eye:
a story of negative karma repaid

This psychic reading exemplifies, more than any other, how what we do in life DOES matter—that the "golden rule" is not just a nice little saying to embroider on a sampler and hang on the wall. A record of our actions is stored and kept track of so that we may balance out the positives and negatives over the course of many lifetimes. A client from the past called me one day to see if I would help a woman who had lost her daughter. Apparently, this lady had gone to several psychics to see if they could contact her departed loved one, and had found that they were either charlatans or not experienced enough in communicating with the other side. One "medium" told her, after taking her money, that she could not find her daughter, but that her son was in danger, and if she would buy some of her potions, he would be alright! My friend, Nancy, had told her about me and what my contact through the Holy Spirit had done for her, concerning the suicide of her brother. "Helen" had turned to her and asked, "What does she charge, and when can I get an appointment?" When Nancy told her that I do not charge any fee, Helen did a double take and said, "She must be the real thing! Please give me her phone number."

Helen called me a week later, and I explained how I contact the deceased and that all I needed from her was her daughter's full name, date of birth, and date of death. While I was talking with her on the phone, Holy Spirit told

Chapter 15

me to tell her about a certain client whom I had done a reading for several years earlier, concerning a woman whose son lived only one day. I had no idea why Spirit wanted this particular story to be told to her, but I complied at once, and Helen was amazed and very touched. Spirit's choice made sense to me later. She gave me her daughter's name and birth date, the day after Christmas in 2002. Then I asked her for the date of "Kaylie's" death.

Slowly, Helen said, "September 26th."

Spirit told me the rest. "2002?" I asked.

Helen began crying, and I felt waves of enormous grief from her. "Yes! How did you know?" (Apparently this was a test for me, as no other psychic had gotten this right.)

"I didn't know," I explained. "But the Holy Spirit does." I told her I would do the reading for Kaylie on her birthday, which happened to be two days from then, and would call her immediately. Then I told her the rest of what Spirit had said to me. "It is okay to be mad at God. He can take it. You need to go into a room and scream at the top of your lungs and call Him a son of a bitch."

"That is *exactly* right," she said. "That is how I feel." She told me she was looking forward to my call.

I began to pray for Helen and for Kaylie immediately. Early the next morning, I had a very strong impression from Spirit and I called her to verify that I was on track with what had happened to Kaylie. I explained that I had not done the reading yet, but because I was praying many times a day for them I was receiving from the Holy Spirit already. This wasn't going to be easy, but I had to know.

"I have to ask you if Kaylie's spirit left her body before she died."

"I don't know. I hope so," she replied.

"Okay, I don't know how to ask this, so I'll just say it," I said, cautiously. "Did you have to make a decision to terminate her life support?"

Chapter 15

There was an audible intake of breath over the phone line from Helen. "You might say it that way," she said, carefully. "Keep going. You are right on track."

A lovely Christmas came and went, and all throughout the day I would say special prayers for Helen. I had the feeling this was VERY important to her *on a soul level*, and was one of the most important readings I was ever going to do. I had no idea that the results of this reading were going to be more difficult for me to relay to a client than any I had ever done.

As I settled in to begin contacting Spirit, I noticed that the dates of Kaylie's birth and death seemed reversed. Spirit had told me the year that she died, which would have put her death before her birth, and Helen had confirmed that date, so I had to trust it was correct and got started. After praying deeply for Helen and Kaylie and aligning with the Holy Spirit, I began to see a past-life review. This was a surprise to me, as I had expected to see her daughter's spirit and receive messages from her, as was usual. Instead, I began to see a scene from the distant past, at least a thousand years ago. I was looking at a primitive village setting somewhere in the northern part of Europe, and the settlement was under attack by some Nordic warriors. The men appeared to be Vikings and were dressed in animal skins and leather. They were fierce men, bent on murder and mayhem, and the villagers were screaming and running for their lives. I saw Helen as one of these warriors, a huge man wearing animal skins and bellowing a scream of rage. He came upon a woman dressed in animal furs who was about six months pregnant. The scene before me became gruesome and beastly, as Helen—the Viking warrior—plunged his knife into the woman's belly and gutted her, killing her unborn child, as the woman screamed in unbelievable horror.

Thankfully, Spirit pulled the plug on the vision and offered this explanation: Helen had lost her infant daughter before it was born to repay this "error" in a past life. She, herself, had chosen this lifetime to absolve the negative karma and this was why she had been so afraid when she was pregnant. On a higher level, she knew what was in store, and had bravely chosen to erase this awful blight on her soul by going through a similar occurrence. Spirit then said the words, "No anesthesia." None of this was making much sense to me. Then they told me Helen was going through a mental torture of great anguish and guilt, and that she was having nightmares.

Chapter 15

Spirit made it clear that this reading was of great importance to her soul growth.

I was aghast. How was I to tell this distraught woman that the death of her child was a result of a terrible act she had done a thousand years ago? I told Holy Spirit that I couldn't do this. They had to tell me something else so I could skip this past-life tie and give her something more encouraging.

"TRUTH IS TRUTH!" they said adamantly.

I couldn't go against that. I figured the worst that could happen was that Helen would swear at me and tell me I was a fake and hang up on me. So many people don't know the truth of reincarnation, and no one wants to hear that the most devastating event in their lives was by their own design. I took a deep breath and called her, hoping she wouldn't answer. She did. I began by telling her Holy Spirit had told me that Kaylie had reincarnated and was continuing on with her own life plan. I figured if she could accept that news then I would continue. It was a coward's way of getting ready to back out if she didn't believe in reincarnation. I'd be off the hook for telling the awful tale that took place so long ago. She asked me to continue.

I prefaced that story by giving her a small dissertation on how we all make a Plan for our lives before we incarnate here, and that the content of this plan takes into consideration the goals and accomplishments we want to achieve, the lessons we have to learn, and the past negative karma we have to make up for. I explained that we make "errors" in many lives that require balancing in another life, and that each soul has been alive many thousands of times, not only on this planet, but on others as well. We must make up the negative karma we have accrued on the planet where we have committed these errors. We don't leave this planet until we are done here.

"So you see, you came into this life with things to do, not just one purpose—I can't tell you how many times people ask me what their 'purpose' in life is. You have several, if not many, reasons you were born. We all came here with the main purpose to remember God, and you are pretty mad at Him right now, so I am sure you don't remember Him. You have been blaming Him for what happened to you, and that is normal, because you don't remember anything except this lifetime, when all the time YOU were the one who decided what important events were going to take place in your

Chapter 15

life. God doesn't require *anything* of you, period. You have total free will; even the freedom to reject Him for life. You used your free will to plan this life, and it became your destiny when you were born," I explained. "Now, what I have to tell you is the hardest thing I have ever had to say to a person. Spirit told me *why* you lost your daughter. First, I want to tell you some things they said so you will know that this is truth. You were *very* frightened to become pregnant."

"Yes! I was terrified the whole time I was pregnant with my son. They had to 'tie' my cervix so I wouldn't lose him," she told me. "Then the doctor did that again with my daughter's pregnancy."

"They also told me that you divorced after this baby died."

"Yes," Helen answered.

"Spirit said the words, 'no anesthesia,'" I went on. "They also said the baby was 'not viable,' although I don't know what they meant by that."

"I do," she said, quietly.

Throwing a quick prayer to Holy Spirit, I began to tell her the details of the vision of the past life she had as a Viking, and the horrific events that had taken place so long ago. She began to cry. After a few moments she was able to tell me she understood exactly why Spirit had shown this to me, and that the awful death of her daughter made sense at last. The story she told me about what happened to her is hard to repeat. Helen had been told, at a prenatal check up, that something was wrong with the baby inside her. The sonogram was not showing any evidence of internal organs, except for the heart, which was beating normally. She prayed and prayed that everything would be alright, and that God would grant her a miracle for her child.

When she was four months pregnant, the ultrasound revealed that the baby girl was missing many of its internal organs. The doctor told her that it would not live if she gave birth, although with the baby's heart beating away, it would continue to grow, not needing those organs while inside the womb. Helen prayed for a miracle, but it was not to be. She and her husband had to decide to terminate the pregnancy and hope for a miscarriage. They injected her with a drug to stop the heart of the fetus, but it did not work.

Chapter 15

They were not successful in getting her body to miscarry the baby and, two months later, she had to travel to another state for an abortion, as the state she lived in had outlawed late-term abortions. The second attempt at stopping the baby's heart finally worked, but when they induced her with drugs to have her give birth, there wasn't enough progress for her to deliver. The doctor finally did a high-risk abortion by dismembering the fetus while it was inside of her. She could not have anesthesia, except for a spinal block, and was awake the whole time.

"I could hear the saw, and I heard the bones snap," she sobbed. "Then they pulled her out one piece at a time and put the remains in a blanket and handed it to me."

I was crying as well, not believing the medieval way this had been performed. It was the most horrific thing I had ever heard of. Helen wanted to kill herself after it was over, and the only thing that stopped her was that she had a little boy at home waiting for her.

"Holy Spirit told me that you have had great mental anguish over this, and that you are having nightmares."

"Yes, that's true," she said.

"Do you understand how brave you were to agree to atone for that life as a Viking, and that your original fear of being pregnant was because your subconscious mind knew this would happen? Do you know that your son came first so you wouldn't kill yourself after this tragedy? God made sure of that because you aren't done here yet," I explained. "I sure wish I was there with you right now. I would hold you and tell you how brave you have been."

"I have had such guilt over this; that I killed my baby," she cried.

"No, you didn't! Spirit was insistent that Kaylie left *before* her body was dead, long before! Her short life inside of you was her gift to you, so that you could repay an error that was weighing on your soul. You did the right thing, Helen." I was desperately trying to help her to see that this nightmare was over, and that she should not carry these feelings anymore. "You will never get over what happened; you won't forget, but you can attain some peace

Chapter 15

about it, after a time. That is why the Holy Spirit had you find me, so that they could explain this to you. They do so want you to begin healing."

"How could Kaylie have been gone before she was dead? Her heart was still beating," Helen asked.

"The body runs on electricity, just like machines do. Coma patients are kept alive for years on electricity, but their spirits are gone. Your body supplied the current to keep the fetus going, and took care of it. But Kaylie was *gone*."

Helen had stopped crying, and we talked of many spiritual things. Before we hung up, she said, "I can't thank you enough for this." I was stunned by her generous and totally unexpected gratitude. She had come so far from the very immature soul that had been the Nordic warrior, over a thousand years ago. Perhaps that is why she chose this lifetime to erase the soul guilt she carried. She was now able, through the soul maturity process of many lifetimes, to do it right, to consciously understand the Law of Karma after she had gone through the balancing event. We closed our conversation with the promise to meet when she had business travel plans that would bring her to my state again. I got off the phone in shock, as I am sure she did.

Never have I had it revealed so clearly to me how the Law of Karma works. *It was self-initiated.* We DO judge ourselves after we die, and we make up for the harm we have done. There was no doubt of that, for I had seen Helen plan for this terrible event to happen before she had incarnated in the twentieth century. I did not understand the horrible vision Spirit had given to me at the time of the reading, but it matched perfectly with what Helen told me later. She would never have to repeat this cleansing, for she had completely changed from the barbaric mentality that caused her horrific actions, and now it was unacceptable to her present consciousness. She had gained *Understanding*. And that was the gift back to her from God, the ability to find someone who could truthfully explain the *reason* why this had happened to her. It was Holy Spirit who put her in the right place at the right time (meeting someone who knew me), so that she would gain Understanding in this same lifetime and begin the healing process inside; to give her soul a chance to find peace, and hopefully, to see that God does not punish people for their transgressions. They take care of that themselves, following the Universal Law of Cause and Effect. Souls eventually learn from their mistakes and are ever growing toward soul wisdom.

Chapter 16

PAST LIVES X 2: COUPLES

How a past-life review can help you see the true colors of others

There are many applications for past-life therapy, and the list goes beyond discovering the cause of phobias, illnesses, problems with drinking and drugs, financial difficulties, and "bad luck." Another very interesting use of reviewing past lives is in the explanation of the dynamics of relationships we have with others. Invariably, most people come back with a person they have had history with before this life to work out past problems or to encourage progress in another. Spirit has told me emotions are like glue, and if you have intense feelings of love *or* hate for someone, you can bet you will go around with them again in a future lifetime. Another reason for burying the hatchet with a person for whom you presently have antagonistic feelings! Many of these stories tug at the heartstrings, for love is like superglue, binding souls across many lifetimes and even different planetary locations that people experience.

Once, after relating a client's beautiful past-life relationship with her current boyfriend, I was asked if all couple reviews were so positive. The answer is a definite no. I recall one channeling I did for a client that ended up being so upsetting that the woman cried in disappointment. I was conducting a life reading, channeling the Holy Spirit, when "Sandy" asked a question that prompted a past-life review. First, she asked Spirit if she would get married.

Chapter 16

"Would you like to?" Holy Spirit asked her. "All is choice!"

"Well, will I marry John?" she persisted.

"That would not be a wise choice," Spirit responded.

Sandy was shocked. "What do you mean?"

"This one was not kind to you in a past life. You were with him in what you would term the 'Old West.' You were left with a younger brother and sister to raise when your parents were killed, and you became a prostitute to earn money. John was one of your favorite customers, and you fell in love with him. Even though he treated you poorly, you had hoped that he would marry you one day. You ignored his insults about your chosen profession and told him that you would make him a good wife. He said to you, 'You are nothing but a f—whore, and I sure don't want any kids hanging around.' This man does not accept the spiritual side of you, and you will not make the progress you could without him."

The woman who had come with Sandy for her life reading gasped, saying, "That is word for word what he says to you now! I told you he wasn't any good for you!" Sandy was crying by now, very upset that she hadn't been told she would live happily ever after with her boyfriend. The channeling continued amidst her sniffles, and afterward I spoke to her. "I know how disappointed you must be, but Spirit always tells the absolute truth. You have two choices now," I said. "Go ahead and stay with him and be miserable for ten years, or cut it off now and find what you really want in life." I also found out that her boyfriend was very uncomfortable with her natural psychic abilities that were coming to the surface, and that his mother thought such talents were "of the devil."

Six months later she sent a message to me. Sandy had broken up with John, and a man whom she had known for some time then declared his love for her, saying he had been waiting for her to grow out of her infatuation with John. He wanted to marry Sandy and have children, and said he could support them without her having to work anymore. I advised her to slow down and wait. It is a fairy-tale ending, but we live in the real world where it is better to really know someone before jumping for the wedding bouquet.

Chapter 16

This also brings up the good advice: be careful what you ask for. Spirit always tells you the truth, so you must be prepared to hear it. That is a good marker for dealing with any psychic or medium: if they tell you exactly what you want to hear, you can bet they are not the "real McCoy." Holy Spirit and spiritual guides are only concerned with what is best for your soul's progress, and they will not mince words when it comes to warnings or critiques of how you are doing so far on this journey called life. Candy-coated readings are a sign of wanting a repeat customer, or of not having a good connection to Spirit. If you receive a reading from someone who goes on and on about how you are light and love and will be wealthy and used to be the Queen of the Nile in another life, head for the door.

Sandy's past-life review came through a "life reading" (where a client prepares a list of questions to ask about concerns in their current life) and was unexpected; however, it explained why Spirit had advised the client not to carry on with her relationship. When people request past-life readings on themselves and another person, the entire review is about them and can include more than one life together if it has been an influence on the current situation. I have found that most people who are involved with another person, whether it be as a couple, mother and son, father and daughter, boss and employee, etc., have been together in several, if not many, life expressions. We like to hang out with certain people, it seems, and we definitely will if the relationship was intense. We can, and do, swap sexes, race, nationalities, and positions of power, all for the purpose of learning to get it right or to enhance another's goal. The guys get a bit squeamish about being a woman before, but if they could see and experience their own past lives they would see that they are the same person with a different costume on for seventy years.

The lives viewed could be from one hundred years ago to eighty thousand years ago. They could be from this planet or another planet. I think it is important for people to realize that everyone here has been around for a very, VERY long time, and that you are a product of all of your memories and opinions and experiences over that time. I laugh when I hear some spiritually-minded people say that they are an "old soul." We are ALL old souls! *There is a difference between a mature soul and an immature soul,* however. A mature soul has learned from their experiences, and makes wise

Chapter 16

decisions, having spent much time in introspection; in contrast, an immature soul has not learned very much from their many life expressions, making unwise decisions, and spend most of their time blaming God or others for their own poor choices in life.

In examining the past lives of the people you are involved with you come away with a unique perspective that leads to a change in your understanding; hopefully, the viewpoint taken is one of compassion. You can understand the reason for the way a person acts in this life, and you can also see why you have certain feelings toward them. This would be a great and useful tool in the marriage and family counseling profession. The couples' past lives that I have chosen to present in this section show the different kinds of dramas that can be uncovered and understood by examining their former relationships together. There is always a correlation from the past to the present of problems that went unsolved in other lifetimes. Intense emotions of love or hate cause the attraction, and we come together again and again to "get it right." Whether that is to sever a bond that is unhealthy, to reunite with an old love, to help a soul overcome temptation, or find compassion for a person disliked before, the goal is always the same: soul growth and progress in maturity. And it *is* fun to see who you were and where you lived before!

Chapter 17

TONY AND SHEILA

A rocky relationship that ends in suicide explained by past-life history

Of the many past-life relationship readings I have done, I think Tony and Sheila's reading exemplifies how this type of psychic sight can explain why couples have problems that seem built-in from the start. They *are* built-in, from their experiences in past lives together. This particular case demonstrates that people repeat life themes over and over, and that an understanding of life's lessons can be gained through Spirit. I had been contacted by Sheila to do a reading in which she wanted to find out about a past life with her ex-husband, who had committed suicide thirteen years prior. My expectation was to have the Holy Spirit present her *most relevant* previous lifetime with Tony. This turned out to be a new experience for me as Tony, himself, came through from the other side to help tell me their story. Another interesting deviation took place: *two* past lives which were the *most recent* to this current lifetime were presented. That was unusual, but perfect, for it explained what had happened to them to create the problems they encountered in this life.

I felt Tony's spirit from the other side as I began the past-life reading. He seemed eager to help present a picture of his and Sheila's history together, knowing that it would help her to make sense out of what had happened to them and to him. He began by giving me a song, as many of the deceased do. I heard one of the songs from the musical *West Side Story* called "One Hand, One Heart," which is all about a profound love that will never die. It was

Chapter 17

his way of telling her, from the other side, how much he really did love her. One of the lines in the song is " . . . even death won't part us now." It was very touching. Indeed, as I was to see, Tony had loved Sheila for hundreds of years, and most likely longer than that.

I began to see a beautiful forest in America, in the Northwest Territory, sometime shortly after the Civil War. Tony had been born in Missouri on a farm, and had fought in the war between the states. When I saw him in the vision, he had decided to get as far away from the aftermath of the war as possible, and had volunteered to go west to a fort somewhere near Cheyenne, Wyoming. One of his jobs was to ensure the safe passage of the wagon trains that were traveling the Oregon Trail to California through that area. There had been many raids on the settlers by the Indians. Most of his days at the fort were quiet and uninteresting, which was fine with him, as he had gone there to get as far away from humanity as possible. The things he had seen during the war had left him hollow, and sleeping alone in the wide open prairie helped him feel clean and peaceful. He often volunteered for scout duty for that reason, to have the solitude his soul needed.

It was on one of these patrols that he first encountered Sheila, who was an American Indian maiden of fifteen years. She belonged to a tribe of Indians that was peaceful, and they were friendly, but distant, to the soldiers of the fort. She was kneeling next to a small river, helping to bathe children, and when he saw her she took his breath away. He thought she was the most beautiful, pure, human being he had ever seen, like an angel in the wilderness. He observed her for a time, without notice, and went back to his camp to record the event in his journal. Tony told me he wrote in his diary that he believed if he could just be in her presence she could take away all the bad memories of the war. It was love at first sight.

The visions continued to show life at the fort, where many of the walking-dead soldiers looked like clones of one another. They were thin, lanky, and weather-beaten, with scraggly hair and long moustaches. Many of them drank alcohol to excess. The war had taken away what they had been inside and hollowed them out. Most of them came west to forget the atrocities they had seen committed in the name of patriotism. The next vision went forward in time to when Tony encountered Sheila again. He was on another patrol, and he purposefully rode his horse to the stream where he had seen her before. She was there again, with several small children.

Chapter 17

This time he boldly came up to her and tried to speak with her, but she was frightened by his presence, and gathered the children to her to protect them. He assured her, as best he could through sign language, that he meant her no harm, and he gave her a gift—his shaving mirror. This was accepted with shy smiles, and he left her there, walking on clouds of happiness for weeks. Tony said that in his journal he called her "my flower," and named her Daisy, the happiest flower he could think of.

Going forward in time to another segment of this life in the West, Tony told me the president of the United States was calling for an end to the "Indian problem," and that his regiment was rounding up the native tribes in their area to put them into land prisons, called Reservations. Sheila's tribe was ordered to move, and the soldiers "escorted them" to land farther north, making them march for days on end. Tony was able to interact with Sheila everyday, which drew racial slurs and comments from his fellow soldiers, as it was plain to see he was smitten with her. Tony could see the intelligence, pride, and beauty of the Indian people, and he preferred them to the soldiers that he was stationed with. After arriving on the Reservation, he volunteered to stay and help set up the new post that would monitor the Indians, so that he could be near Sheila.

The tribe was shocked to have been forced to leave their sacred land, and some of the men made plans to run away from the land prison and the demeaning soldiers. Talk of war on the white men was fueled by the alcohol they had learned to like, given to them by the post's soldiers, who watched and laughed at the drunk warriors. Brave from the liquor, the deported Indians attacked the post to gain their freedom, surprising them in a night raid. Tony showed the scene very clearly, and many soldiers were killed, but the natives were no match for the guns that were kept near the beds of the men in the army barracks. Sickened again by the bloodshed of war, Tony unfortunately had to stand by as retribution was taken by the commander of the post. The commander told the soldiers this would be a deterrent to any future uprisings, trying to justify the hangings of the tribe's young men and their chief.

Viewing past lives can be tough for me, as I feel everyone's feelings and see all of the events as clearly as what is real around me in this lifetime. It was truly sickening to watch. The elders of the tribe began to die from broken hearts, having no will to live and see what was to become of their

Chapter 17

people. Sheila had become deeply depressed and sullen, and would not look at Tony, seeing him now as the enemy, the cause of her tribe's suffering. She died that winter, as did many of her people, of pneumonia. Tony was later killed in the line of duty, being called to round up Indians in what became a big battle in South Dakota that same year.

I could feel that there was much more to the review than this one lifetime, and two days later I was able to continue with the reading, which now leaped forward to the very next lifetime Sheila and Tony had together. Again, I was immersed into the movie of their lives, and saw an incredible sight before me: a gigantic wheel, high in the air. I was not sure what I was looking at, and went to a different angle to look at this immense thing. It was a Ferris wheel, and it could be seen from miles and miles away! I found myself at a fair, and the people were dressed very fashionably; men wore bowler hats, with suit coats and starched white shirts. Ladies wore beautiful full-length dresses, with large floppy hats and carried parasols. It appeared to be in the very early 1900's, and I heard the tunes of ragtime music played on a piano. This was no ordinary fair, however; it was immense, and the buildings that housed the exhibitions were enormous. There was a waterway, like a river, with boats upon it where people could purchase rides, and towering above it all was that enormous Ferris wheel, many stories tall. Then I heard the song "Meet me in Saint Louis, Louis." (Researching this later, I found out that this had been the 1904 St. Louis World's Fair, and that the original Ferris wheel, which had been built for the Chicago World's Fair, had been rebuilt one last time. It was two hundred sixty-four feet tall, and had thirty-six gondolas, each of which could hold sixty people!) What a fantastic scene!

Tony worked at the fair, as did Sheila. Tony was a mechanic and carpenter, a jack of all trades who was hired on to help build and set up the World's Fair, a project which lasted a few years. Tony told me with some pride that he had helped "Mr. Edison" set up a special display of his electric lights. Sheila was a young lady who worked for a hat designer, and she managed a shop in the fair. She was a sharp businesswoman with a keen mind and a talent for design and seamstress work. She met Tony at the fair, and it was a whirlwind romance. In short order Sheila was pregnant, and in those days having a child out of wedlock was scandalous. They married right away and had a baby girl, keeping their jobs at the World's Fair. Sheila's mother helped out by watching their daughter, but she disliked Tony at once.

Chapter 17

Although Tony and Sheila did love each other, they had opposite views on life. Tony had a tendency to drink (carried over from the previous life as the Civil War soldier) and was moody. He was irresponsible with money, which caused many arguments at home. After the fair closed, Tony went to work in a factory, which he hated, and Sheila again became pregnant. Soon, another girl was born, and Sheila had to quit working at the hat store to take care of two daughters. She began to create her own designs of dresses, hats and accessories at home, and sold these to local shops to help bring in money for the family. Tony's drinking continued, and he became violent with Sheila when he was drunk. He hated his life and felt penned in by fatherhood, eventually abandoning his wife and the girls. He became a merchant sailor, traveling all over the world. His ship was sunk as it carried supplies for the government at the beginning of the First World War. The vision ended showing Sheila's parents contributing the money to open her own dress shop. She did quite well in providing for herself and her daughters. She eventually had Tony declared dead, and went on to marry a prominent businessman, one of the first men to own an automobile dealership. They did very well financially, and had two sons together.

After receiving the two past-life readings for Sheila, I looked up the information on the Saint Louis World's Fair, and was astonished by the accuracy of the details that Spirit and Tony had given to me. Not only was the giant Ferris wheel present, but the enormous buildings that housed the exhibits were there, called "palaces": the Palace of Education, the Palace of Liberal Arts, the Palace of Electricity, etc. It took ten thousand workers several years to build the World's Fair, which was called The Louisiana Purchase Exhibition, in honor of the one hundredth anniversary of the Louisiana Purchase in 1804. It was magnificent in its scope, and was open to visitors from the entire world from April through December. There were over five hundred concession stands, which sold everything imaginable; including the latest fashions, where Sheila would have worked. I also found that Thomas Edison was a notable guest there, and it was the highlight of the fair when the exhibits were lit up at night with thousands of electric bulbs.

I called Sheila the next night to read to her what the communication with Tony had brought, and she was simply amazed. She began to recount the similarities between her life with Tony in the present and the past.

"We had a lightning-fast romance, like before, and I became pregnant. We had a daughter," she explained. "Tony did drink a lot, and he was abusive when he was drunk. He was terrible with money, and spent twenty dollars for every ten he had in his pocket. And my mother didn't like him from the beginning. She wanted me to leave him."

Tony left her after their second daughter was born and Sheila was left to raise them alone. She put herself through school, earned a degree, and found work to take care of the family. "Tony was in the military, and was terrified to go overseas. I guess that was left over from the fatality at sea in the World War I life," she said. "He eventually remarried and then committed suicide. It was very sad. He would call me and cry, and I knew he still loved me."

Another very interesting point in Sheila's life was her compulsion to visit every World's Fair location in the United States. She said she had been to every site in America that hosted a Fair, and that she always felt a need to go to the highest point in these cities at night, whether it was in the Space Needle in Seattle, Washington, or the Arch in Saint Louis. She also said she cries when she hears American Indian drumming ceremonies, and wants to dance and chant with the native people as they perform. As a child, she would run and join the dancers in these festivities that she witnessed with her father when he worked for the Bureau of Indian Affairs. "They were kind enough to let the little white girl join in," she told me. "It was in my heart."

Will Tony and Sheila be together again in another lifetime? I cannot say, for I do not know if the lessons they wanted to learn were completed. The draw, the magnetic attraction of love and the need for healing, is very strong for these two souls. An understanding and the beginning of healing took place for Sheila after this reading, and it was given to her by Holy Spirit and the spirit of Tony, who still cares about her very much on the other side.

BRIAN AND AMANDA

A past-life review reveals a surprising reversal of nationality and true love

One of the most convincing and surprising pieces of evidence for reincarnation for most clients of mine is the perfect mapping of their personality to a former life. Mothers are astonished when Spirit tells them of their children's dispositions, matching them to the traits that were most prominent in another life long ago. Family and friends delight in learning that someone they know in this lifetime was once their mother, father, sibling, or dear friend of another time, and laugh at how "Uncle Fred" is the same as before. This is made even more believable because I know nothing about most of the people I do readings for. They often live far away from me, and the only way that this knowledge can come to me is through the Higher Mind of God. The repeated life themes are also great clues that we have existed before, and with the same souls. Readings for couples are especially interesting. They help us see that we created a PLAN and made soul agreements before reincarnating, to continue on with unresolved lessons and to enhance the life of someone we love. Somehow we manage to find that other person in all of the billions of people on the planet. This next story of Brian and Amanda shows how they crossed culture barriers, continents, and religions to be with someone they had loved through several lifetimes.

I received a call from Amanda in Nevada, after she had talked at length with a client I had worked with a few weeks prior. Like many young women, she wanted to know if her current boyfriend was "the one" she would marry.

Chapter 18

I told her that Spirit always honored the free will of any soul, and would not tell her if he was her future husband, but that we could ask for a past-life reading that would highlight any problems they may have had in another existence. Perhaps this would help her understand their personal dynamics better and tell her more about his soul's character. She was excited about this idea, and gave me her birth date and her boyfriend's information as well. I explained how I receive this review from the Holy Spirit, and that I would call her with the reading soon.

Two past lives were given for Amanda and Brian, and interestingly, Brian was the focal point in both lives. I always pray to receive the most influential past-life experiences relative to their current life expression. In this case, their past lives spanned a short length of time, the 1500's and the 1700's. They most likely have been together before these particular centuries in history, but these lifetimes were the ones that were influencing them today. I immediately saw Brian as an early American settler. Dressed in attire from the 1700's, Brian was short and thin, with blonde, curly hair, sporting a short beard and moustache. I saw him striding with very determined steps through a forest. He was going to a meeting in "town"—a small settlement somewhere on the East Coast of America—which had been called to talk about the British influence on the colonies. Brian was very unhappy about the way things were being handled.

Spirit presented his soul to me as a man of great honor and great personal character; he had confidence in himself and a strong opinion on most things. He and his wife were very religious people, possibly Quakers. His wife was Amanda. I saw her as short and of medium build, with very long brown hair that was usually pinned up with a small white cap covering it. She had a round, sweet face, and Brian adored her. One of the things he loved about Amanda was her high moral character, as well as her goodness and sweet nature. She was a talented seamstress and had a beautiful singing voice. Music was important to both of them, and Brian played the violin. And here was something I had never seen in any reading of couples I had ever done—this couple never quarreled. They had immense respect for one another, and a very deep love.

Then Spirit showed me that they were farmers in upstate New York. It was beautiful country, and they had both been born in America from settlers who came over from England. They had a family of six sons, and

Chapter 18

Amanda was pregnant again. She prayed to God unceasingly for a daughter this time, a wish that was granted. Brian and Amanda had American Indians for neighbors, and befriended them and admired them for their knowledge of farming. They both learned the language of their native neighbors, as well as French from the fur trappers who came down from Canada. This life was about family, self-sufficiency, and starting a new country. They worked very hard physically in that life and were genuinely grateful to God for their blessings.

The next evening I asked Holy Spirit to check this reading for accuracy, to make sure I had not made any errors in translation or had left anything out that they wanted to present to Amanda. Instantly, I began to view another past life of theirs, this time in an earlier time period. Again, Brian was the focal point. I saw him onboard an old sailing vessel, standing on deck in a uniform that was from the 1500's, as a Spanish conquistador. He was enthralled with the sea and the wind whipped his shoulder length hair back behind him. Spirit allowed me to view his mindset: he was an officer in the Spanish military, was very intelligent, strong, precise and logical, and he had a sense of personal honor that was very high. He was a devout Catholic. The ship was sailing a long way from Spain, and it took me a few moments to understand where they were heading. It was the Philippines. I eventually saw the islands with their sandy beaches and palm trees and crystal blue waters. Beyond this was a jungle of green.

There was a Spanish settlement on this particular island already, and Brian and his men had been sent to contain a small uprising of the native Filipinos. This was done in very short order as the island men were no match for the larger and stronger men of Spain with their superior weapons of the day. Brian had no personal feelings toward the natives, at first. He and the other men thought of them as animals, not human beings. He observed them as an anthropologist would. As an experiment to alleviate boredom, he decided to see if he could teach one of the natives to read. He found no interest in drinking and bedding every Filipino girl available, as his men did, but was attracted to one young woman in particular: a beautiful house servant, Amanda. He wanted to see if she could understand the intellectual concepts of language, writing, and mathematics. She proved to be a very quick pupil, and her inner beauty and delightful character helped him view the people of the Philippines as members of the human race.

Chapter 18

Many months of teaching brought them closer together, and Brian fell deeply in love with Amanda. Brian converted her to Catholicism. Most of the natives were being taught, or forced, to accept Christianity by the missionaries on the islands. He was quite a bit older than her, perhaps ten years or more. Amanda became pregnant, and Brian petitioned the Church to marry her, but was told mixed marriages were not acceptable. This enraged Brian, and he left the organized church and the military to be with Amanda. They lived near the beach. Brian adored his wife and new son, whom I saw him playing with on the shores of the island. He decided to build his own community and church, and set about to educate the island people. All who wanted to learn were welcome. He became revered among the native people, who recognized a soul of truth. Many of them had been treated badly by the Spanish soldiers and missionaries, and loved this Spaniard who was kind and respectful of their people. Amanda was the link of love and innocence that caused Brian to see all people as souls of potential. Her kind and loving ways balanced the agitation and energy of the warrior spirit in Brian and they complimented one another's nature.

The review ended there, and I went downstairs to confer with my husband, Joe.

"Say, do you know anything about the Philippines?" I asked him.

"Oh, a little. What do you want to know?" he replied.

"Did Spain try to conquer the Philippines?" My ignorance of world history was showing.

"Of course they did," Joe said.

"Are the people Catholic there?" I asked further.

"Practically the entire nation. Why?"

I told Joe about the reading, and then hit the encyclopedias (we still have ours) to confirm what he had told me. Indeed, Spain had gone to the Philippine islands in the mid to late 1500's, and brought with them Catholic missionaries. I called Amanda to read the notes that I had taken during the past-life reading. She was quiet throughout the story, and then

Chapter 18

burst out with words of joy and amazement. She said that their past-life characterizations matched their current personalities to a tee, and that in this life Brian is Filipino! He is also ten years older than Amanda and he is Catholic. Amanda converted to Catholicism shortly before she met Brian. They are both very spiritual people as well, and they have never had a cross word between them. People say they are perfectly suited to one another. We had a wonderful conversation about Spirit before hanging up the phone, and about the idea that Brian had loved the Philippines and the people there so much that he decided to be born there in another life. Then he had to find Amanda in America. Just thinking about all of the things that had to occur to make that happen is enough to occupy your mind for months. Life is complex. God is complex! That night, as always, I gave great thanks to the Holy Spirit for providing this wonderful tool for waking up souls to the truth of reincarnation.

Chapter 19

BRAD AND LAURIE

Spirit gives an unexpected past-life review and a lecture about attracting chaos

Two friends of mine had been having a real rough time in life, with one bad thing after another happening to them. It ran the gamut of illness, financial problems, family trouble, legal issues, betrayal, pets dying, the loss of employment, catching an unusual disease, and an addiction to prescription pain killers and alcohol. Brad and Laurie were wonderful people, so why was all of this "bad luck" coming to them? Brad called me to see if the Holy Spirit could provide some answers. What follows is a very comprehensive and thorough reading. It begins by examining one of the past lives that they have had together and then concludes with a special message from Spirit as to what it means and how they can improve their circumstances in this life.

After deep prayer for Brad and Laurie, and a request for the Holy Spirit to show me the reason why they were having such difficulties in this life, I was immediately shown images of each of them as different people in different lands and in different times of the past. They were both in ancient Rome, and were American Indians, and there were scenes of them as other people in separate lives as well. These visions came as a slide show to me, and then Spirit settled on one life in particular: the 1860's of America. This lifetime together had a great influence on their present-day relationship and current circumstances. I saw Brad as a Civil War soldier, dressed in a Confederate Army uniform with gray colors, a gold shoulder braid, hat and boots—all very polished and sharp looking. He was tall with dark hair and a moustache

Chapter 19

and goatee, a well-educated southern gentleman who spoke French. He was from Louisiana, but had been to school in the East, studying law. He was very ambitious, hoping to be elected to a seat in the government, and had his eye on becoming governor of his home state someday. He was an excellent horseman and marksman, and like all true southerners, believed that the South would win very quickly over the North, perhaps in a few months' time. He saw the war as an opportunity to make a name for himself, and he rose to the rank of colonel without much effort.

The presentation of his personality continued, as Spirit viewed the lifetime for me. Brad's family owned slaves on their plantation back home, but he had no real feelings about slavery as right or wrong. He treated all people kindly, regardless of color, but was indifferent to the issue of owning a human being; that was just the way it was in the South. Brad was very much into appearances and image, and searched for the perfect wife of grace and beauty, with a family of great social standing and wealth. He found her in Virginia at a dance that was held to support the South in the Civil War. Laurie was indeed a beauty, her heritage of Swedish and English ancestry showing in her delicate features and blonde hair. She was raised to be a lady: quiet in public, always proper, and devoted to her family. She came from a background of money, her father being a wealthy and prominent rancher who raised some of the finest horses in the state. There was a tremendous attraction between Brad and Laurie right away, which was a draw from another previous life together as American Indians, before the white man had come to this continent. They were engaged quickly, but Laurie did not want to move to Louisiana and leave her family during the war. She faithfully wrote letters to him every few days while he was away fighting for the Confederate states.

Contrary to the short time frame the Colonel and all others had been sure of, the war dragged on. What they had once believed would be a quick victory of honor by Southern superiority had become a nightmare of true horror. Brad was shot in the leg during a battle and, although he recovered from the wounds, it left him with a permanent limp and the need to use a cane. Deeper wounds inside caused nightmares for years about all of the carnage and agony he had seen during the war. He married Laurie at last and took her back to Louisiana, where they quickly got started on having the first of five children. They adored their sons and daughters, and took great care in rearing them to be beautifully dressed and on their best behavior in

Chapter 19

public. I was shown a scene of the five little children dressed in their finery and lined up according to age, with Laurie beside them in a beautiful gown. Brad was never elected to office, and he was restless in not fulfilling his dream of power and prestige. He was outspoken, entertaining, and very controlling of the entire family. He set his sights on having one of his offspring go into politics in the future.

The future, it turned out, was grim indeed. Spirit moved the vision forward in time to the 1870's when a terrible disease was sweeping the nation, and this illness claimed the lives of all but one of Brad and Laurie's children. It was shown to me as a type of fever and a rash, and I saw Laurie giving sponge baths to her children in desperation all night and all day, collapsing in fatigue. Even in meditation, I choked up with tears, feeling her fear and ultimately her deep grief as four of her children died. Brad and Laurie dealt with their personal agony in different ways. Brad became enraged at God for allowing such a tragedy to strike their family and he loudly railed against the Creator, having no enemy to battle with face-to-face this time. Laurie was inconsolable, becoming addicted to the laudanum that well-meaning relatives had given to her to dull the pain of her heart. She eventually committed suicide, leaving a note that said she had to go to Heaven to be with her children. The coroner, in spite of the evidence, ruled her death as an accidental overdose, because of the family's high standing in the community. The colonel felt he had nothing to live for with Laurie gone as well, and shot himself shortly after her death.

This was going to be a difficult report for me to give to my friends, and I knew it would be upsetting. I could see some similarities in their present personalities to those of the past, but I didn't know them well enough to see what else this past lifetime could mean to them. I found it interesting that in their current lifetime, both Laurie and Brad were very much into health and body building after that life where disease had caused so much heartache. Laurie was a nationally known bodybuilder, a state champion, and was a weight lifting trainer. They were dedicated to eating healthy foods and taking care of themselves. I had looked up the history of the 1800's and had found there was a Typhoid fever outbreak in the South during the 1870's that would account for the fever and rash that took the lives of their children. There was no cure back then. Brad's personality was very close

Chapter 19

to that of his counterpart in the 1860's, as was Laurie's. I decided to call Brad with the reading and ask for verification of facts that fit both of them to this past life, and would then proceed with the life reading by the Holy Spirit that would answer the question of why this current life was fraught with bad luck.

Speaking with Brad later helped to unravel some of the mysteries of the past-life reading. He was astonished at the similarities between that life in the past and his current experiences.

"This is amazing!" he exclaimed. "I grew up in North Dakota, about as far north as you can be in the U.S., and I was always fascinated with the Civil War. I had a Confederate flag on the ceiling of my bedroom, and always thought of the South as the good guys. That wasn't normal for a boy in my part of the country. And I loved the uniforms of the Confederate soldiers." He went on to explain that he and Laurie loved hot climates, like that in Louisiana, and they both felt they should be wealthy in this life—a goal he had worked for, but not attained and was disappointed over. Brad and Laurie had also felt sad that they did not have any children together, but they met late in life, and each had families separately. He admitted that he still felt lost as to his true vocation in this life, which compared closely with the previous incarnation in the 1860's. Brad was tall, dark, and handsome, and had a charisma and charm that would lend itself well to a public office, just like the colonel.

Laurie tended to be shy in public, and was very patient and kind, but worried about her children to the point of sleeplessness. I believe that worry stemmed from the horror of losing her children before and being helpless to save them. It all made sense. Now to see if we could make sense out of what was causing them to have so many problems in this life. This was where an explanation by the Holy Spirit, to see if past negative karma still faced them, could be invaluable.

The next evening, after going into a deep meditation, I asked questions for Brad and Laurie of the Holy Spirit, and a Master Teacher appeared to give this dictation for them:

Chapter 19

* * *

SPIRITUAL TEACHER:

"When there is an inordinate amount of chaos being magnetically attracted to a person, it has two meanings: (1) that he has not outgrown the NEED for chaos, and (2) he has karmic lessons to clear up. *A need for chaos is the need to feel ALIVE. When a person does not feel alive in God, the emptiness creates a desire for proof that one IS alive, that one has a life. By attracting chaos—excitement, good or bad—the ego feels alive.* If one draws bad or undesirable chaos, then the soul has beliefs and karma to clean up. Unfortunately "bad luck" breeds more of such events and circumstances into one's life, because the person is then putting out the thoughts of 'What's the use anyway?' and 'I knew it wouldn't work!' By the Law of Attraction, these thoughts will attract more of the same. These thoughts begin to fill the mind, and if they go on long enough, the heart.

"Negativity is like a leprosy. It eats away the good beliefs until only the ugly sores of anger and disillusionment can be seen. And everyone runs from them, in case it is catching. True friends see through this superstition and support such people. It is time to STOP the diseased beliefs with which you are attracting all of these undesirable circumstances. Let us look at some of them:

1) God is not to be trusted.
2) Mankind is evil and should be obliterated from the earth for their stupidity and selfishness.
3) I don't know what I want to do with my life.
4) I am sick and I have no money.
5) I do not have to tolerate people who disagree with how I think and do things. They need to change.

"There are many more, but we will take these first. They condense down into fear, anger, fear, anger, etc. Do you see the pattern? All negativity and sickness, all anger, weakness, intolerance, and sorrow are ALL caused by the belief that a person is separate from God.

"The answer to it all lies in the reunification with Creator. How to do this? FIRST, admit you have no idea what to do, and think about how the

Chapter 19

God Who created this universe surely knows what to do with you! THINK ON THAT until you can accept this possibility as true. See how logical it is to expect that Creator really does know the answers you need. Now, drop ALL thoughts that oppose this idea, and imagine that He WILL help you! FEEL the hope that this thought brings to your heart. Tell God, 'Let's start from this point forward. I'll stop all negative thoughts I have in their tracks, to give you the room you need to work.' You must get out of your own way and allow God in. As GREAT as God is, His Law of Free Will is the Law of the Universe, and He will not violate it. Why doesn't God DO something, you ask? *Because you are in the way.*

"*Stop all negative thoughts now!* This will take a great deal of effort because your thoughts are like a train going off a cliff, out of control. This technique absolutely WILL work. You will see how terribly abusive your mind can be to yourself, for every negative thought harms YOU. Intolerance for others truly hurts you. It closes your heart, and that is the only place God can enter. Do not shut the door by being intolerant of others, no matter how immature their souls may be. You do not have to live with them, just be kind and gracious to all. Truly evil persons are not common, and with those ones intolerance is justified.

"*Watch your speech!* It is an outpouring of your thoughts. Spoken thoughts carry a tremendous power and energy. By spreading the negative vibrations around yourself, you attract exactly the same negativity back to you. Much of your 'bad luck' comes from this problem of speaking your negative thoughts. Speech is as a command to the Universe. If you see your life and your world and your nation and your people as evil, stupid, incompetent, and lazy, you will attract MORE of these types of people and circumstances to back up your beliefs. Thus, you inadvertently perpetuate the problem and the belief.

"Believe differently, and you will attract the opposite of what you are now. Why did you attract an illness? Because your LIGHT was dim. Your immune system is tied to your belief structure. CHANGE the way you SEE things and ALL around you and inside you will change. If you *treat this as an experiment and ACTIVELY control your negative thoughts*, taking notice of them, you will see the proof of the power of the mind to alter one's life noticeably. Catch yourself as you speak, then before you speak. Catch yourself as you think!

Chapter 19

"GIVE THANKS TO GOD AND MEAN IT! Find the things you are fortunate to have and express from your heart of hearts your gratitude to the Creator.

"It will take time to undo all YOU have set into motion. So, as you go, remember that you will have residual events and circumstances coming at you. Say to yourself when this happens, 'It is just a part of the cleanup that is leftover from before,' when your errant thoughts were out in the Universe unchecked. It is not personal, it is impartial. It is the Law—the Law of Cause and Effect, the Law of Attraction. You forgot about it—now, don't forget!

"The past life that was given through Losara to you was but one of many you have had with your dear Laurie. Do not give up as you did in that life. Triumph over your own negative attractions. The loss of your children in that life was a karmic debt from another life in the past where you took the lives of others' children. It was cancelled out by that sacrifice and sorrow. You can think of this in negative, angry terms, or you can say, truthfully, 'I do not understand this, Lord. Please help me to understand.' Remember, anger closes the heart, and the heart is God's doorway to you. Always pray to be shown the way, to understand the truth. As you clear your negativity and fear, clarity comes. You are lost because you cannot see the path you were meant to be on. Clear the path, and ask to be shown where your ideal situation is. IDEAL, not in your mind, but God's! The more diligent you are in truly stopping the negativity, the faster you will see the results of getting out of your own way."

(I interrupted the Master Teacher to ask about the family problems Brad and Laurie were having with her children.)

"Laurie and her sons have had many past lives together that they are working on to clear. Selfish manipulation through fear of withdrawal is the game they play with her, and she must refuse to participate in the drama. You may be loving and supportive to a degree, but once children become adults they must leave the nest and assume full responsibility of their lives and actions. Not allowing a person to grow by being overprotective is a karmic mistake, for you stunt a person's soul growth by imprisoning them to your ways, even if your ways are correct. CHOICE must be allowed, and if a person chooses to dishonor you or your house they must be responsible for the consequences of violating the honor of the individual.

Chapter 19

"This is what God does, you see. He practices *the true form of unconditional love*, which is not 'I love you no matter what,' it is 'I love you enough to allow you to make mistakes and suffer the consequences of your choices.' In this way one can learn from his own mistakes and mature in soul growth to make wiser decisions next time. Done in love, NOT anger, this method of honoring the Law of Free Will does get results, although some souls take many lifetimes to mature into the beginning of Wisdom."

* * *

Brad was then given a reminder to read highly spiritual lessons everyday, as sustenance for his soul. Just as a plant needs water, the soul needs God, meditation, and the study of higher values. This practice will help keep his thoughts off of negativity, and elevate his state of mind and heart.

When I contacted Brad and Laurie to see if they wanted me to use their real names in this chapter, or use the names "Bonnie and Clyde" to assure anonymity, Brad wrote to me and said he had no problem with people knowing about his life, past or present. This is very gracious and giving of them, for this is a very personal reading. We all have these same issues, and it is wonderful that they were willing to show their laundry to the public so Spirit's answers can be shared for the benefit of all. Learning about the Law of Cause and Effect can undo a lot of bad things in the works, and can explain why some people seem to have a dark cloud covering them at times. Sometimes the cause is in another lifetime, but there is a way to remedy that, and it is in aligning with the Creator that those answers come. The main points of the advice were to stop your rampant negative thoughts and speech, be truly grateful for what you do have, and get out of your own way so God can get through.

Chapter 20

TYLER AND KIM

You can't hide things from a psychic Mom

My children have grown up knowing about what I do. They have always kept my "weirdness" to themselves; after all, no one else's mom talks to dead people and to the Holy Spirit. They kept it at arm's length, enduring my lectures about karma and how the consequences of your actions and thoughts go further than this lifetime. I never saw any eye rolling because they had seen enough proof of psychic phenomena, and how people were helped by spiritual readings, to know that this was the real deal; but they didn't inquire further or study metaphysics. So, when my son called me from college and asked me for a reading I almost fell over.

"You want me to what?" I asked him to repeat the question.

"Can you do a past-life reading on me and a friend of mine?" Tyler asked again. "I told this person about you, and we thought it would be interesting to see if we ever knew one another before."

"I'll bet it feels good to finally have someone to talk to about your mother," I replied. "Sure, I'll do it tonight. Just give me her name and birthday. I already know yours! I still remember those nineteen hours of labor!" (It was a joke between us; I have always told him he owes me, big time, for that day.) Tyler gave me Kim's name and birth date and I promised to call him as soon as I had anything.

Chapter 20

As I finished preparing for the past-life reading that night, entering a deep meditative state, I saw Tyler and Kim. I knew nothing about Kim, and was excited to see her, for if the physical description was correct then the entire reading was correct. Tyler is six feet two inches tall, has dark hair and hazel eyes. I saw Kim as much shorter than he, perhaps all of five feet tall, and she was a beautiful young woman. She had brown eyes, dark, shiny hair, and looked Polynesian. In the vision they were holding hands and smiling. That told me that they were dear to one another, and had been together many times in other lives.

I was drawn immediately back in time, standing on a street corner of a city that was in the eastern part of the United States. It was the Boston area near the harbor, Spirit told me. I could tell that the timeframe was around the 1860's. There was a light snow falling, and the gas lamps were lit over the cobblestone street. There, across the street, was Tyler, looking very elegant in his gentleman's coat and stove pipe hat. He sported a beard that looked like Abraham Lincoln's. At once I knew that he was wealthy, the son of an industrialist, was about twenty-two years old, and had an older brother. He lived on a large estate, complete with servants, and was highly educated and well spoken. He was a conservative, and was very much into appearances. He had a cane in his right hand—not for use, but for show—to complement the wardrobe.

Walking down the street toward him was Kim, called Amelia in that lifetime. She was a tiny thing, a Bostonian of genteel breeding, who was dressed in a magnificent gown with hoops, a matching parasol and button-up shoes. A hat with a wide ribbon under her chin covered perfectly coifed hair. She was the daughter of a very wealthy shipping magnate and was about eighteen years old. They were meeting to go to a party together. Amelia was Tyler's brother's fiancée, and he often escorted her to balls, parties, and the opera or theater. His brother helped run the factories the family owned, and did not have the time to take his future wife around to these frivolous affairs.

At first glance, Amelia seemed to be the spoiled debutante, attending scores of parties and dances, without a care in the world or a thought in her head. The vision leaped forward to show what she was really doing at these soirees: she was using them for cover as she passed secret information about the Underground Railroad. She was an abolitionist, helping to get runaway slaves from the South to the North. Tyler had no idea what Amelia was up

Chapter 20

to, but he was so in love with her that any chance to be with her was taken. It wasn't long before he discovered what she was really doing, and he was aghast. Not only was it dangerous, but he was sure that his brother would not approve. Hopelessly devoted to her, he swore his secrecy about the meetings, and was soon involved in the cause himself. One vision showed Amelia with an abolitionist newspaper or brochure in her hand.

In viewing past lives, I understand everything about the person: their thoughts, beliefs, motivations, and background. Amelia's father ran a shipping company that sailed all over the world, bringing luxuries from other lands. He had also brought slaves from Africa and Jamaica. She and her father had gotten into heated arguments about the slave trading that went on, and although he indulged her enough to hear her point of view, he sternly dismissed the subject when she went too far in her criticism of him. Amelia was a grand keeper of secrets, and he never knew what she was involved in.

The past-life review brought with it the feeling of great prosperity in America, a time of new innovations and inventions. Steam ships were replacing sailing ships, railroads were crossing America, and factories were supplying items of necessity and fancy. Men were in charge of the country and they loved their importance; women were still struggling to have a voice in anything. A woman revolutionist, taking on the rights of the Negro people, was unheard of. A feeling was given to me by Spirit that Amelia knew Frederick Douglass, the famous freed slave who so passionately and tirelessly worked for, and was the head of, the Abolitionist movement of that time.

The Civil War broke out, and Amelia and Tyler were thrown into important roles: she married Tyler's older brother and helped the northern cause, and Tyler went to work supervising the changeover in the factories to ammunition and cannon production His status as a gentlemen and son of a wealthy industrialist assured that he avoided the draft. These were busy years for them. Amelia had two sons over the period of the Civil War's four years, and Tyler worked hard manufacturing Union Army supplies.

Amelia continued to help the runaway slaves, donating food, clothing, and money to those who made it to Boston. She told her husband that these things were going to help the poor, which of course they were. Tyler was exceedingly careful not to associate himself with the abolitionists openly. I saw a vision of him in a "gentlemen's club" where the clientele was very

Chapter 20

fashionably attired, smoking pipes, and talking politics. I was surprised to see many of the men there did not support President Lincoln, and that they were not as concerned with the slavery issue as they were with the audacity of the southern states to secede from the Union. Tyler remained carefully neutral on these issues in the club. Then Lincoln was assassinated. The men had mixed feelings about the change in leadership, but were appalled that a president could be assassinated so easily. They formed a delegation to petition the government to have better protection for their leaders.

Amelia was absolutely distraught over Lincoln's death. He was a hero to her. Although she was married to Tyler's brother now, she saw Tyler frequently, as he was always finding an excuse to visit. He had married the appropriate woman of good standing in society by then, but his heart always belonged to Amelia. He remained devoted to her for the rest of his life.

When I called my son the next day and gave him the description of Kim that Spirit had shown me, he was incredulous. Not only was Kim just under five feet tall, but she was Filipino! Then I recounted the past-life reading for him, and there was a prolonged silence on the other end of the phone. He asked me if people could repeat lifetime themes. I told him that they absolutely can and do. I knew what was coming.

"Mom," he said, quietly. "I love her." He then told me that Kim was his roommate's girlfriend.

"You can't help but love her," I told him, feeling awful about his predicament. "You loved her before this lifetime." I promised to send him a copy of the reading that day.

Then my usually conservative son did something daring. He showed her the reading, and confessed his love for her. What a mess! To make a long story short, they became a couple, after much distress for Kim, and were happy together for a year and a half. They parted ways in a respectful and friendly manner. His unspoken love for her in that Civil War lifetime has had a chance to be experienced fully in this life. They remain good friends. Now, Kim has begun the study of metaphysics, and Tyler has a whole new perspective on, and appreciation for, his mom.

Chapter 21

MEDICAL IMPROVEMENT FROM PAST-LIFE REVIEW

Spirit heals my shoulder

The body cannot differentiate what "time" is, and the mind feels all things in the "now," making it very real. For instance, think of a time in your life when you were very angry from an injustice that had been done to you. If you think long enough on what transpired you can make yourself as upset as you were at the time the event occurred. You can also cry with tears of joy over the day your child was born, and relive the euphoria as if it were yesterday. Our emotions have a very powerful energy, and they mark us deeply with memories, even from events that happened in another lifetime. Our bodies react to our emotions: excess stress can cause high blood pressure, shingles, heart attacks, and so on. Sometimes mysterious illnesses can be a clue that we have not completely processed a belief or emotion from another life, and we carry it forward to our current one.

I had a sudden problem with my right arm in 2005. My right elbow and shoulder wouldn't move correctly, and I had pain that aspirin wouldn't take away. I strained to remember what I had done to it. Did I lift something too heavy? Nothing came to mind, and I tried to ignore it, but the pain and loss of mobility got worse. I went to my chiropractor for several months. An adjustment helped for a day, then it came back just like before. Eventually, I was walking around with my arm hanging like a rag from my shoulder and was taking lots of painkillers. I tried massage therapy. Nothing worked. This went on for months and my husband suggested that I ask Spirit what was

Chapter 21

wrong. It's a funny thing about people who have spiritual abilities—when they are stressed or worried they can't hear a thing! You can only connect with Spirit in a peaceful state of mind. That was really frustrating, for I knew Spirit would know what was wrong. During one session with a massage therapist I began to cry when she worked on the right shoulder. It didn't hurt enough to cry over, and I was embarrassed.

"I have people cry all the time," she reassured me. "It means there is emotion stuck in there."

A few weeks later, during a channeling session I was doing for my husband, Joe asked Spirit a question that caused a huge reaction in me. I am not fully present when channeling, allowing the Holy Spirit to take over my body and speech centers, so this reaction was very unusual. I found out later he had planned this in advance, knowing that if he told me about it I might psychologically block it, so he kept it to himself. Smart man! When he had talked with Holy Spirit for awhile on various topics, he asked the question, "What is wrong with Losara's right arm?" Spirit always answers with the highest truth, and immediately threw me into the past-life origin of the problem. I found myself reliving my most recent past life:

I was a young Jewish girl with long, dark hair, about fifteen years old. I was standing in a train yard with hundreds of people, and there was great chaos everywhere. Great screams and cries of anguish and pain permeated the air, and a feeling of panic choked me. I was holding onto my family for dear life. Nazi soldiers with machine guns were herding people into train boxcars, separating fathers from wives and children, and children from mothers and siblings. When it was my turn to get into one of the crowded train cars, I grabbed onto my mother with all my strength, and as one of the soldiers brutally ripped me away from my family I felt my shoulder separate agonizingly from my arm. I began to scream and cry hysterically while in the trance state, and my husband tried to calm me down. It was as real as if it had just transpired moments ago. The life review jumped forward in time to the concentration camp, where I was crammed into a barracks that had bunk beds three tiers high. There was no food, no water, no sanitation, no warm clothing, and no hope. It was full of the living dead: people in such shock that they could barely exist. To keep alive, I submitted to sexual abuse by the camp soldiers, no longer caring about anything except seeing

Chapter 21

my family again. The life viewscreen went forward to the day when we all lined up to take a shower . . .

Holy Spirit permitted me to see what happened when I died in that life, and I saw my spirit rise up out of my body, something I had not seen in any previous life review. A JOYOUS reunion with my family of that life took place, as they had already died in other concentration camps. The relief of being out of that hellish place and the joy of reuniting with my family was overwhelming, and the tears flowed. I then turned and looked back at the earth, and cried out to the people there, "What are you doing?! This is not who you are!" I vowed that when I returned to Earth for my next life, I would devote myself to telling people who they really are: precious souls of God, full of glorious potential. I would help them wake up from the sleep of ignorance and amnesia caused by their lack of connection to God.

As I came out of the past-life review, I immediately knew why my arm had been bothering me for months. The pain was triggered by a present-day occurrence, which brought back the subconscious memory of that life as a Jewish girl during World War II. Back in January of that year, my oldest son was accepted as a freshman into a university in Pennsylvania and would be leaving the following fall. All my life I had been the one who cried the most when people were leaving on trips or moving away. It was a joke in the family . . . "don't take Losara to the airport!" I was always afraid that I would never see them again, that something terrible would happen. Having my entire family ripped away from me in that last lifetime explained my fears. Now my son was moving far away from Colorado, and although I was very proud of him and very happy for him, the subconscious mind felt the dread of the separation and recreated the pain I had experienced in my shoulder during World War II.

Within two days the pain that had been so debilitating for months was gone. My conscious mind now recognized that the pain was not caused by a current situation, and released it totally. I can now say goodbye without falling apart, much to the relief of my family, and I know the person will return and I will see them again. Not all physical problems stem from past-life situations, but some do, and when all else fails, it can be a wise alternative to check into.

MEDICAL MIRACLE FROM PAST-LIFE REVIEW

Hypnosis heals a woman's tumors

My husband's ex-wife had this experience in 1984. The year he met her, she had surgery for a bone spur on one of her femurs. She recovered completely, but was left with a scar on her upper leg. Then, sometime later, the terrible pain came back; this time in both of her legs. They went to their chiropractor for treatment. He took x-rays, which revealed that a growth had appeared on the leg that did not have the surgery, as well as on the one that did. This was, of course, very frightening, and they went to see the orthopedist who had done the original surgery the previous year. He was quite concerned, but callously said, "In the worst-case scenario we would have to amputate your legs." Mary (not her real name) was understandably hysterical after that comment. Joe was determined to find an answer, and hearing that there was an expert from the Mayo Clinic visiting their area, made an appointment to have him look at Mary. This doctor also took x-rays, but from several different angles. He said he had never seen anything like it, and advised that the growths not be touched, fearing it could trigger a more rapid growth or cancer.

Mary was in chronic pain as the bone spurs continued to grow. Prior to this time, Joe had been delving into hypnosis and had met a professional hypnotist in Denver. He asked him if he thought hypnotherapy would help Mary, and the therapist agreed to try regressing her to see if there was something locked away in a childhood memory that might be causing the

Chapter 22

physical problem. She was desperate to find an answer that did not involve surgery or amputation, so she agreed to undergo a session of hypnosis. After a long process of relaxation techniques and visualization, the therapist was successful in getting Mary into a light hypnotic state. He was convinced that a childhood trauma was responsible for the bone growths in her legs, but he inadvertently asked the open-ended question, "Go back to the incident which is causing the abnormal pathology in your legs."

Immediately, Mary saw herself standing on a raised, wooden walk in front of a general store in the Old West. The town was small and dusty, and she could see she was clothed in a long, calico dress. She saw herself actually IN this life, not as an outsider looking in. She then saw a man dressed in 1800's-style clothing, whom she recognized as the ex-husband in her present life. He had also been her husband in the 1800's, and was a violent, jealous man. She began to see little snippets of that lifetime, mostly about her relationship with him. He was very controlling and went to extremes to watch her, fearing that someone would take her away from him because she was so beautiful. She saw in the vision that she had once tried to leave him. To keep her from running away again, he broke both of her legs across the femur with an ax handle. The hypnotic visions showed that she eventually had a child by this man. In her desperation to get away from him, she left the small baby and ran out across the desert. It was the last thing she was shown during the hypnosis session, and she did not know if she made it out alive.

As you can imagine, it was a traumatic experience to see that lifetime and to realize that her ex-husband had caused so much pain and anguish over a hundred years ago. In this life the couple had been drawn together again to resolve their karma with each other. Mary had absolutely no desire to have children and was uncomfortable around them. In this current life, however, she had successfully left that husband without secretly running away and without violence. The painful bone spurs were in the same place in her legs where they had been broken in that previous lifetime. After her hypnosis session, all pain left that very day, much to everyone's surprise. The hypnotherapist was astonished at what had transpired, realizing if he had not asked her subconscious mind to go to "the incident" that caused the problem, they may not have had such an incredible result. A week later, still pain-free, Mary had another set of x-rays from her chiropractor. The growths were completely gone, and never returned!

Chapter 23

PAST-LIFE THERAPY—A STORY OF HEALING ANGER

Spirit helps a five-year-old with a past life review

Cathy contacted me one day out of desperation. Her five-year-old, Tyler, had been having problems with anger that came up out of the blue, and he would swear at her, hit her, and demean her with taunting language. She had taken her son to several doctors and a child psychologist, and they were suggesting mood-altering drug therapy. Cathy did not want to put her son on drugs, as he was usually a happy child, full of energy and fun, and she was afraid of what the medicine would do to his personality. She asked me if I could help find out why her son was acting this way and what could be done to take away the anger. I told her the Holy Spirit can do anything, and asked for Tyler's full name and birth date.

I entered meditation after prayers for Tyler and Cathy, and immediately saw Tyler standing under a tree. Next to him was an ancient-looking man, like the figure of Father Time, and his grandmother, who had died the previous year. The old man symbolized that his problem was very old, and his grandmother was there for support. Behind Tyler stood a knight in full armor, dressed for battle, sitting upon a horse. This was from a past life as a fierce warrior in the fourteenth century. Spirit told me that Tyler had been taken captive by the Moors, and was treated badly by them, somewhere in ancient Turkey. They said that he had been a soldier in many lifetimes, most recently in the war in Vietnam. Spirit then directed me to write down their counsel.

* * *

HOLY SPIRIT:

"This heart has seen and experienced much atrocity by humanity, and chose Cathy as his mother for her loving character, hoping to heal his own. He carries anger at humanity and at God for allowing war. Tyler becomes very angry at displays of weakness or cowardice. Lifetimes of training in the art of war have left him with little in the way of tools to cope with disappointment or anger, and violence is a strong compulsion in him. Frustration at being small and not in control of his own life leads to outbursts of rage. If he finds a figure to give his 'allegiance' to he will be devoted and protective of that person. He respects strength. The removal of the past-life influences would help greatly, as well as centering the soul back to his aspects of love and understanding. Even though he is a child in body, his Higher Self saw the possibility of attaining healing by being born again to his mother, Cathy, who has been his mother before. Great love is there between these two."

Holy Spirit continued, with advice on how to help Tyler: "Just as this one falls asleep, have his mother say to him, 'Tyler, your lifetimes of war are over. This time you will experience healing for your angry heart. Allow the Grace and Peace of the Divine Mother to flow into your soul, and treat your mother with respect, for she is a reflection of Divine Mother.'"

* * *

The next day I read what I had been given by Spirit to Cathy over the phone. She was astonished that his problems stemmed from past lives, but said it all made sense. "He is always playing soldier and war. He uses phrases about the military and procedures in combat that he could not possibly know. This year, for his fifth birthday party, he wanted everyone to dress up in knights' costumes." She agreed to read the message from the Holy Spirit to Tyler every night as he fell asleep. Ten days later she called me in amazement. Her son was a totally different little boy; kind, loving, respectful, and in control of himself. "It's a miracle!" she said. She was now concerned that Tyler was going to spend a week with his biological father,

Chapter 23

who was aggressive and a poor disciplinarian with their son. I told her to read the message after she knew he would be asleep, that the Holy Spirit knew where to find him, and he would hear the words delivered by his mother. This worked very well, and she has had no problem with this type of behavior since then.

The words of Spirit were a holy command that Cathy read to her son each night. It was a command for this boy to remember who he really was, and that this lifetime was not one in which he had to prepare to do combat with another person. I have often seen that reminding a soul they are not in that past lifetime, where pain or horror had taken place, serves as a trigger for the mind. It snaps them out of a reaction that leads to experiencing the negative consequences resulting from a former life. In this case, Spirit reminded Tyler that his allegiance was to his mother, who is a symbol of the Divine Mother, and warranted his respect and love. Spirit helped to balance the warrior aspect of his soul with the aspects of love and understanding. Balance is the key, and finding out why this boy was unbalanced brought understanding and relief for this family.

THE DARK SIDE

Chapter 24

THE EXISTENCE OF EVIL

My personal encounter with the Dark Side

There has been a tendency in the recent decades of the New Age movement to dismiss the notion of evil, calling it the expression of "opposite polarities" or "the shadow that allows us to comprehend Light." I have always thought it was an ingenious trick by evil to convince these well-intentioned people that it does not exist. What better place to hide than out in the open, having people believe Satan is a myth? Spirit has told me evil most definitely exists, and that "Satan" is a consciousness, not an individual. (As opposed to Lucifer.) This satanic consciousness pervades all over the Earth, and its followers are most definitely real. In the spiritual world there are indeed demons, hideous creatures of energy, who can and do interfere with the people of Earth for the purpose of keeping them away from God and His Divine Energy.

I have had my own encounter with a demon, and will relate that story here. It is imperative that people know they MUST protect themselves when doing meditation or spiritual work, as you are opening yourself to all energies at those times. There are "tricksters" in the spiritual realm who love to masquerade as highly evolved spirits, and they will give "information" to a person who tries to channel, do automatic writing, Ouija-board messages, or spiritual readings. They are not easy to identify, but there is a way to make sure that you are not being bothered by a negative or evil spirit. ALWAYS pray for protection from God before you engage in any spiritual activity. If a spirit comes before you, demand that he or she "present thy soul" and watch what happens. It is rare that one can pretend to be of

Chapter 24

Light for long when they are not. You will see them darken in light or leave you. Demand that they leave if they are not of Light and do not serve God. They can appear as radiant beings, so do not be fooled. Putting on a costume of light and piety is not hard for them. Call upon the name of a holy being that you believe in if you need help. Holy beings are of the Divine Energy, and their very names vibrate with that holy frequency, so it is a powerful tool and aid. Do not ever be fearful. *Divine Energy rules over all energies* and cannot be beaten. (See the chapter in this book on how to clear negative entities.)

In a reading I was doing for my husband, Joe, the highly evolved spirit who came through me that evening asked, "Would you like to know why Light always wins over Darkness?" Of course, my husband said yes. "When Darkness faces Light it has to keep looking over its shoulder, like this," the saint said, turning his head around to illustrate the point. "Darkness is always waiting to see who will try to be the king of the mountain and knock them off of their position. Arrogance hides the fear that they are not really good enough to be on top, and remember, evil attacks its own. But Light, knowing that God Almighty stands behind it, stands firm and confident, assured that the Highest Power in the Universe is with him. There is no fear. There is absolute confidence in Light."

I learned the lesson of evil masquerading as Light the hard way, and was very blessed to have an intercession by a great Spirit of Light that saved me from my own folly. In meditation one evening many years ago, a magnificent spirit, radiant in appearance, came before me. He was incredibly handsome, with a smile that dazzled me. I was so dazzled that I forgot to ask him to "present thy soul" as I had been taught by Holy Spirit. I could see every facet of his beautiful face, right down to the hair in his eyebrows. He was dressed in a magnificent robe and was quite tall, with a dark, closely trimmed moustache and beard. Convinced that this was a spirit of some importance, I welcomed him. He asked me what my heart's desire was. I told him that above all else, I wanted to remember God and to achieve enlightenment. He told me he could help me with a shortcut to that noble dream. All I had to do was to give him my spiritual sword and he would put it into my heart, "completing the energy" that I needed to progress instantly to enlightenment. I, thinking that the Holy Grail of my quest was about to be given to me by an enlightened being, said yes.

Chapter 24

A note about the spiritual sword: I am told that everyone has one. It represents the true nature of a soul and is colored in various hues that match the frequency of the person. There are times when I have asked that a spirit present their sword, for I can instantly tell if they are of the Light by the color of it, and by it's brilliance. In my personal prayer that I say every day, I have included the words, "I carry forth before me my sword of truth and integrity." It is a very real thing, although it cannot be seen but by the spiritual eye.

I manifested my sword for the being, which in my case is turquoise in color and very bright, and handed it to him. He motioned for me to lie down in front of him and he stood over me, holding my sword high above my spirit body with both of his hands, ready to plunge it into my heart. I prayed that God would accept me and bless me with enlightenment, and was very excited that my long wait would be over. Suddenly, the look on the Spirit's face changed, and I saw the most evil smile crawl over his handsome features. In an instant, I realized that I had been tricked. As he began a mighty thrust with my sword, I saw a hand and an arm materialize to his side, and with the strength of the Divine, the hand of Christ Jesus reached out and grabbed the devil's wrist, stopping him cold! I was instantly thrown out of the trance state. The Christ used one portion of his arm to defeat Darkness. Such is the Power of God!

I was mortified at what I had allowed to take place. I was grateful beyond description for the Divine Intercession on my behalf. And I was greatly humbled that even when I was unaware that I was in danger, *God was not unaware of me.* There is no doubt in my mind that had that dark being actually impaled me with the sword, I would have died, most likely of heart failure. Grand energies were involved here. I learned a lot that night. I learned how foolish we can be when we want something so badly that we will entertain the way of a shortcut to get it. I learned that you NEVER give your spiritual sword to anyone, and that a being of Light would never ask you for it. A being of Light would not have had to ask what my heart's desire was, either. *A being of Light would never offer a shortcut to enlightenment,* knowing that all experience is designed for the growth of a soul, and that the lessons of enlightenment must be understood to their depths, taking root as *wisdom* in the spirit itself. I learned never to assume that a spirit is of the Light, even if they are beautiful and radiant. I believe that my inner prayer to God, before the evil entity had a chance to impale me, saved my life. My only thoughts were of being one with God. It remains one of the most important lessons I have ever had.

Chapter 25

A DANGEROUS ENCOUNTER

A psychic friend's dangerous visit from an evil entity

My husband, Joe, and I have been blessed with knowing a woman of great psychic ability, integrity, and intelligence. She is also the most blunt person I have ever met. The combination is priceless, to those who appreciate honesty and a sharp eye for stupidity. She was Joe's spiritual teacher during his early adulthood, and I met her shortly before we became engaged. I will call her Francis. She told Joe all about me, over twenty years before we met. During one of their lengthy talks about Spirit he sighed and said he wished he could meet someone like her, because all of the women he knew were shallow and uninteresting. Francis told him that he would, indeed, meet someone who had gifts of the Spirit, and that she would have very blue eyes and reddish hair. Joe was very excited. "Don't look for her, though," she said with a chuckle. "You won't meet her until you are in your forties." He was disappointed in her predicted timetable, and looked for her anyway, finally giving up when he was in his thirties. We met when he was forty-three.

Of all of the stories we have heard from Francis of her remarkable experiences over a lifetime of listening to Spirit, the one that is the most incredible to me is her encounter with a truly evil being. There are great similarities between the being she met with and the devil I was saved from. Francis is now eighty-four, and I called her for permission to tell her story, so that people would realize there IS an evil force out there.

Chapter 25

"Hell *yes*, there's an evil force! You mean people are so stupid now that they don't even know that?!" she asked. "Okay, just don't use my name, for God's sake!" I assured her that her privacy would not be compromised. She, like me, does not charge for her spiritual work, and like most psychics, she feels other's emotions. These can cause pain for her, physically and mentally, when she is near someone who is having problems. At our wedding rehearsal dinner she could not eat because of the inharmonious emotions of the people sitting across from her. She told us later that the man who was near her had unresolved issues from a previous marriage. We didn't even know our friend had been married, but found out he had been, years ago. Francis keeps her talents under wraps unless Spirit pushes her to say something. Then watch out!

Years ago, as she was getting ready for work one morning, her husband turned to her and said, "If someone tries to push you off the road, hold your ground." She looked at him in shock. This was a totally uncharacteristic thing for him to say, and had nothing to do with anything that was taking place in the usual morning rush to get to work. She asked him to repeat it, and he said, "I don't know why I am saying this, but hold your ground." Francis had been around the psychic block long enough to know that Spirit can and does use any means possible to get a message to someone when it is important, and she filed it away in her mind. Later, as she was driving to the doctor's office where she was employed as a nurse, she took her usual route that crossed a very narrow two-lane bridge. The bridge had a stone wall three feet high on each side, and when there was traffic in both directions the cars would pass within inches of each other. As she began crossing the bridge she saw a blue car on the RIGHT side of her car. This was defying the laws of physics, but there it was just the same. She could see the driver plainly, as they both had their windows open.

He was incredibly handsome, with dazzling eyes and a perfect smile. His dark beard and moustache were closely trimmed to his face. His smile then changed into an evil, arrogant grin that said, "Gotcha!" He began to go over into her lane, trying to force her car into the oncoming traffic. Ahead of them was a semi-tractor and trailer coming down the other side of the narrow bridge. Gleefully, the man yelled, "It's time to die!" and edging his car over even more, he pushed her over the dividing line. Francis remembered her husband's strange warning that morning and, thinking of him and her

Chapter 25

four children, held onto the steering wheel for dear life. The semi-truck came screaming past her, no more than two inches separating them from a head-on collision. Terrified, she looked to her right to see that the blue car had vanished. She pulled to the side of the road after crossing the bridge, shaking badly from the experience.

She was the first to arrive at work, and let herself into the back of the office to begin the morning duties of opening the front door and turning on lights. The office was arranged so that the lobby was separated from the receptionist's desk by a wall with a sliding glass window. As she began getting ready for the morning's patients, she looked up to see the man who had tried to run her off the road, grinning at her with that evil smile from the front desk's window.

"I don't give up so easily," he snarled.

"Neither do I!" she shot back at him. She quickly rounded the desk and went out the office door to the lobby, but found that he had vanished. Sitting in the waiting room was the first of the morning's patients. "Did you see that man who was just here at the window?" she asked him.

Puzzled, the man replied, "What man? There's been no one in here but me."

Francis maintains that this was a very real occurrence and that it happened in broad daylight. There is no one more truthful than this woman, and I fully believe her story. It is interesting that this evil being was able to create an illusion so realistically that he could have forced her into the oncoming traffic, certainly causing her death. Evil seems concerned with getting rid of spiritually talented people who have pledged themselves to absolute truth and integrity. I have read of other instances where highly honorable psychics and persons of great faith have had close calls with evil beings. And it is their faith in God, the Supreme Energy in the universe, that kept them safe. Light knew about the intent of the evil being that tried to kill Francis, and warned her. Light is the more powerful of the two forces, and they take care of their own.

Chapter 26

CLEARING NEGATIVE ENTITIES

Using Spirit to clear evil entities from people and haunted houses

Some souls do not go on to the Astral World when they die and they become earth-bound, roaming the world and attaching themselves to unsuspecting pedestrians. They are literally energy vampires, feeding off of your personal energy. Some of these lost souls are very negative spirits and they cause the person they hitch a ride with to feel irritated and run down. Sometimes your mood will take a nosedive for no apparent reason, and you ask yourself what happened. There are also lost souls who hang around the bars and taverns and drug alleys of town, all for the purpose of attaching to people who drink or do drugs. In this way they may enter into them (possession) and enjoy the habit they used to partake of when they were alive.

It has been known that a person under the influence of alcohol or drugs may not remember what they have been doing for a time; there is a good chance they were hosting a spirit who craved that "high" feeling, and a negative spirit took over the body of the addict long enough to actually be present in the consciousness. Plenty of material evidence suggests that it is not wise to consume alcohol and drugs, but the spiritual evidence is frightening. The claim of insanity while committing a crime under the influence of alcohol or drugs actually may have validity when you consider that possession from negative entities during these times is possible. You can pick them up anywhere—the grocery store, at work, school, the theater—in short, wherever there are people.

My Master Teacher, who is in the spirit realm, gave me more information about where these negative entity attachments come from. Not all of them are discarnate souls, he said, in fact the majority are not. His explanation follows:

* * *

SPIRITUAL TEACHER:

"Negative energies abound on this third-dimensional plane. THOUGHT FORMS can become creatures, and many negative attachments are these. They are difficult to keep away because the World Consciousness feeds them. Truly 'lost souls,' or souls who have not returned to the Astral Plane after death, are stuck in the third dimension. They are mentally deranged and very needy, like starving, wandering beggars. Having the angels of Light assist them back to God is the best way to help them and to rid these spirits of their vampirish need to take energy from you. Demons and evil spirits have an agenda to harm other beings and they delight in creating fear in people, thus weakening a soul's connection to God. NEVER show fear to these dark ones; always call upon a Christed Being (a being who is one with the Christ Consciousness) to keep them away. In this way Divine Energy will take care of them."

* * *

While attending a birthday party two years ago, a friend of mine was regaling me with the adventures of her vacation to the ancient ruins of Machu Picchu in Peru. As Lee was showing me the photographs she had taken, I could feel that something was wrong with her and I asked how she had felt lately. She admitted that she felt terrible since coming back to the United States, and was very run-down.

I looked at her and said, "Are you having nightmares?"

She was stunned that I knew. "Yes!" she exclaimed. "They have been really awful."

Chapter 26

I asked her if she had been ill while she was in Peru, and she answered that she had. I asked her if she had been depressed for no apparent reason. Again, Lee answered in the affirmative. "I think you have a negative entity attachment," I told her. "I will ask the Holy Spirit to cleanse your aura tonight." She told me of a native woman in Peru who had tried to warn her to beware of evil spirits at the ruins, as these spirits would be attracted to her Light. The native woman, who was quite old and did not speak English, wrote her a warning letter in Spanish. Lee, who spoke very little Spanish, did not have time to have it fully translated until she returned home.

That night I petitioned the Holy Spirit to cleanse Lee of all negative or evil soul attachments, following the procedure that is printed after this narrative. It turned out to be very difficult, and this indicated she had picked up a very bad spirit. Absolute faith in God and His ability to clear these negative entities is imperative when you are undertaking a cleansing. I get mad. They have no right to do this, and cause undue suffering to the unsuspecting victim. I also asked Spirit to help my friend sleep that night, and gave great thanks for the cleansing. The next day she called and said, "Wow! I slept great, and today I feel so much better!" The nightmares stopped and her energy level returned to normal, which for Lee was high gear. It was clear that she had picked up a very negative spirit while she had been in the ancient ruins, just as the old woman had warned her of doing.

I once had a call from a client in another state who was concerned about how her sister's house felt to her. She was convinced something evil was in that house, and asked if I would clear it. I assured her I would ask the Holy Spirit to do so that evening and asked for the names of the people who lived there, wanting to be thorough and cleanse their auras, too. That night I prayed for the clearing and was surprised at the resistance I was feeling in that house, particularly around her niece. This resistance felt evil, not just negative or lost. It was deliberately trying to cause harm. I knew something was causing this negativity, and it would return to her if she was not made aware that she should protect herself against attachments. I called my friend the next day and told her what I had sensed.

"What in the world has your niece been doing lately? Where has she been going that she could pick up such an awful spirit?" I asked.

Chapter 26

"Well," she answered quietly, "she goes to the bars a lot and plays pool there. And that's not all; she told me that one night an incubus attacked her in her room, and that it tried to have sex with her. She said she slapped it away, and could actually feel it trying to penetrate her."

I was simply aghast. "She slapped it away? How could she even keep sleeping in that room?" I exclaimed. "You call her and warn her that these things are not to be fooled with. That a demon even thinks it can try this with her is an indication she needs a *serious* change of personal vibration, and she must stay away from that bar!"

No wonder my friend had felt bad in that house! She had left the bedroom and slept on the sofa in the living room, rather than endure the foul nightmares she had experienced the previous night when she had stayed in her niece's room. The fact that the niece could refer to this demon by its proper name, "incubus" (a male demon who attacks his victims sexually), alleges that she *was* aware of what had attacked her, and that frightened me for her mental comprehension of what she was dealing with.

I have cleared the auras of my children when they suddenly become belligerent or grouchy, and it helps every time. (Works well on husbands, too!) Remember, these things attach all the time, wherever you go. If you hug someone who has a host of negative spirits hanging on, they can transfer them to you. It is best to protect yourself before you enter the workplace, or shopping mall, or any public place by asking the Holy Spirit to surround you with a white Light of protection. I had inadvertently picked up some negative spirits one day, and SAW them later when I entered a deep trance for a reading that night. They were truly frightening to look at and appeared to me as black manta ray-like creatures with mouths that were literally feeding upon my Light aura. Holy Spirit took them away and I was able to continue on with the reading.

Until I had actually seen them, I hadn't truly understood how real they were. The clearing of negative energy around a person or in a building has terrific effects on how much lighter and more positive people or the atmosphere of places feel. To see these negative forms was very sobering and it helped me to focus on my intent to engage the Holy Spirit to take them away. I knew that "thoughts are things," and that mental energy was literally the creative factor for everything in our lives; but to learn that we,

Chapter 26

as a group or as an individual, can create a conscious creature who lives in the fourth dimension was a big surprise. These creatures can become what Spirit calls "tricksters" who delight in fooling around with people's consciousnesses. They can become "guides" to people who are attempting to channel without the great discipline and intense meditation it takes to truly tap into Divine Energy.

I know of several delusional people who have "received messages" from the spirit world who were actually listening to lower-energy souls or tricksters. Sadly, these people would not listen to the possibility that the pages of "information" they were writing were lies. They would tell anyone who questioned them about the inconsistencies of their writings that they were just jealous of their ability to communicate with Spirit! I call this childishness a case of "my channel's better than your channel" and maintain that it is not hard to spot a fraud. The delusional person's need to feel special overrides the common sense alarm that would normally go off when you "hear voices" that are coming from your own mind or the consciousness of a trickster energy. It is wise to guard yourself from these negative energies, and to clear yourself every day. I also recommended that you cleanse your entire house of negative energies that build up over time, especially after a family argument, or when you have had guests over. People notice the difference right away, and you will be amazed at how light everything feels. Children love to be a part of a house cleansing and it helps make them aware of the invisible energies in our world.

Chapter 27

DIRECTIONS FOR CLEARING NEGATIVE ENERGIES

How to clear yourself and your home of negative spirits

The MOST important thing to remember is that we are incapable of doing this alone.

With great reverence, you must acknowledge where the power to clear negative energy comes from: God. Never be afraid of negative or evil forces, for Divine Energy is far stronger than these. Treat these energies as the nuisance that they are—they have no power over you unless you give it to them or are unaware of them. Most people are unaware of them and do not have a high enough vibration to keep them away. You can pick up negative attachments anywhere: the grocery store, school, work, or from someone else who has them. It is a very good idea to cleanse yourself everyday, and especially after you have been in a crowded area, like an airport, a business meeting, or a concert. Always ask the Holy Spirit to bless someone you see who is obviously in a negative state of mind or is having a bad day, for they will attract negative energy and will give it away. The best way to do this is to pray for the person and imagine a pink bubble of Light around them, as you ask the Holy Spirit to aid them.

Remember, God is the One with the power. You must center yourself and know that the Holy Spirit HEARS you, because they do. You may use

Chapter 27

any prayer that you feel confident in and can say with great sincerity, but this is the prayer that I use:

"I put forth the intent and the prayer that the Holy Spirit will, through the Grace of God and with the help of the Angels of Light, release and remove all negative entities and evil attachments from me (or fill in the name of someone you wish to clear). They are NOT allowed to be here! Take these attachments far away to their proper place in God, and heal my (his/her) aura with Divine Light. Bless me (him/her), and bless me indeed! I give great thanks for this service."

Then picture the angels literally taking away these attachments, and see a golden-white Light around yourself or the person you are cleansing. Be sure that you are at peace, not anxious about the negative entities you are trying to remove. *The power is in the peace.* I always ask Holy Spirit to take them away to their proper place in God because they need healing, and you do not want to just set them loose to attach themselves onto someone else. If you are dealing with an evil Spirit always call upon a high energy, such as Christ, or one of the saints. To invoke the name of a Divine Being carries the Divine Energy needed to rid yourself or others of evil. It's true! Claim it as your right as a child of God. Evil can be stubborn, but they will leave if you demand it with Divine Energy. If you are unsure that you did it "right," do it again. It certainly won't hurt, and everyone needs as many blessings as they can get.

Your results will be as good as your confidence in God. That is why some people need someone else with experience to do this. Then there are times you cannot get into the peace and you may need help. The more you do it, the more confidence you will have. You CAN do this! You will see the difference in yourself when you do it correctly, for you will feel better within minutes. And when you see it, you will know this is real and that God hears you.

When you are clearing your house of negative energy you use the same process, but go from room to room to truly get the great effect of Light in your home. It is not required that you move at all, but psychologically it helps you know that you have completed the removal of lower energies. To really create a lighter atmosphere, light candles in each room and ask Spirit to bless the rooms as you move through them. Light your favorite incense to carry with you. I often sing hymns throughout the house and open the windows. You are creating higher energies as you do this, and your focus

Chapter 27

will be strong in attracting higher frequencies. Kids love doing this with you, and their high and festive vibrations help as well.

A friend of mine uses Native American techniques to bless houses, and uses a special chime that she gongs into the corners of each room. She helped me clear a haunted house one spring, and we cleared each member of the family as well. We also did the entire grounds of the home. I had identified the spirit of a man who had taken up residence in the large detached garage, and was told by the homeowner that a man had been shot and killed on the property by his wife over fifty years earlier. I also detected a very negative entity in the teenage boy's bedroom. Interestingly, a large three-wick candle had been split down the middle as the boy slept, and he had been having nightmares for weeks.

I also identified a recently departed soul who had been hanging around the house trying to get a message to the client by causing the chair in the family room to rock by itself. He was a friend of the owner's and wanted him to get a message to his widow and two children that he was okay. He correctly gave me the name of his son, Adam, whom he said was five years old, and told me that he also had a new baby. All the information proved to be true. Two weeks after the clearing, the owner called to say that he could not believe the difference in the feel of the house, and that the strange footsteps, the rocking of heavy chairs in the living room in the night, and the bad dreams had all stopped happening.

For those who wish to use a pendulum to help with the focus of positive energy, I highly recommend reading a book by Raymon Grace called *The Future Is Yours*. I was privileged to meet him several times, and not only is he the coolest human being on the planet, he is also of the highest caliber in character and talent. He refers people to the great material on dowsing instruction on the Internet called the "Letter to Robin," which can be downloaded for free by going to *www.dowsers.org*. It is helpful to use a pendulum, if you have one, only because it is a good tool of focus. We have a tendency to lose focus very quickly, thinking about the next thing we have to do or what to make for dinner. The pendulum itself is useless, so don't designate powers to it that it does not possess. Always remember that your INTENT is everything, and what you are focusing on is what you will attract. Keep yourself in tune with the Highest Energy and you will not be so susceptible to the negative energies all around you. Make spiritual cleansing as habitual as taking a shower every day.

A WORD ABOUT HELL

Mother Mary takes me to "Hell"

In all of the thousands of readings I have done over the last eighteen years, I have yet to see anyone in "hell"—that place of fire and brimstone that has been preached about from many a pulpit in our religious society. I can even attest to the fact that people who commit suicide do not go to such a place, because I have spoken to them. One of the readings I did on a young man who ended his own life is in this book. It is a remarkable story. I have, however, seen a place that would certainly be a hellish place to be, and was taken there by a being of incredible love. This place would be what is described as a "lower astral plane," where souls of very low frequency can become trapped by their own unrecognition of God.

One evening during meditation, I beheld the Lady Mary, earth mother of Jesus the Christed One. Her radiance was unlike anything I had ever seen. Her Light filled my entire sight, and the love that surrounded her was complete and total peace. I was awestruck, to say the least. She held out her hand to me. "Come. I want to show you something," she said. "Hang on tight, and do not let go of me."

We were suddenly sailing through space (by way of astral projection), and even without a reference point, I could tell that we were far from where we had just come. Mary's Light surrounded us as we glided effortlessly through unimaginable vistas of stars. After a time, we literally descended into an area that was completely black. It was a place void of light, and I had no idea what we were doing or where we were. Off in the distance, I could see something

Chapter 28

fast approaching us: a yellow-green glow. As the strange illumination came closer, I could see shapes in the greenish light. Then suddenly, there they were: hideous creatures that appeared as a mass of sticky, foul blobs. They had bulging eyes opened in terror, and huge, gaping mouths of sharp teeth with which they tried to bite us. They screeched and cried in agony, and glommed onto one another, unable to become free from the mass. It was a truly terrifying sight, and I held onto Mary's hand for dear life.

She was perfectly calm. She told me that these souls were far removed from God by their own choices, and that their agony was caused by not being able to receive or to remember the Light. Mary's Light protected us from the pitiful beings, and she sent love to them. Far off in the blackness, I saw a stationery ray of bright Light that remained fixed on one point. A being was descending down through the ray, but it was not one of the globular creatures below us. "Behold, a Rescuer!" Mary exclaimed. It was an angel, she told me, who had volunteered in great compassion to come down to this low astral plane to bring up one of the beings who was stuck there. They take a very great risk to do this, for they can become trapped there as well in their attempted rescue. Tears came to my eyes at the sight of Divine Compassion in action before me. Mary and I then ascended to another plane, and I have no recollection of what we spoke of afterward.

After I had been married to my husband for a time, I told him of the visitation with Mary and where she had taken me. Joe was astonished, for he had been to this very place in a remarkably vivid dream the year before we met. He had been keeping a dream journal on and off over the years, and had recorded this one because of its intensity and feeling of realism.

In his dream, he found himself suspended and floating in space, not outer space, but a dark space where there was absolutely no light. He felt a searing emotional pain that went from his throat to his heart and solar plexus. The feeling was of a tremendous loss and an unspeakable agony. Breathing was difficult, and he found that he was enclosed within a large cube whose walls were composed of bluish humanoid beings. These creatures had eyes that were wide open, staring as if they were in a constant state of shock. Their bodies were mashed together to form the walls, intertwined in a tangled fashion, and he was bound within this space. He could feel their pain, and as he tried to escape he began to feel frantic because there was no way out of the agony. The agony was of loss, hopelessness, suffocation, and constraint,

Chapter 28

and it was all internal, all within. Joe began to feel panicky, for as he tried to move to a different part of the space, or change his perspective in any way, he found that there was no way to escape the searing pain and horror. He suddenly sat up in bed, gasping for air. Reflecting upon this later, he said he felt that he had visited a place of absolute agony and hopelessness, and he was amazed at how debilitating it was. He had no idea why he had been shown this terrible scene. And he was very glad he woke up.

As I was told by Mary, this is a place where beings who have shunned the Light of God go when they are not incarnate. There are many levels of existence in God's Universe, and we choose where we will reside, not by signing up for a spot we want to live in with friends, but by attracting the matching area of frequency that our soul vibrates with. We are beings of energy, and we each vibrate at a certain frequency, depending upon our soul growth. Those souls who have a lower light frequency will automatically be drawn, by the Law of Attraction, to one another in the dimension that suits where they are in vibration. Those souls who have higher frequencies will be drawn to a place of higher vibration. It is the same as on any planet: like attracts like, and just as in a non-physical state, you will be drawn to people who are more like you here on Earth.

I was very shocked to experience such a place, and was very grateful to Mary for showing me this. I was reminded of the scene in the movie "Ghost" where the man who had lived a life of crime and had a total disregard for human life found himself hauled off by black demons when he died. More than anything, I was touched by the love and courage of the angel who was "the Rescuer," trying to save a tortured soul from that awful existence. By the Law of Free Will, we have the right to reject God and the Light, and by the Mercy of our Creator Father, we have the assurance that He will never give up on us, no matter how many lifetimes it takes.

SPIRITUAL ADVICE

Chapter 29

INTRODUCTION TO SPIRITUAL ADVICE

Be careful what you ask for: the humorous, touching, practical, and profound words of Spirit

Most people go to psychics to see into their future, to help them make decisions, and to receive hope that things will be better than they are experiencing currently. Some go to see if psychic phenomena are real, to answer deep questions man has not been able to answer, or to find cures for ailments. In my opinion Edgar Cayce, the seer from Kentucky, was the best psychic of modern times. His communication with Spirit was incredible, and his readings, now archived in Virginia Beach, Virginia at the Association for Research and Enlightenment, are national treasures for the whole world to share. He was an impeccable trance channeler, and the information that he received literally fills volumes.

If one has access to an impeccable channel, one of very high integrity and accuracy, only the highest truth is given to the seeker from that medium or channeler. If the person seeking truth follows through with the advice given, wonderful results can be had. It is a *choice* to follow through, and therein lies the catch. Results rely on the free will participation of the seeker. Spiritual advice, when given by a high source, is never given lightly and it is a privilege to receive it. The goal of the Holy Spirit in giving advice is always the same: to create change for the better, to promote the growth of a soul, and to ease suffering.

Chapter 29

Spiritual advice ALWAYS involves the teaching of the Laws of Spirit, for *everything* is influenced by these Laws. These readings invariably point out the transgression of a Law, for that is where all problems we have on this Earth lie; whether it be about finances, health, relationships, or employment, Spirit will use the inquiry to teach about God and the Laws. I will include in this section stories about spiritual advice that astounded me or made me laugh or cry. The one consistency I have found in all of these readings for advice is that you could give them to any human being on the planet and they would understand them and see themselves in them. We all have the same problems and failings, and we all need help.

Some of these readings for advice are very short and sweet and to the point, and these are my favorites. I have collected many of these and joke that someday, when I am an old lady in a rocking chair, I will stitch each one of these sayings on a pillow and fill my whole house with pillows of wisdom. As an example, during one channeling session with a grandmother who was having trouble reaching her granddaughter with logic and reason, she vented her frustration and asked the Holy Spirit what they advised. Without missing a beat, Spirit said, "Stupid is stupid, and you may say so!"

Often, when I am just doing routine things, Spirit will offer a pearl of wisdom to me or admonish me for a weakness that I have. One day I was mumbling and complaining under my breath about all of the impossible tasks I had to do, when my spiritual teacher yelled in my ear, "Don't tell me what you can't do—tell me what you CAN do!" Well, that sure got my attention! Spirit is always very compassionate, however, and one evening in meditation, after going through a very traumatic series of events and feeling completely hopeless, I heard the very comforting voice of the Holy Spirit say, "A day is not a life." I have said those precious words to myself as a reminder many times.

Questions from my clients can result in a dictation of many pages from the Holy Spirit or from my Master teacher. These readings are fascinating, covering topics that range from how the Law of Magnetism works to how to discipline a belligerent child. What I have found is that God is concerned with everything, whether it is a problem you are having or whether you were just wondering about something. This truth is what I feel is most important for people to understand: God is HERE—right here—all the time!

THE DEFINITION OF INNER HARMONY

A dissertation from a spiritual Master about personal chaos

During a prolonged time of unease and chaos in my life, I sought the advice of the Holy Spirit to see how to address my problems. What follows is the dictation I received during a meditation session from my spiritual Master teacher, who is currently on the other side. It remains one of my all-time favorite pieces of spiritual advice to pass onto friends and clients who feel overwhelmed with life.

* * *

SPIRITUAL TEACHER:

"*Inner harmony does not come from a lack of chaos from the outside world.* This kind of false harmony is temporary and will be shattered upon the re-entry of chaos. True harmony comes from within; an all-pervading peace of confidence, authority, and silent power. True harmony cannot be moved, interrupted, or shattered by outside circumstances. It is at rest, and can, at the same time, focus intently. This is power!

"It knows all situations have a solution, and settles only for the best solution. All answers come from God to a harmonious heart, as all hearts

Chapter 30

in harmony only seek God's answers. ALL problems can be solved with God, but only a harmonious, still mind and heart will hear His response. Concentrate on God, the perfect stillness, as you meditate, not on the problem. Listen and expect an answer. KNOW it comes, and *be appreciative*. Do not judge the length of time (to hear the solution) as a difficulty of God's, but as a poor reception by you.

"Fear, anger, sorrow, anxiety, and depression are as a storm upon the sea, and the dove cannot land upon a ship tossed on the waves of emotionalism. Invite the dove, the answer from God, and still the waters so it may land upon your ship. Then set sail in earnest for the course suggested to you. A mind always in harmony can receive all the time, no matter how diverse the trip, as its sails are always open to receive the wind, the Holy Spirit of God.

"As you know, Losara, you can hear the Holy Spirit whenever you have a need, even when you are unaware of a need, and it can be loud and clear, instantaneous guidance. You are NEVER, ever alone. Clear the lines in your mind, and calm the seas of your heart, and think of God. The Law of Attraction will bring you to Him."

* * *

Chapter 31

TRYING NOT TO THROW UP ON AN AIRPLANE

Spirit diverts my attention from sickness by telling a story

God is everywhere all the time, and He is concerned with your every situation. I was shown this yet again as I returned to Colorado with my oldest son, Tyler, after visiting his university for orientation. As we were boarding the flight from Pennsylvania, a very loud and angry passenger was getting seated across the aisle from me. Not looking forward to sitting around this woman's negative energy, I prayed that the Holy Spirit would calm the irate woman and send her healing, positive energy. Within seconds she was smiling and pleasant, and settled in for the flight. Then an infant in the back of the plane went on a crying jag, and everyone groaned, knowing that it would be a very long flight indeed if the baby kept that up. I sent pink light and love to the little guy, but the screaming continued on and on. How come it didn't work that time?

I prayed to know what went wrong, and my Master teacher appeared in my spirit vision to answer my question. He pointed out to me that in the first case with the angry woman I had asked the Holy Spirit to calm her, whereas in the second case of the unhappy baby, I had tried to send Light myself, forgetting to ask Spirit to do it *for* me. "'Of myself I can do nothing,' remember?" he reminded me, referring to what the Master Jesus said about how "the Father within" Him was the Doer of all things. My

Chapter 31

spiritual teacher calmed the baby at once, and a collective sigh of relief was heard throughout the plane.

Immediately after takeoff we encountered heavy turbulence, and having weak stomachs, Tyler and I were both contemplating reaching for the airsick bags in front of us. I decided to see if my spiritual teacher could help me focus on something else. With that thought, and already being tuned in to him from a few minutes earlier, my teacher instantly took me (by way of consciousness travel) to a place where we were standing underneath a cypress tree that was covered in Spanish moss. I couldn't figure out why we were there, so I just looked around a bit, feeling sorry for the poor tree that was being smothered by the ugly moss.

My teacher read my thoughts, of course, and said, "No, no! Don't feel sorry for the tree. It has an agreement with the moss, and it gets just enough light to stay alive."

I still felt sad for the tree, thinking how much better it would be without the moss. My teacher continued on with his discourse, showing that he had not chosen this location on a whim.

"People are just like the tree with the Spanish moss," he said. "You have an agreement with the World Consciousness which covers you in a veil of ignorance and allows just enough Divine Light through to keep you alive. When you renounce the veil, the World Consciousness, you will remember God and throw the veil away to receive your full measure of Light!"

I sat there in astonishment, my nausea gone.

"Focusing on the World Consciousness causes you to be afraid of everything," he continued, "because you do not remember that Creator Father and Divine Mother will take care of you. When you focus on Divine Consciousness you see the truth, and you fear nothing."

Chapter 32

THE LESSON OF BETRAYAL

Why we must all suffer from betrayals in our lives

This lecture from Spirit falls into the unsolicited category, and came as a result of an experiment I was trying out during an elementary school meeting. An election recall was being put up on the agenda, asking parents to vote on whether or not a board member should be asked to step down for actions and remarks made that were not consistent with school policy. The meeting had turned a bit ugly, although those in charge were doing their best to keep it from becoming so. As I was sitting and watching the proceedings, I silently asked Spirit about the character of the man accused of wrongdoing, trying to practice the art of discernment.

Immediately, I heard from the Holy Spirit, "This is a lesson for him and for all concerned. It is about betrayal."

I didn't have paper with me to write anything down, and I was hearing a great lecture on this subject, so I asked Spirit to hold it until I could get home and copy the dictation. The man in question was recalled at the end of the evening's vote, and we adjourned for the night. After putting the kids to bed, I was finally able to sit with pen and paper, and my spiritual teacher came in to tell me about the Lesson of Betrayal.

Chapter 32

* * *

SPIRITUAL TEACHER:

"There are certain Universal lessons that all souls must learn, and the condition of betrayal is one. They must see BOTH sides of betrayal, so a person becomes the betrayer and also the betrayed. The lessons are given in degrees of severity, and are repeated many times throughout the lifetimes of the soul until it is completely and thoroughly known and understood. This is not simply a matter of experiencing both sides a few times. If it is not UNDERSTOOD in its ENTIRETY it can recycle again and again. Some souls have many lifetimes of betrayals; in fact most do.

"The goal is to understand both *why* the betrayer betrays, and how it feels to be betrayed. Karmic Law has a hand in it, because if the full measure of the lesson is not learned, it will be repeated. Why is it important for all souls to understand betrayal from both sides? To obtain an understanding of God and the Dark Ones. Not only for the sake of learning the value of honor, but for the value of forgiveness. In this way the abhorrence for betrayal becomes permanently bound to a soul, along with the ability to see and understand the cause of the betrayal, the 'why' of the equation.

"Most all betrayals are for greed and power, and are fueled by arrogance. Some betrayals are done to end an intolerable situation, and the perpetrator sees no way out of a situation he feels helpless to change. (For instance, a person knows a friend has committed a crime or has dishonored another person and feels he must tell the truth.) The impact of a betrayal can be so deep it must be worked on for more than one incarnation. In having ALL souls experience both sides of honor God hopes to eliminate forever the desire to betray anyone.

"Christ Immanuel demonstrated the betrayal lesson by allowing Judas to betray him to the ultimate penalty. He understood the lesson entirely and allowed the crucifixion—also a betrayal—and rose above it all tremendously and with Grace. The betrayal from Lucifer was a very deep wound to God and to the Universe. In ordering all souls to attain understanding He avoids a repeat of that circumstance, adds to the maturity of each soul, and teaches that betrayal, the ultimate insult, leads to war.

Chapter 32

"In order for healing to take place one must practice forgiveness of self (for allowing the betrayal in the first place, as we attract all circumstances to ourselves) and resolve hatred. A person must experience both sides of betrayal in the interest of true understanding. Highly evolved souls have no capacity to betray another (it is unthinkable) and understand that the lower vibrations of arrogance, greed, fear, and the drive for power fuel those who betray another. The betrayers are not one with God, and desire what another has because they do not share or feel God's pure love or power which will provide all they need. They are separated in their states of mind and heart from God.

"Fear is the root cause of all betrayals. Fear is the condition of feeling less than, left out, of not being loved, or being unaware of the true nature of BEING—where one is afraid of annihilation or the end of existence. (They fear death so much that they will betray another to save themselves, not realizing that they do not "die.") When betrayal occurs the REAL cause IS fear. Find the reason for the betrayal and you will see, for greed is the fear of lack to a severe degree, being power hungry is a fear of having anyone in control of you, and arrogance, when broken down, is a fear of truly not being loved or recognized. Arrogant ones need recognition, fearing that others are better than they are, even though they proclaim that they are superior. Ones who feel superior are afraid of inferiority and that it shall taint them. They do not go beyond their arrogant disgust of beings weaker than them (or less educated, poorer, or mentally deficient) to the healing light of compassion for all. The finest example of compassion was, of course, Jesus Immanuel.

"A lesson in how to avoid betrayal—both aspects—is learned when a society holds TRUTH above all things, for the fears behind betrayals will be spoken of and misunderstandings can be dealt with. Arrogance, greed, and the lust for power, all reasons for betrayal, can be healed in a society which recognizes the value of each soul and honor is the only way of life. The material universe has a long way to go in its healing of betrayal. On the astral planes all thoughts are known, and truth is the order of life. If one were to plan a betrayal or harbor evil intent, he would literally wear it for everyone to see."

* * *

Although this dictation on betrayal was terrific, it left me with a lot of questions, and after talking with a friend who was in the middle of a doozy of a "lesson on betrayal," I asked my spiritual teacher to explain it further. This woman, "Judy," had been left by her husband for a younger woman, her church had turned its back on her, she was being thrown out of her house, and her children did not believe that their father was living with another woman. (The mistress would go to a friend's house when the kids came over for their weekend visits.) Judy's lawyers had taken $60,000 from her to help win the case against her husband in court, and they were no help at all. She was now broke, and broken in spirit. "The lawyers promised me everything, and I got nothing! They only told me what I wanted to hear," Judy said. She was understandably bitter. I have seen people suffer worse betrayals, too. I was curious about several things. For example, if we have thousands of betrayals over hundreds of lifetimes, when is one done with that awful lesson? Being betrayed is one of the most hurtful things in life. If there was a way to get out of the cycle of betrayal, I wanted to know about it. I presented this question to my Master teacher one afternoon during mediation. Here was his response:

* * *

SPIRITUAL TEACHER:

"To show one has completed the lesson on betrayal, he must so thoroughly understand the nature of, or cause of, betrayal that not only is it impossible for him to contemplate, let alone perform, an act of betrayal, he also KNOWS that any act of betrayal against him concerns a lesson FOR the betrayer. Christ, upon the cross during his crucifixion, said, 'Father, forgive them, for they know not what they do.' The betrayal act could not touch his soul, though it could destroy his body for a time, and he knew all of these souls would accrue terrible karma for killing an Avatar, *so he asked God to lessen their karma, to forgive them, because in their lower state of evolution they did not understand their error.*

"Christ himself could not forgive, *meaning change*, their karma, but God could, so he petitioned the Creator to consider doing so. Therein lies the lesson, Losara, not just in avoiding betraying anyone, but in understanding why it happens in the first place; to see the REASON behind such an act and say, 'You are doing the best you know how from the level of soul growth you have attained.' *To not hold a grudge after one is betrayed is of the highest order of soul maturity, and is rare indeed.* This is why I always say to you,

Chapter 32

'Take no prisoners'—take no EMOTIONAL prisoners—after personal disappointments occur, for you only tie yourself to these people for future karmic interaction by using the cosmic glue, emotion, to attract them to you later, in other lifetimes.

"Your own regrets of the errors you have committed in life show that you 'knew not' what you were doing at the time. So it is with all souls. Seeing people as SOULS, not mother, father, son, daughter, boss, spouse, neighbor, or friend helps tremendously in forgiving others as they disappoint you. Not all souls are mature, and these ones are learning through the errors of their life experiences, just as you do. It does not mean that you have to invite your betrayers to dinner, it means that you truly wish them well on their journey to a higher state of being, and you discard thoughts of revenge or anger, which only hurt YOU by attracting negativity your way.

"This is a hard lesson, to be sure, for reaction to such a blindsiding event against you stings to a high degree, and being emotional creatures, your first response is rage and disbelief. It is your SECOND response that is the most important. You have a choice in how to respond to the betrayer. That response is an indication of your soul's growth and your personal character. One can choose wisely or unwisely in his reaction. 'Turning the other cheek' can be a response of cowardice or of true understanding, depending upon the circumstances. (Are you doing so because you are afraid of confrontation or because you know that further involvement is not needed?) It is a fine line, forgiveness, and is measured by the INTENT of the person wronged.

"When a person has REAL knowledge of the oneness of all life, he sees how retaliation serves no one, and only harms himself. This is not to say that dangerous souls should be let off for crimes committed. Responsibility for one's actions must be addressed. I am speaking of emotional attachment of a negative nature which, as an example, tattoos that other person's vibrations onto you to resolve later. Much 'food for thought' for you on this issue!"

* * *

DEALING WITH BULLIES IN THE WORKPLACE

Spiritual advice regarding an employer whose tactics were hard to endure

An old friend of mine had just started a new job in his field of technology, and called to have me ask the Holy Spirit to advise him on how to handle his new boss. The manager of his end of the project was arrogant and demeaning to his employees, and "Peter" did not want to speak his mind and lose his job, nor could he endure the awful treatment he saw everyone else cower from. He had wanted to write a scathing rebuttal letter to the manager who had been overly critical and rude to him in front of other employees. The response from my teacher in the spirit world was immediate, wise, and practical. I did two readings for this man on the subject of bullies in the workplace. Here is the first dictation from Spirit:

* * *

SPIRITUAL TEACHER

"If honor is maintained with a degree of graciousness, these ones (bullies) can be circumvented and may even become allies instead of adversaries. Always is such a person, the arrogant know-it-all, suffering from fear and a feeling of unworthiness. Do not fall into the role of liar, one who falsely presents an agreeing attitude to smooth out irritations, because all respect is lost and

Chapter 33

the tyrant takes advantage of such fools easily. The art of diplomacy here must have the sharp edge of TRUTH at its throat so as not to misinterpret or mislead the level of awareness of all parties involved. Mistakes cannot be permitted to mollify an inept 'superior,' for the worker suffers the results of the outcome of the mismanaged work. [*Author's note*: The employees were scared to point out the manager's errors in procedures.]

"Always remember that all wars begin with an insult, so use care and tact in correcting an overseer's error. Ask the Holy Spirit to put an aura of Divine Cooperation around all parties, yourself as well, who are included in the project. Remember that you must ask the assistance of Divine Beings to move Divine Energy. Weaker and low-frequency beings can be helped or moved by Divine Energy if you state your intent to God first. *Intent is ALL!* This carries the emotion behind the visualization of your request. Make your intent of a noble cause—not to get your own way, but to truly serve your new work-place—and request the IMMEDIATE help of the Holy Spirit. Then give thanks that it is being done. The words will come to you as you pray, 'Show me how to write a letter that defines the way I expect to be treated without insulting anyone concerned.' Then expect inspiration within the time you need it."

* * *

The letter my friend wrote was a beauty, but I took a pen and edited out all of the insults (sentences that started with "you") as this had been a direct piece of advice from Spirit. It was logical and very well thought out and stated his position without being adversarial. He delivered it to his boss, and his boss's superiors, by email that next day, and around 6:00 p.m., as I was making dinner, I heard another dictation begin from Spirit for Peter. I grabbed a pen and wrote down this message:

* * *

HOLY SPIRIT:

"Intellectual bullies are no different than physical tyrants; when they see a weaker individual they will continue the abuse as long as it is tolerated by the 'victim.' A stronger soul who demands change in that person's ways will win because bullies always run from a true challenge. Cowardice is the core

Chapter 33

element of a bully, for arrogance is very afraid of not appearing to be the king of the hill. You will see a change in this manager's attitude toward you, but not toward the others. To run away (change jobs) or meekly surrender is not the choice of a person of honor. To bully a bully never works, for arrogance is present in both parties and usually a war erupts.

"Now that you have delivered your statement to your manager, foster cooperation, treating your 'superior' as an EQUAL, and use the invitation given to discuss all issues you need to. He sees your strength now, as do others there, and he will want to appear as a comrade, equal in strength, reason, and logic. You were wise in seeking Spirit's wisdom to tame your usual response of rage, and in centering yourself to allow for a clear and factual response to the unreasonable and unprofessional 'style of management' your boss pushes on everyone. Now proceed with focus, and always align in PEACE with the Divine Energy so insight can be used each day."

* * *

When I read this last dictation to Peter that evening, he was amazed. Not only did his manager respond positively to his email, but he used the exact wording that the Holy Spirit had quoted above. The boss had excused his own bad behavior toward his employees by saying that others did not agree with his "style of management" (which was to shout at and belittle people in front of others) and that it was "a miscommunication" to Peter when he thought he was being accused of not handling his work appropriately. He told him that his door was always open for discussions. The next day, Peter's boss was *very* cordial to him, and all the other employees were in shock. They asked him what he had done to get on the manager's good side. He had stood up for himself in honor, and had made sure to bless everyone he worked with, calling upon Holy Spirit to douse the building with Divine Cooperation.

Chapter 34

PURPOSE AND FREE WILL: THE GIFT OF SELF-DETERMINATION

Spirit answers a client's questions about the "unfairness" of life

People often ask me about the difference between free will and destiny. Every soul has been given the gift of free will, and they use this when they plan a lifetime on Earth before incarnating. They are coached by higher beings and angels before they are born, and once they are here physically their plan becomes their destiny (i.e., destination). I explain that they have the right to ditch the plan they made, exercising their free will, or to follow it. There is always a "Plan B" in the wings, so to speak, and as Spirit has told me countless times, "The Plan is perfect, because it is flexible." That refers to individual plans as well as the Plan for all of Earth. Yes, the Earth has a BIG Plan, one that will affect the entire universe. For now, I will concentrate on an individual's life plan and how free will and destiny mix together to form a complex life pattern.

A client came to see me about something that was really bothering him. He was very unhappy about how his life had turned out so far. He had experienced some failures in the business world, and after beating himself up, turned his anger on God for not helping him succeed. Once he got started down the path of negativity, his anger went out to anyone who was successful or wealthy, and then all of life looked grim and unfair indeed. Why were some people lucky? It wasn't fair! God should have blessed him with parents who were rich, etc. I posed a question to him: "What is more fair than the Law of Free Will? What is unfair about 'Do whatever you want?'" When people do not understand the Law of Attraction and how they bring everything, good or bad, into their own life, they look for someone to blame. Free will is the first rule of the Law of Attraction, but there is also another important factor in this equation—desire. As I was listening to this client go on about the unfairness of the world I was also hearing Spirit in my head, beginning a dialogue in answer to his comments. When I could find some quiet time and a paper and pen, the dictation from my spiritual teacher began to flow rapidly.

* * *

SPIRITUAL TEACHER:

"Desire in a soul is the fuel to the potential each one was created with. *Your purpose is to realize your potential in and with God!* All things ARE possible in God. The desire to be great *at* something is different than a desire to *be* great. Greatness is measured by a social meter stick; it is someone's opinion of you. To become great at something is a measure of proficiency, determined by practice over a period of time. Desires are necessary to move forward in existence. Stagnation occurs when there is no forward momentum. The kind of desires one has is a mirror to that soul's maturity. Desires are NOT implanted in a soul; they are not cultivated for, or given to, anyone. Desires are purely an individual choice.

"CHOICE determines all stages of your life. Choice determines how far a soul goes in accomplishing his desires or goals. *PURPOSE IS THE CHOICE TO FOLLOW ONE'S DESIRES, SO PURPOSE IS SELF-DETERMINED.* If Spirit advises that a person has a purpose to fulfill, on a given plane in a given lifetime, they mean that the soul has the POTENTIAL to fulfill it's desires through choice! There is no promise that any one soul will become this or that (as in a destiny for one to become great). Some people have a greater potential to fulfill their desires because they are more mature souls who will make wise decisions in their lives. Then there are souls who learn about the lesson of free will in life *by making unwise choices that cause the decrease in their potential to succeed* in fulfilling their desires.

Chapter 34

"THE LESSON IS SELF-RESPONSIBILITY: SELF-DETERMINATION.

"Yes, all desires are possible in God through the ENTIRE EXPANSE of a soul's existence. This one lifetime is but a small space in your entire span of life as a soul. So, you have not succeeded in becoming what you thought you could years ago. So what? *So, what will you do now?* Do not think that you are done in this life, and do not think in terms of this life only. If you have only one year of life left, or fifty years of life left, before you cross over to another plane of existence, what will you do with it NOW?

"The gift of self-determination is priceless, and it is your responsibility to DECIDE how to pursue the desires you have, to see them develop into your highest potential! Your OPTIMAL DESTINY is what YOU decide it will be!

"GOD DOES NOT DO ANYTHING TO YOU EXCEPT ALLOW YOU TO BE FREE AND TO LOVE YOU WHILE YOU BECOME SELF-REALIZED.

"The predictions given to you by Spirit [in a life reading this client had years ago] were determined by your potential and by the path you were on at the time. You can alter this path by limiting your potential through poor choices. Everyone makes unwise choices in life. What you do *after* making an unwise choice is a mark of your character, your soul's maturity or lack of maturity. Experience is a grand teacher, but be careful of the opinions you form as a result of these lessons of experience. Are your opinions those of anger and blame, or are they of contemplation and planning? Is the course you have set in error? Were the choices sound and wise, or were they made in the haste of anger, panic, self-pity, or arrogance?

"Do not hold onto negative opinions once the truth and wisdom of an experience that was not pleasant or fulfilling is contemplated. The Law of Attraction is ALWAYS functioning. Take the lesson, learn from it, and *decide* to correct the course in thought, speech, and action. Become the Master of your life! A Master learns from all choices, and does not blame others for his mistakes. There are other lives that cross your own and influence your life with their choices. These people can affect your life for two reasons: karma

Chapter 34

(positive or negative) from a previous incarnation with you, or you allow their decisions to conflict or harmonize with your own choices. Remember that Divine Energy rules over ALL energies. A Master uses, and listens to, Divine Energy.

"All experiences in this life have an effect on your next life because you form an opinion and keep a memory of them. Think BIGGER—think in terms of infinity, and how long your soul will be alive. All knowledge, all experience, is valuable, so do not throw away future experience in the study and understanding of deep concepts, such as the Law of Attraction, because your desired end result is not here yet. Will you deny your potential? Will you have a tantrum and stop your forward movement?

"Have the tantrum, let it go, and DECIDE to move toward your optimal destiny. If your ultimate desire for greatness in your field is not completely fulfilled in this lifetime expression, it will be carried forward to another lifetime, and your maturity of character will determine your choices in the next life, and we shall see if you attain your goal then.

"BE THE MASTER OF YOUR *ENTIRE* LIFE!"

* * *

My client was hoping to hear that the Lord would help make him a success now, in this lifetime; but the truth is, the buck does stop here, right at your own front door. *It's fair, it's the Law, and it means you can change your attitude whenever you decide to.* A new choice is only a second away. When you see people who are naturally good at something—they do things with ease that you work very hard at—remember that they brought this ability with them from a previous life. They worked very hard at it in another lifetime, which is why it seems easy for them, and why it seems God gave them "more" than you. Everyone is good at something. You have been alive, as a soul, for a very, very long time. Everything you practice on in this life will be that much easier for you the next time around. As Spirit said, think BIGGER! Take responsibility for where you are now, use that free will to choose to work hard toward your desires, and tap into the grand potential of your soul.

Chapter 35

THE CAUSE OF PHYSICAL PROBLEMS

Clients ask Spirit about ailments that their doctors cannot cure

Educating the public about the real cause of physical illnesses or problems is a task long overdue in the world. Modern medicine can set a broken bone, restart a heart, transplant a kidney, remove a tumor, and get rid of wrinkles, but they still do not know why people get sick and why others stay healthy. Diet and exercise have something to do with being healthy, for sure, and everyone knows it is unwise to smoke or overeat, but so many diseases are a mystery to the medical profession. That is because they do not look at the heart of the issue—literally the issue of emotion—where the root cause of all physical and mental problems stem from. There are some very good spiritual books out now that show the correlation of a mind that is not in harmony to a body with disease, and these should be studied at universities along with all of the textbooks on anatomy, pharmaceutical remedies, and operational procedures.

Here are a few stories that illustrate how chronic physical problems can be caused by psychological stresses and negative beliefs. In these cases, modern medicine had not been able to detect the cause of these problems nor help them alleviate the symptoms. For anyone who is interested in helping themselves heal physical illnesses, I highly recommend the books by the spiritual intuitives Louise Hay and Caroline Myss. Taking responsibility for where you are in every aspect of your life, including your physical condition, is vitally important in the healing process. The Universal Law of Attraction includes the fact that you create how you feel physically, not just how full your bank account is and how your love life is doing.

One client emailed me to find out why he was still having physical problems after seeing many doctors and receiving treatments that ranged the gamut of drugs, physical therapy, and even energy sessions from a "miracle machine." He would get rid of one symptom to have it replaced by another set of problems. He was weary of being constantly sick with one thing or another and not having any answers. Here is part of what my spiritual teacher had to say during a dictation I did for him one evening:

* * *

SPIRITUAL TEACHER:

"The trials of the body are ALWAYS a result of past karma or current psychological beliefs. These beliefs are a result of the *state of mind* concerning past, present, or future events. An examination of what is going on presently which causes anxiety, anger, frustration, or fear will highlight the areas or beliefs causing the physical problems. Pain-killing drugs mask the effects long enough for the cause to be ignored, which in turn becomes the trigger for the body to find another way to bring this need of emotional resolution to the attention of the person; hence more physical problems on top of existing ones. One MUST deal with the erroneous states of mind causing the imbalance of energy, for it will not just go away. Surgery and painkillers (though sometimes necessary) only move the manifestation of imbalance elsewhere, or it can return to the same area later.

"Ask yourself these questions:

1) What am I anxious about, upset over, or fearful of at this time?

2) What long-standing negative beliefs am I carrying? (For example: It is hard to succeed in life. It takes money to make money. I am fat. Other religions are wrong.)

3) Can I release these beliefs truthfully and never revisit them, or do I intend to hang onto them so I feel vindicated in my point of view?

4) Can I really trust God?

"Write down the answers to these questions and study them carefully. Honesty is the key to discovering what is making you ill, for it comes from you, yourself. Your reactions TO others can also make you ill. Define the emotion behind the beliefs you carry that are negative, and be determined to cleanse them from your heart and mind. *This takes work. This takes discipline.* When you are ready to be well (and some are not, for they like the attention they get from being sick) make a pact with yourself to do these exercises and begin focusing on wellness. In your DAILY meditation time, visualize yourself as being whole, as being energetic, and being grateful for your health.

"Do not sabotage yourself and your results by throwing in the logical thought of 'but I am not well now.' Discard that immediately. When you know the emotional reason or issue that is causing you to have physical problems you can reverse the emotion by picturing the *opposite* feeling. *Every cell* in your body carries what we call 'the emotion wave' inside of it, and it responds to your vibrational frequency [see chapter 40]. It is saturated with your feelings, and it responds to them intimately. Visualize the Light of God flowing to each cell in your body and they will pass it between them and take the Divine Energy they need to become whole and healthy. Negativity throws your cells out of balance. Pour in positive energy!

"These exercises in releasing negativity take many sessions; do not become discouraged over a seeming lack of progress. You are working on getting rid of years of negative emotional imbalances. Resentment is a particularly difficult imbalance to get rid of. *Resentment is disappointment tinged with hatred.* It hardens over time, like tartar on your teeth or plaque in the arteries of the heart, and can cause kidney stones and growths in your body.

[*Author's note:* This client was very angry that people he had loaned money to could not pay him back. Spirit addressed this specifically, since he asked if he should have given money to those who had petitioned him

Chapter 35

for funds.] "God works through people, so if you pray to be an instrument of His Will, He will draw to you those whom He can help through you. In prayer and meditation in the Peace (the state of mind in absolute peace) you shall know whom to help financially or otherwise. 'Blind intuition' is only guilt—'I should be giving and nice to all'—that seeks to feel better immediately. To seek the sound guidance of Spirit is best. It will come as a knowing, as a deep intuition of what to do. It can be an instant knowing, if one is attuned with God, but most often requires thought and prayer.

"The Mind of God never leads one astray. Keep in mind that God is aware of karmic debts to another, which you may owe, and what lessons you may need to experience. The Law of Attraction is always on, so these are not simple matters. TRUST in God to guide you, if you ask, in the direction which will benefit your soul. That requires a great acceptance of all kinds of lessons, good and bad, for your goal is soul progress, not material riches in particular, though some lessons are gained in the handling of riches. It all comes down to the following: What is your goal in this life? How will you achieve it? The answers to these questions will show you where you are in soul growth. You ask if you are on the right path? Answer the questions above."

* * *

Another client I worked with had been having trouble with her sinuses for three years. She had been to several doctors, none of whom had helped her. The drainage every morning was so bad that she frequently became nauseous, and she even feared that she was pregnant because of the "morning sickness." She called to ask for some spiritual advice on the problem. Once again, the personal reaction to, and the perspective on, outside circumstances were the culprit.

* * *

HOLY SPIRIT:

"All sinus problems are a rebellion to what is happening around a person—they are sick of a situation in their life. Vomiting or stomach problems are caused by not being able to stomach a situation or environment. These are reactions to where a person is or what they are having to endure.

Chapter 35

The remedy, psychologically, is to change the situation or environment. The *cure* is to conquer the feeling or perspective WITHIN one's self, or they will attract it again, once they have changed the situation. First, identify the situation or environment you are 'sick' of. Then see it from a higher perspective. Will change alter the actual emotional response to the root cause? It may for a time, but is the root cause or belief strong enough to attract the same scenario, type of person, or environment into your life?

"When an emotional response creates an actual physical problem, especially a chronic condition, the belief or emotional tag is very strong, and will repeat if not addressed in truth.

"Sinus problems are an inner crying about a situation or person, or both. Unhappiness and a feeling of being helpless to change that situation is at the root cause. Fear of change, even when conditions are unacceptable or demeaning, leads to great unhappiness and a feeling of powerlessness. Feeling stuck and wanting to cry, but withholding tears, also can lead to sinus misery. (Not grieving fully over a loss, not seeing a way out of a job you hate, etc.) Refusing to perform a change needed, where there is an inability to look truthfully at an incorrect belief or environment, leads to stomach ailments. Fear of taking responsibility to create the change is the cause of stomach ailments like nausea, pain, or disease. This type of fear is the fear of letting go of being right or letting go of the familiar.

"The familiar thing can be a person, place, or belief. Each one must dig deeply within to find the truthful answer. When one can do this, the relief can be found, both physically (sometimes through the sudden contact of a correct treatment or an instantaneous healing), and mentally (through a true change in one's perspective). Often, when the self-realized truth about the cause of the condition is found, the outward environment changes. It must, for the lesson is no longer needed. This can be a change in occupation, home, supervisor at work, spouse, living or working arrangements, etc. The focal point of the lesson will alter.

"Self-introspection on a deep level, in great and open truth, is the key. Asking for Divine Inspiration as you earnestly look at your feelings about where you are is the quickest way to reveal truth and get resolution. Reverent prayer to the Almighty One (Who IS Truth) for help will be given to any honest seeker. *Sincerity* aids in the pursuit of truth. The cause of your illness

Chapter 35

must be identified by yourself to be effective. You will KNOW if you have found it. *There will be no question, because at first you will resist the answer.* Denial roots the cause into your being, and sets up the pattern for sickness, pain, and the attraction of continued negative circumstances.

"Very deep-rooted beliefs will eventually cause cancers, if they are of a negative or untruthful bent. The body knows the harmony of truth, so untruth is disruptive to its balance. Simply put: write a list of why you are unhappy in any area. Make a DECISION to CHANGE it and see the mind rebel in fear. Or find a reason to change how you feel about that topic and see how your mind justifies your negative opinion. Seek Divine Inspiration on how to change yourself or to be shown how to change the condition or situation. Then, using visualization, see and feel yourself as healed. The outside help you need will then be suddenly available or known. If you are successful, change the thought pattern or state of mind which prevented the original change needed, so you do not attract it again. Harmony and balance bring health."

* * *

In each of these cases, truth was given to them through a dictation by the Holy Spirit. I have found that very few people actually try the suggestions that they ask for. It is hard work, and takes discipline. You have to take responsibility for where you are and how you feel, and that is not something we humans do well, nor were we taught to do that growing up. We followed the example of blaming others for whatever is wrong in our lives. Once you understand this concept, you can use these techniques for conquering any dysfunction in your life, or for overcoming any lesson or test you are involved in. Spirit says to remember that you set up these lessons and tests before you incarnated, and that you believed you could triumph over them.

Spirit also says: "LIFE IS AN OPEN-BOOK TEST . . . YOU CAN ASK FOR ALL THE HELP YOU NEED!"

Chapter 36

TEENAGERS: SUICIDE, GANGS, AND DRUG USE

What is wrong with our society's children?

Just before this book came to print, I received a call from a grandmother (I'll call her Margaret) whose fourteen-year-old grandson was stopped from committing suicide in the nick of time. She asked me if the Holy Spirit could find out what had gone wrong with "Andrew," and what the family could do to help him. They were understandably distraught, and had taken him to a juvenile center where he was being treated by a psychiatrist for depression. Andrew had been placed on drugs and was under observation for a few days. Margaret explained that Andrew was a good boy who did well in school. His father was a minister, and their lives were typical of the American family: both parents worked, they had bought a home two years prior, and they had three happy children. The real circumstances were different than appearances, it turned out, and my Master teacher in the spiritual realm saw through the family mirage presented to the outside world. I asked him to advise this worried grandmother and to comment on our society's teenagers.

* * *

SPIRITUAL TEACHER:

"Suicide is an attempt to stop the pain of feeling worthless or to end an intolerable situation. It is always thought to be the only way to rid one's self of PAIN. In very young people it is the pain of never being 'good enough' that pushes the thought of non-existence into their minds. What they do not understand is that this pain is a *mental anguish*, and if the body ceases to exist it does not matter, *for the Mind continues on* in its torment. They do not escape all of their pain by crossing over into the astral world.

"During the teen years a male's hormones are wild, and can cause all manner of unbalanced chemical reactions. Some males have a harder time than others, and parents, as well as past-life influences, play a major role in how successful the boy or young man is in controlling sexual and combative urges. In times of long ago, young males were training for their careers by the age Andrew is now, and all of that 'steam' was funneled into hard work.

"In these 'modern times' boys have nothing to focus on or work hard at to expel these extra energies, therefore they become sexually active earlier and are aggressive, for they are not plowing the fields, becoming warriors, or sailing the world on clipper ships. This is why there are gangs: too much testosterone going nowhere. The boys have urges to prove their maleness and worthiness and cannot express them in work or in sex, so they form clubs to test themselves against other males. Left unsupervised, because of working parents and extended family living away, they seek out packs of peers to engage with.

"When such a boy also has a father figure who does not teach much-needed wisdom, but berates and finds all manner of fault with him (preferring to denounce rather than show the child how to perform well) there is a death of self-esteem and trust. A parent's role is to TEACH, NURTURE, and DISCIPLINE WITH WISDOM. If a parent uses shame, ridicule, and tyranny on a child, the child will turn OFF to all role models that are adults and seek the comfort and advice of his peers.

"When you add the very unfortunate ingredient of religious disapproval, the youth believes God is also against him and that he does not deserve to live, wrongfully thinking he is of no use or value to anyone. His pain is complete and all consuming, and a satisfaction of revenge with the suicide act (to hurt those who hurt him) makes the plan to end his life perfect. In his eyes it is a way to get out and get even.

Chapter 36

"Redirection of the NATURAL surge of testosterone levels is what is desperately needed in these boys. The drug epidemic is caused by teens trying to soothe these normal flare-ups that have no outlet. If the teens do not have a passionate outlet, like sports or other physical regimens, they will burst with hormonal craziness. City life is most detrimental to a teenaged person, especially when parents are too busy to help them cope. The raising of the age at which a youth can legally attain work is also very counterproductive, as it stops what is often a very good outlet and learning opportunity for them.

"Stuffing teens into classes or sports or religious clubs *that do not interest them* creates more restlessness, and an anger of not being listened to grows. Their opinions are not worthy of notice, they see, so a feeling of 'what's the use?' begins and depression sets in. Past-life suicides influence a depressed person greatly, and the temptation to end an unsatisfactory life is great. Each avoidance of this past-life pull is a victory, especially if a turnaround in attitude and external conditions can be made.

"Further condemnation by parents or teachers MUST STOP. Hatred can be rooted into a soul by abuse, physical or mental, and this can take lifetimes to heal. While bad behavior cannot be condoned and discipline must be taught, *the key is to teach self-mastery, through the example of the adult!*

"In the separation of grandparents from most children, a very valuable resource is lost, because most older adults have had a lifetime to learn from their own foolishness and now have at least some discipline and wisdom to share from a perspective of kindness and conviction.

"Andrew has a poor role model in his father, and has no passionate outlet that *he* would choose to channel the raging hormones that cause his anxiety and the feeling of wanting to escape and be free. The added tension of not living up to his religion's version of Christianity and the reminder that the 'gates of hell' are waiting for him is cruel and suffocating. He needs to be thought of as a young man and NOT AS A DISOBEDIENT CHILD. Some freedom and trust must be given to him, even if he makes mistakes, and he must find an outlet for his energy, which will only increase in the next few years.

Chapter 36

"This religious stranglehold must loosen, for it impinges upon his free will, and he will rebel. God loses many young persons to fearful, controlling parents who believe that saturation in religion will make their children 'good.' Andrew will either become what he hates (his father) for self-preservation, or he will denounce vehemently what he hates and express the polar opposite of his father and his domineering ways. If he is ALLOWED to speak and express himself now, he will find the middle road and attain some soul growth."

* * *

A few days after delivering this reading to Andrew's grandmother, I received a phone call updating the family's status. Things were definitely not what they had seemed to be. Margaret had traveled to Andrew's home, volunteering to tidy things up while the family was in another city where they had taken their son for treatment. What she discovered there shocked her. As she opened the front door with a spare key, the stench coming from the house sent her reeling backwards. Covering her nose, she entered the living room to find a total disaster.

"It looked like it had been ransacked, but apparently these were their normal living conditions," Margaret told me. "The smell came from allowing the dogs to use the carpeting as a toilet for a few years. Dishes were piled high everywhere in the kitchen. There was trash on the floor, along with toys, games, books, clothing, etc. A child's writings and drawings were on the dining room wall in markers. The smell from the children's rooms was unbelievable, and I had to throw out their bedding and buy new covers, sheets, and pillows for them. It took me hours just to clean enough to be able to stand the smell, and I refused to even go into the master bedroom.

"The garage was even worse, and the door opener didn't work, so I was unable to air it out," she continued. "The dog kennels were in there, and I cannot imagine how they could keep their pets in that place for any length of time. Andrew was sharing a bedroom with his eight-year-old brother, and he still had children's bed sheets on his bed. Underneath his bed I found a pile of letters from his girlfriend. They were disgusting, full of vulgar and offensive language and extremely suggestive writing. I switched the children's bedrooms around, put Andrew into his own room and bought him masculine

Chapter 36

bedding that was more in line with his age. His little brother and sister are now sharing a room.

"In talking with my daughter, I found out that the maid they had used over a year ago quit and someone has turned them into Child Protective Services. The father spends half of his day at home, and yet does nothing to clean, cook, or take care of the children, while my daughter holds down a full-time job. Her husband spends most of his time at home on his computer, and yells at her and the kids. More truth came out when my daughter told me that after Andrew had run away to see his girlfriend one night, they had called the police. Andrew slipped out the back way at the girl's house, and his folks called the police again when he arrived home. I am not sure what was said by the officer, but Andrew planned his suicide a few days afterwards." Margaret sounded both sad and disgusted. "Obviously, the church counseling that my daughter and her husband are receiving is not doing any good."

Some hopeful signs appeared after the grandson was released from the treatment center, Margaret reported later. Andrew's father called Margaret to apologize for his antagonistic treatment of her over the last three years, and he has decided to leave the clergy. Andrew was reportedly very happy about his dad's decision to go into another field of work. Therapy will continue, and I am sure Margaret will keep close tabs on what is transpiring in her daughter's family. Unfortunately, due to the narrow religious background of the parents, she cannot share the reading from Spirit with them, as they would not accept this form of communication. Perhaps she will be able to use the information to guide her daughter, however, and suggest some alternative approaches for Andrew's well being and development.

I attained permission to share this story in *Divine Contact*, with the hope that parents of teenagers and pre-teens would see that it is very important to engage their sons (and daughters) in meaningful, honest dialogues about what *they* would find interesting as constructive outlets for the very real problem of raging hormones. Most importantly, *teaching self-mastery by example* will offer healthy role models they can follow without feeling belittled or worthless. These children will one day rule our world. It is in our best interests to help them balance themselves.

Chapter 37

DAN GETS A LECTURE FROM SPIRIT

A college student asks Spirit how to "get rich quick"

Several years ago, I had a very vivid dream in which I was waiting on my front porch for someone. I didn't know who it was, but I was told by Holy Spirit that he was coming soon. In the dream, a young man about twenty years old came walking up the sidewalk, carrying a trunk on his back. He was nearly doubled over from the weight of it. He saw me on the porch and walked over to me, asking if I had a room to rent.

"I have been waiting for you," I said. "Come on in."

"I have no money to pay you," he told me, hesitating on the step.

"You don't need to pay me," I answered. "God sent you here, and I have plenty of room."

I remembered the dream the next morning, and knew that it was a message from Spirit that I would meet a young man who needed my help. He would have a "trunk load" of problems. A few months later I met this young man at the gym where my husband and I worked out. Dan was nineteen years old, very shy, and had a wonderful, honest face. He also had a shining soul. We became good friends, and soon I introduced him to my husband, Joe. They shared a passion for science and math, and Joe began tutoring him in physics and calculus. Dan was soon a regular member of the family, and

Chapter 37

was at our house more often than at his own. We tutored him in Life 101, as well as college courses: how to set up a checking account, handle money, write a résumé, shop for clothes, how to cook, how to present himself for an interview, and so on. Many spaghetti dinners later, we decided to adopt him, informally, and he began to call us Mom and Dad.

During this time he also learned about what I do, and we had many, many discussions about God and all things metaphysical. He couldn't get enough! What a delight to meet a young person who was so interested in everything and who cared so deeply about people and the world. Dan was, and is, a sincere spiritual student. When it came time for him to decide what his next step in life would be, he asked if I would do a reading for him and ask the Holy Spirit what to do. His grades in college were average at best, as he had some learning challenges, and he was really unhappy at home. He loved school and had dreams of becoming an engineer.

"Before I do the reading, you must change your question," I told him.

"But I really want to know what I should do. I can't decide," said Dan.

"Holy Spirit will rarely tell you what to do. 'There are no shoulds,' they will say, and you will get a lecture on how free will is the Law of the universe," I explained. "They will say, 'ALL IS CHOICE.'"

"Then how do I get an answer?" he asked, frustrated.

"Ask what the WISE choice would be for you," I said with a smile. How many times had Holy Spirit told clients this! They are sticklers for vocabulary.

Dan could see now that his choice was between what was wise and what would be unwise, not what he "should" do. He wrote a question with the proper wording and understanding and I went into a meditative state to ask for spiritual guidance for him. My spiritual teacher came through to have me write a dictation to help Dan see what he really wanted and needed at this time, and proposed that the WISE choice was to obtain his freedom from a situation at home that was causing immense depression. This depression was causing him to have difficulty at school and was stunting his personal

Chapter 37

growth. It was time for him to leave the nest and live on his own. This meant that he would have to postpone his education at the university, as he could not afford school and an apartment. Spirit even showed me where to have him apply for full-time work. After some coaching on our part, and teaching him that persistence pays off, Dan did get employment at the facility Spirit had recommended. When he had gained his freedom and was out on his own, his entire life changed for the better, and he began to make his own decisions and experienced a happiness he had never known. When his job was terminated, Spirit again told me where to send him, and he became employed that day.

A year later, Dan was again unhappy about his life situation. He missed school and felt that he SHOULD be back at the university, studying engineering. He had learned enough about how to live, he felt, and now if Spirit could just tell him how to quit work and get enough money to go to college he would be happy. Remembering the advice from a year ago, he very thoughtfully worded his question for Spirit and sent it to me by email. I asked Dan if I could print the answer he was given by my spiritual teacher in this book, as it pertains to almost everyone on the planet. It is a personal reading, so I thank Dan for allowing his life to be an example to others on how Spirit looks at the cause of issues in your life, and how they can be very frank in their advice. The truth given by Spirit can always be applied to other people. It is Universal Truth. Here is the question written by Dan, and the answer given to him by my spiritual teacher:

DAN:

"I want to go back to college free from the restrictions of financial instability, while also having the time to develop more understanding of the principles of engineering and physics, science in general, through the liberty of money. Also, I want to have and maintain the best possible health attainable. I would prefer this in the form of having a farm so that I know the foods I consume are free from toxins, [are] fresh, and provide the best nutrition. What would the wise courses of action be in order for me to realize this desire?"

Chapter 37

*　*　*

SPIRITUAL TEACHER:

"Remember that BALANCE in life and God-Awareness are your goals, not an 'easy' existence. A very great sage of long ago said, 'Before I was enlightened, I chopped wood and carried water. After I became enlightened, I chopped wood and carried water.' What needs to change is YOU, if you desire to change your financial status. A noble cause does not attract prosperity! [By the Law of Attraction, you attract your financial situation by how you feel about money.]

"Change your opinion, your perspective, and change your bank account. Losara has told you about how your every thought and word attracts EVERYTHING into your life. Just because you neglect to remember that the Law of Attraction is *continually on* does not mean that you are not subject to it. You *believe* that you must have no financial responsibilities to be able to go to college and do scientific experiments—and so, since you have no money now, you create no opportunity to study science, see? You limit several ways to further your education.

"Instead, BE OPEN TO THE DIVINE IDEA FOR YOU, WHATEVER THAT MAY BE. Strive for *balance* in life, which encompasses work, study, meditation, service, and joy. Your priorities must be balanced and you must believe you can attain them all. Holy Spirit advised you to postpone your studies in order to gain experience in LIVING first. A year and a half is hardly enough to say you understand life or how to manage your responsibilities. Do not run away from life, embrace MORE life!

"It would be *wise* to continue to work, to raise your own food in your new garden, to cultivate friends, and to study and meditate. A course or two at the university will keep your mental skills sharp as you continue to hone your life skills in self-reliance. Focus is a challenge for you, and discipline is a problem for all souls here. As you become self-reliant AND disciplined, you will attract what you desire—IF you also use the tools of manifestation correctly. All of these issues must be balanced and worked on. In this way

Chapter 37

you will get the habits of procrastination, self-pity, and wishing for unrealistic goals out of your head.

"On third-dimensional Earth money is a necessity for man: it is a tool to acquire goods and services. Unless you are Self-Realized in God, you must work to gain this tool called money. [Masters naturally attract all that they need, as they realize it all comes from God.] Work is not an unworthy way of life, nor does it have to be hated. To like what you do for work and to attract an enjoyable, fulfilling life, APPRECIATE what you have now, or the Universe will see that you really do not want to work at all. You will attract the termination of your job. [You send out the thoughts that your job makes you unhappy and the desire not to be there creates the end of employment.] It is GOOD that you are employed. It is GOOD that you can pay your bills and buy food. It is GOOD that you have the mental clarity and the physical stamina to perform your job. If you are bored at work it is because you are LAZY! Find work to do, or do mental work while you are idle. If you are stressed, overwhelmed, or overworked at your job, ASK for help from the Divine Mind Who has all solutions. You attract what you focus on! Your 'focus' is what you THINK, FEEL, and SPEAK EVERY MINUTE of the day, whether you are aware of it or not.

"God does not rescue you. He gave you all the tools you need to create a good life on your own. You are not helpless, nor do you need to fall into wealth to attain your goals. Many people waste time on wishing for the big lottery prize. [Wishing is weak-willed and carries no belief behind it.] Focus on the prize of Self-Realization and actively create what you need. Balance your life and attain peace and purpose and fulfillment. It is, literally, YOUR CHOICE."

* * *

This reading was right on target for Dan. Spirit would advise similar, but different ideas for someone else. (Not everyone needs to postpone their higher education.) The important things that I wanted to get across here are that we, alone, are responsible for where we are in life, and that God understands our situations very well. Dan appreciated this reading by my spiritual teacher very much. "Spirit told me what was wrong and how to fix it," he said with admiration. Sometimes being pointed in the right direction is all that we need.

Chapter 38

GOD THE TYRANT OR GOD THE PHILANTHROPIST?

Why doesn't God fix your life?

This piece of spiritual advice is one of my personal favorites and addresses a topic that often puzzles people: is God truly all loving, or do we also experience the "wrath of God" as well? This question came up in a reading for a man who was full of anger at the seeming lack of God's presence in his life. God sure wasn't fixing anything for him, even after prayers and supplications for a few small favors to be thrown his way. "Alex" was so busy at work that he got to spend very little time with his wife and young daughter by the time he got home. He missed his wife, who was sometimes absent when he did get home, as she did volunteer work for the needy. He had to keep his job, and to keep it he had to work overtime, while all around the world's criminals and drug lords got filthy rich and had time for vacations! It seemed that God was on their side, not his. When I told him he should be grateful for the time he did have with his family and that he was attracting what was wrong in his life, he really got mad. I let him vent his frustration about the ways of the Almighty.

"God wants us to fail! He enslaves us with these unfair Laws. We are set up from the time we come here with no instructions to barely survive, and we're supposed to be grateful to a God Who takes credit for the little good you receive, but YOU are to blame for the bad things that happen!" he raged. "If God is not responsible for the bad in our lives, why thank Him for the good, which He has nothing to do with?" (It particularly irritated

Chapter 38

him that athletes thanked God for any victory they had, when they were the ones who trained day and night for success. How was God to choose which team won, he thought, feeling it was ridiculous.)

He had a very good point, actually. We are taught in our religions that God rewards the good souls and punishes the evil souls, but in real life, it sure doesn't seem that way. This is a main point for atheists as well. There is no evidence that there IS a God, they say, and morality is just a point of view taught to people to keep our society civilized. I addressed these questions in my evening meditation with my spiritual teacher. What was I to say to people who did not see the goodness of our Creator in this world, and saw God only as a tyrant to please, or who did not see evidence of Him at all?

* * *

SPIRITUAL TEACHER:

"We are dealing with two different concepts here: Fact and Truth. The FACT is that Alex has only two hours a night with his family on weeknights. The *TRUTH* is that ALL IS CHOICE, and in choosing to retain a high-paying job he accepts greater responsibility which demands more time to solve problems. A step down in his rank of employment would mean a decrease in wages, which he chooses not to do. His wife uses some of her free time to help the needy, which reduces the time she can spend with Alex. That is a FACT. The *TRUTH* is that this is part of the reason why he loves her so much—she has a giving heart. His resentment of her time spent away from him is a choice, a perspective of self-pity.

"Should Alex be grateful to God for those two hours of time with his family on weeknights, or is he justified in sneering in his disgust, saying, 'If God is not responsible for the bad things in life, He is not responsible for the good?' The FACT is that God is *not* responsible for the good in your life, and He is *not* responsible for the bad, either. The *TRUTH* is that you reap what you sow, the Law is binding, and *you* do attract all of your circumstances, good or bad. The *TRUTH* is also that by His Grace you have become enlightened (have knowledge of) the existence of the Law of Attraction, and have been given instruction in it so that you may choose *wisely*. The Law of Attraction is a FACT, and the *TRUTH* is that Alex's negative reaction to events he attracted in the first place is causing his health problems, his time with his family to decrease perceptually, his financial dissatisfaction, and his inability to focus on important work.

"Alex knows about the Law and is not using the tools of manifestation. That is a FACT. The *TRUTH* here is that he is angry that he cannot manifest what he wants quickly, so he gives up in anger. He perceives his wife's cheerfulness as denial of the negative world around them. The *TRUTH* is that she is using the Law wisely, and is focusing on what she wants, not on what she doesn't want. The *TRUTH* is that Alex is perceiving her incorrectly. It is not uncaring or naïve to look on the bright side of life, it is *wise*, for the Law of Attraction is constantly working.

"The Law is fair and that is a FACT, for all evil shall be returned to those who do evil, all negative persons shall have more negative things to complain about, all goodness shall be returned to those who do good. The *TRUTH* is that all of these reciprocal Laws take time to come full circle in this third dimensional world, according to the Law of Balance. Every soul's agenda is to reunite with God. Every soul has a Plan that they, themselves, set up to gain certain experiences from for their progression of Spirit. It is a FACT that wisdom is gained through direct knowledge or direct experience. *And the TRUTH is that some souls choose a life expression that includes negative events for the purpose of gaining wisdom* about a particular negative issue for that experience or lesson.

"The repercussions of evil, or negative expressions in life toward others or toward self, seem slow to most people here. They view time by Earth standards because it is all they remember. They say Hitler didn't pay for his wickedness. That is a FACT, but the *TRUTH* is he will. He must, for he has sown evil, and it will be returned to him. That he didn't come to justice (in the life in which he expressed the opposite of God) is the trump card the arguers against God play, but they do not remember the rules of the Law of Cause and Effect, so the FACT is that they are ignorant of the *TRUTH*.

"Should one be thankful to God for what seems to be man's accomplishment? The FACT is that *man is responsible for his own accomplishments*. The *TRUTH* is that *man could not accomplish anything without God*, for He is your very breath. An ungrateful heart is closed, and God can only reach you through your heart. Be Ye, therefore, grateful and He shall come unto you and show you His Wonders!"

Chapter 38

* * *

Sometime later, as my husband was reviewing this reading for inclusion in the book, he asked if Spirit could explain the actual definition of the difference between *fact* and *truth*. It is hard to articulate this, I found out, when I tried to explain it to him myself. I have the added advantage of my spiritual Master sending me an ethereal wave of *knowing* when we talk together, and this helps in my own understanding of new concepts. I decided to see what Spirit had to say on this question, and in meditation I asked my spiritual teacher to give us a further explanation on how to tell the difference between fact and truth.

* * *

SPIRITUAL TEACHER:

"A fact is a result of following, or rejecting, the Truth. A Truth is a Holy or Universal Law: the rules which God created to keep order in the chaos of Creation. So, you see, a fact is a representation of whether one is in harmony or disharmony with a Universal Law. It is the effect of the cause: the outcome of the belief or action which upholds or violates 'the rules.' Every soul has the free will to follow or reject these Laws, and they are self-serving; meaning that if a soul follows the Law he will naturally attract the higher conditions of that rule, and if one violates a Truth he serves up the consequences to himself.

"For example: The Law of Free Will dictates that all sentient beings are free to live and express themselves as they wish, no exceptions. If a being were not in harmony with this Law (he rejects the Truth of free will for everyone) he may become a person who enslaves others. He may believe that free will concepts only apply to the elite, educated people of wealth, or of a certain race. This is not in harmony with the Law, and as a consequence of thwarting this Law, his personal vibrations lower, attracting a lower level of frequency equal to his belief in either this lifetime or his next incarnation.

"Perhaps in that subsequent lifetime he becomes a person who is discriminated against (thus fulfilling the Law of Cause and Effect). He, not remembering his past actions, is outraged by the 'unfairness' of the other group or society. The *FACT* in that life is that he IS discriminated against;

Chapter 38

but the *TRUTH* is that he drew to himself this prejudicial treatment because he was unfair to others before, as a slave owner. To learn the lesson of Cause and Effect, and to experience the unfairness of his own prior lifetime, his soul chose to 'walk in the shoes' of those whom he mistreated previously. Hopefully, he will learn the error of his ways and change his belief to harmonize with the Law of Free Will.

"There is a REASON for the circumstances one finds oneself in. Look at the *facts* and ascertain the *truth* behind them through the Holy Spirit."

* * *

Chapter 39

STUCK ON THIS SIDE OF HEAVEN

Night terrors in a neighborhood of children

Releasing spirits who have not gone on to the Light in the Astral Realm after death is a very special kind of service. There are those who "haunt" houses or other buildings or pieces of property, there are negative souls who attach onto unsuspecting people as they go about their day, and there can be evil entities whose purpose in attaching to a person is to cause them harm. Each of these situations is handled differently, but always with the same tool: the Divine Energy of the Holy Spirit. In this chapter I will tell about a case where I, with the aid of God's Energy, cleared people and places of spirits who were "stuck" and were causing problems. It is usually only when problems crop up that the lost souls are noticed.

About thirteen years ago my youngest son, who was two years old, began having night terrors. These are not nightmares, they are TERRORS, and are very distressing to the child and to the parents. Cody would begin screaming and yelling at the top of his lungs, not quite awake, yet not asleep, and nothing would console him. Often he would talk gibberish at nothing in the room, and the crying and screaming could last a long time. My husband and I would try everything we could think of to quiet him. The little guy's horror was real and we were very upset over not being able to help him. I read all I could on the phenomenon of night terrors, but nothing was helpful or useful during these episodes. I had done a past-life reading on my son, and it was good to know where some of his problems were stemming from, but it did nothing to alleviate the terrors.

Chapter 39

He had been, in his last incarnation, a Jewish woman who had been put into a Nazi concentration camp in Poland during World War II. He was experimented on medically, and kept in solitary confinement. The things Spirit showed me were horrendous. It was no wonder that this child had, from infancy, been terrified of doctors to the point of having to restrain him for any examination, and he did not like to be alone. After months of having the night terrors, I called a psychic healer, as I was not versed in healing and was desperate to find something I could do for my son. As soon as we walked into her office she gasped, saying, "My God, his aura is wide open. *Anyone could walk into him.*" She went on to say that he had been tortured by the Nazis in Poland in a concentration camp. This was a validation of what I had already been told by Spirit, but her next statement was quite important to what I found out later. She told me that he had made a pact with the souls of the concentration camp victims. Whoever was able to heal first would help the rest on the other side. He was keeping his auric field open so that these souls could experience his healing during this life. The healer did some work to try to close his aura.

This did explain an amazing thing that had happened a few months earlier when my family was in the living room watching a PBS special on television. Cody had been sitting on the floor playing with toys, when a commercial came on for a documentary on the Nazis. A picture of Adolf Hitler came up on the screen and he turned, pointed a tiny finger at the image, and said, "Bad guy!" I was dumbfounded.

Unfortunately, this did nothing to lessen or relieve the night terrors, and one night he had an enormous episode that truly frightened us. It was at 2:00 a.m. (of course) when we heard screams of unspeakable terror coming from Cody's room. Although he was not completely awake, his eyes were wide open, and he was crying out in horror and slapping himself all over. "GET THEM OFF! GET THEM OFF!" he shouted over and over. Even when my husband tried to hold him, Cody continued to flail around and slap at something invisible to us. When we were able to get in-between yells, we asked him what was on him. "BUGS!" he screamed. "THEY'RE ON ME! THEY'RE IN MY MOUTH!" He was hysterical. He acted like a drunk going through the D.T.'s. Then he began to see them on me, too, and desperately tried to stop them from crawling up my arms. I was crying by now, and we took him outside to show him the stars, trying anything to get him to focus on something else. It took over an hour to calm him down.

Chapter 39

The next day I called our pediatrician and scheduled an appointment. By the time we were able to get in, Cody was perfectly normal, like nothing had happened. I explained what had been happening to the doctor, but his exam revealed nothing unusual. The doctor felt very sorry for me and believed what I had told him, but there was nothing he could do. Just as we were leaving the exam room, however, the doctor said to Cody, "I am glad all of those bugs are gone."

"No, they're not," Cody said, turning to him with an open hand. "There's one right here."

The doctor didn't hesitate. He grabbed the invisible bug off of Cody's open palm and put it into his lab coat pocket. "There," he said. "All gone." I could have kissed him. Cody smiled and ran down the hallway. This attempt, however, did not erase the night terrors, and in desperation I appealed to the Holy Spirit for more help. Entering a deep state of meditation, I petitioned God to show me what was wrong with my son. Immediately, I saw the form of a girl dressed in clothing from the late 1800's. I was looking at the soul of a child who had died just over a hundred years ago.

"Hi!' she said. "My name is Penny." She had on a calico dress with an apron, wore high-top shoes that buttoned, and a bonnet that tied in a large bow under her chin. She was about seven years old. "My brother says I'm a baby because I have a dolly." She showed me a rag doll with a matching bonnet. "He's twelve. He's a big boy." She looked furtively over her shoulder and then whispered, "Want to see something?" Digging her hand into the front pocket of her apron, she brought out an object to show to me. It was an Indian arrowhead. "I'm not supposed to have it. Mama says that the heathens made them. I found it on the ground."

She began to ramble on, being glad to be the one who had news to tell. "We're from Black River, Kentucky, and we're going to Denver! Mama doesn't like the wagon master. She says he's a drunkard, but I like him. We stopped at Fort Collins yesterday. Bye!" With a wave of her hand, she was gone. Thoroughly confused, I asked Holy Spirit to explain what I had just seen. They gave me the images of Penny walking back to her camp of covered wagons that were stopped for the night in my neighborhood of one hundred years ago. The settlers were very excited that they would most likely

Chapter 39

reach Denver in the next day or two, and they had a party to celebrate the end of a long journey. They built a large bonfire and got out their musical instruments to accompany their singing and dancing. I saw the wagon master, whiskey bottle in hand, getting thoroughly plastered. He had been warned the previous day at Fort Collins that there had been "trouble" with the local Indians who were upset over an "incident" with the U.S. Cavalry recently. The soldiers had killed Indian women and children in eastern Colorado in cold blood, and the natives were retaliating. He had been told to be on the lookout. On the plains of Colorado on a warm, clear evening, the singing and playing of the settlers could be heard from miles away, and they aroused the interest of a band of Indians in the area. The unsuspecting pioneers were attacked and slaughtered in savage revenge for the atrocities that the U.S. soldiers had committed against their people. Penny and her brother hid in what looked to be a type of bench built inside one of the wagons, but it only postponed their deaths. The boy was tortured for fun.

These images were sickening to view, but now I understood what was happening to my son and, I found out, to other children in the neighborhood. The horror of the pioneers' death had trapped them into the ether, the band of energy surrounding the area, and they could not release into the Light of the afterlife. Their emotional trauma and their belief that they were still on their way to Denver was keeping them locked into place. The wagon master had entered Cody's open auric energy, and caused the horror he was seeing (alcoholic hallucinations) to become Cody's. Other children in our neighborhood were also experiencing night terrors, too, and there were plenty of spirits that were trapped who were also attaching to these kids at night and causing problems. One toddler, in particular, had reported to his mother that he had seen a "man with candle" in his basement on several occasions.

This was overwhelming to me. What was I supposed to do now? I contacted another psychic I knew who said she could cleanse Cody's room and the basement underneath and get rid of the spirits. She used some type of fire ceremony with Epsom salts and incense. It looked pretty, but did no good whatsoever. I again sought the guidance of the Holy Spirit, asking to be shown what to do. They directed me to do a similar ceremony outside. "You want me to go into the middle of my cul-de-sac and light a ceremonial fire?" I complained. "My neighbors will think I am nuts!" I was determined

Chapter 39

to try anything to help my son, however, and enlisted the aid of the neighbor whose small son had seen the man with the candle.

Much to my surprise, on the morning we were ready to clear the spirits from the area, all of our neighbors suddenly left the cul-de-sac. With a prayer of thanks for that miracle, we set up a fire ceremony like the one the psychic had done in my house. Every time I tried to light the Epsom salts recipe, the wind came out of nowhere to blow out the matches or lighter. Frustrated, I sat down on the concrete to meditate and ask Spirit what to do next. They let me know that this was not a physical clearing, it was a spiritual clearing, and had to be done in that realm. Suddenly, by Divine Grace, I knew exactly what to do. Going deeper into meditation, I contacted Penny, and there she was with the wagon train. She ran to me, shouting, "The angel's here!" Apparently, I looked like a being of Light in her dimension. She yelled for the others to join her and see "the angel" and I asked them to start a big bonfire because today they were going to go to Denver! They cheered and ran to get firewood for the blaze. I told Penny to have her brother light the fire, and when he did so, an enormous spiritual blaze swept around the neighborhood for a quarter of a mile in each direction. The heavens opened up and angels poured down from the Astral Plane to attend to each soul, telling them that they were going to Denver. What a sight!

All of the people cheered in joy, but none of them moved, for the wagon master, their leader, would not budge. The wagon master was the only one who realized they were all dead. He was standing by himself, looking haggard from the guilt of every day of that one hundred years that had gone by. He felt responsible for what had happened and he refused to move, thinking he did not deserve to go. I knew that the pioneers would not go without him, and I prayed for the Holy Spirit to do something to help him. A shaft of Light appeared in the sky and focused directly behind him. A figure emerged from the Light and tapped him on the shoulder. It was his mother. He turned to see her, and he released a torrent of tears as great, heaving sobs came from his chest. Suddenly, all of the souls began to fly heavenward with the angels into a hole in the clouds, and I cried with joy for their release.

The next morning my neighbor called me on the phone in great astonishment. "Get over here right now! You won't believe what is in my basement!" I grabbed Cody's hand and we ran across the street to her house. She excitedly escorted us into the lower level of her home, which was

Chapter 39

completely sealed and had only one access door. On the wall was the biggest butterfly that I have ever seen in my entire life. It was as big as a dinner plate. "Butterflies are the symbol of transformation!" she practically shouted. "The soul who was in my basement is free!" Later, we would bemoan the fact that neither of us had thought to take a picture of the butterfly, and that our only witnesses were a handful of children under the age of four. We took it outside to set it free, marveling at its size and beauty.

All the night terrors for all of the children stopped. The "man with candle" disappeared. Ten years later, after telling this story to some new friends, I discovered that their son had been having night terrors during the same time frame. His night terrors had ceased during March of that year, the same month I did the clearing. They had lived one street behind our cul-de-sac!

I did some research and found out that there was, indeed, a Black River Kentucky, where Penny said she was from, and that a significant massacre of American Indians had occurred in Sand Creek, Colorado in 1884 by U.S. soldiers. I was unsuccessful in trying to find out if there had been a retaliatory attack on a small group of settlers by a band of Indians near where I lived, but I was elated that the problems with the children had ceased. I was also happy to learn that Spirit can help you do ANYTHING, if you ask the right questions!

Chapter 40

THE CREATION EQUATION: MANIFESTING DESIRES

How to attract good things into your life by using the Tools of Manifestation

Much has been written about the Law of Attraction recently, and how to use the tools of manifestation, the mental process of drawing to yourself what you desire by using thought, visualization, and action to gain results—or what Holy Spirit calls "The Creation Equation." Spirit first told me of this in the 1990's, and wrote it for me as an actual equation: Thought + Intent (Faith) + Action = Results. I have read many good explanations of the Law of Attraction, but have been disappointed that these other revealers of the secret to consciously creating your life have left out one very important ingredient: God.

I am not sure when the word "God" became politically incorrect. In books about spirituality, I have noticed a trend for authors to apologize for using the name God. They will say, "or whatever you wish to call the Spirit," as if they have made a socially unacceptable blunder by calling the Creator of the universe "God." I have heard other generic names: the Source, the Origin, the Light, the Cause, etc. I have issues with these labels because they are impersonal; they represent a force that is more mechanical than sentient. This is precisely what I wish to correct in this book—to reverse the thought that God is impersonal. God is closer than your thoughts. My spiritual teacher says that God is your very breath. Atheism has become popular in

Chapter 40

our culture that treasures logic above all things. Yeah, well try holding your breath, Mr. Logic, and see how long you live. "Oh, well," Mr. Logic says, "Breathing is involuntary." Really? Whose idea was that? Good thing God thought of that, or you would have to think about breathing all the time. Nothing would get done.

And I cannot call My Father, the Creator of all that is, the Source. When I want to have a good long talk with God, it just doesn't flow to envision a "Source" listening to my deepest thoughts. I like to picture God sitting next to me on my bed, and we are having a great conversation. Make God personal to you. You will get along better with Him, and you will believe that He cares about you and can hear you. One night, as I was about to do a meditation, my teacher in the spirit world came to see me. He asked me to write him a letter to tell him how I felt about everything that was going on in my life. "Why should I do that?" I asked him. "You can read my thoughts all the time, and you already know how I feel."

"Yes," he answered, smiling. "But YOU don't."

I wrote a long letter, and felt so much lighter. Then I tore it up. Write a letter to God, the REAL God, the Father of the Universe, and the Creator of every soul and everything in the cosmos. When you get all of that out of the way, then you can be ready to receive His ideas on what the wise choice for you will be in whatever situation you face. How do you receive the answers from God? It's called *intuition*. To receive intuition, you must be at peace in your heart, for a heart and mind that are in chaos or panicked are closed to the whisperings of the Holy Spirit.

Here is where we get back to the topic of manifesting what you desire. There are three kinds of energy at work in the Universe: neutral energy, demonic energy, and Divine energy. Neutral energy is the stuff that all things are made of. I call it God Stuff. Everyone uses neutral energy all the time, without even being aware of it. The Law of Attraction allows us to create with this neutral energy every second of the day; it's how things work. You send out a thought (energy) that goes to the Universe (neutral energy) and it comes back to you EXACTLY the way you ordered it. Picture yourself sitting at a table. The Heavenly Waitress, order pad in hand, pencil ready, writes down your every thought and your every word. She takes this order to the Heavenly Kitchen, where the Cook serves up exactly what your free

Chapter 40

will has commanded. So, if you are sitting there thinking *and feeling*, "I am so fat and broke," the Heavenly Waitress scribbles in her pad, walks over to the Heavenly Kitchen and yells, "One order of fat and broke!" The Cook will serve you whatever you want, so back to you comes an order of being overweight and financially stressed.

This is why it is imperative that you watch what you say and watch what you think at all times. It is hard in the beginning to do this, and you will find that at first you will catch what you say after you say it. That's okay, because you can say to the Heavenly Waitress, "Wait! I didn't mean to order that!" after you have mumbled "I feel like shit today." You know what will come back from the Heavenly Kitchen after that order is put in! *Words are vibrations, they are energy, and they are powerful things.* They are the commands to the Universe, to the neutral energy. When you can catch your words after they are spoken (having a coach helps here; they will catch your negative words for you), the next step is to catch the negative words AS you speak them. Then you can change them as you go, and order the opposite of what you were going to say.

When you are really getting the hang of this, you will catch your thoughts BEFORE you speak. Now you are remembering that the Heavenly Waitress is right there beside you, all day, every day. She doesn't care what you order, that is entirely up to you. So choose WISELY, and order (focus on) positive things. My brother-in-law was trying to practice this concept and my sister was his coach, catching him on every negative word he uttered. One day, after cursing a blue streak at a man who had cut him off while driving, he quickly looked at Sue and said, "But I mean that in a nice way!" It has become a family joke now, and we all use that phrase after we goof up the no-negative speech exercise.

Once you have committed to watching what you say and think, and are beginning to realize that you send these commands out to the Universe continually to be filled by the neutral energy, you are ready to really begin manifesting what you truly desire. This is where the Creation Equation comes in and where the use of Divine Energy can propel you further than you imagined. Thought + Intent (Faith) + Action = Results. To break this down into concepts that are easily understood, I will define in very simple terms what this equation means. Thoughts are IDEAS. You start with an idea of what you want. An intent is a feeling. Emotion is the fuel to the fire of creation. Action is, of course, doing something. It is the legwork needed to set things into motion in the Universe.

Two of the best books I have read on the Law of Attraction are *Ask and It Is Given*, by Esther Hicks, and the *Power of Intention*, by Dr. Wayne Dyer. I highly recommend these books to everyone who wants to take control of where they are going in their life. They highlight the need to think about the desired RESULT of what you want FIRST. Focus on how you want to *feel*, not on what you don't want to feel. If you hate your job, don't think of your demeaning boss and the long work hours, think about how you would *like* to feel in your job. Perhaps you want to feel more appreciated. Visualize what it would feel like to get a compliment from your boss. You would feel proud. Are you broke? Think about what it would feel like to become prosperous, to pay your bills with ease, and to buy what you need. What would you feel? Relief! How would you feel if you liked your job? Satisfied! Do not focus on the thoughts of what you don't like about your job (remember that the Heavenly Waitress is taking it all down) and visualize what it would be like to go to work with a smile on your face, looking forward to your day. Now you are using thought and intent to create (attract) something positive instead of attracting the same old drudgery every day. Do this visualization after you have settled yourself into a place of peace and quiet, and no one is demanding your attention. *The place of power is in the Peace.*

Here is where the use of Divine Energy comes into play. Once you have decided how you want to feel, how you want to express your life in joy and do interesting work, and pay your bills with a smile, call upon God for help. If you imagine the exact job that you want, you will limit what God can help you attract. Let's say you need a pair of brown shoes and have envisioned them in detail. You will attract the brown shoes, but what if you could have had two pairs of shoes? What if you could have more than what you envisioned? I often say that those who feel that they should not ask for too much are limiting God. God is abundance! When He was creating the Universe, He didn't say, "No, no; only two planets! I don't want to overdo it." He expresses Himself abundantly, and that is what He wants us to do, also.

Getting yourself into the Peace is a vital component of creating the vibration that will attract the positive things that you are focusing on. Spirit told me that emotion is a key factor, and strong emotion is like gasoline to a fire. So watch

Chapter 40

what state of mind you are in when you are praying and creating. Negative emotion will only attract more negativity. When you are in the Peace you are in the presence of Divine Energy, which has an innate wisdom living inside it. It is this wisdom that you want to tap into. Spirit has told me that when you pray, *ASK FOR THE PERFECT SOLUTION* to whatever you need. Now, in asking for the perfect solution, you must not limit what God can do for you by putting conditions on your desires. For example: you want a new job and you make a list of things you desire from a different employment situation. If you state to the Divine Energy that you want to make $XXX a year, you have set a limit that the Heavenly Waitress will record and have the Cook order up for you. Instead, envision a lifestyle that you want to attain and feel how it would be to have that prosperity. You can bet that God's perfect solution will be superior to what you can think of. Guaranteed!

Once you have settled your mind into a state of Peace, put forth the feelings that you want to feel. Visualize that you have what you desire RIGHT NOW—that it is already yours—*and ask God "to perfect this idea in action."* This tells God that you trust His ideas are probably better than your own, and He can take your idea and improve on it. Truly feel this, and you will become light-hearted for a time. Do this often, and take care not to sabotage yourself by becoming negative afterward. *Take action on your desire*: do you need to get some résumés out, look for a new place to live, or contact someone who can help you with what you need? You must do the legwork to get things into motion. Sitting and wishing on a star won't get you anywhere. Make a list of what actions you can take and DO them. Then there is one more thing to do, and this makes the wait bearable, for it can take time for the Divine Energy to put all of the things into place for you. This is a dictation from my Master teacher in spirit about having *Divine Expectation*, the final step in Manifestation 101:

* * *

SPIRITUAL TEACHER:

"Remember that spiritual guidance and direction are things to ask for DAILY, continually. In that way you are remaining open at all times to this direction, and people, events, and inspiration appear for your benefit. It is not to then just sit and to forget, but to be actively expectant of Divine guidance through any possible means. In this way discouragement cannot

Chapter 40

take root, for you find yourself thinking, 'How will God present the answer to me?' or 'I wonder how He will do this?' It turns out to be an expectation that holds excitement instead of worry.

"You will then recognize His hand in your life everyday and carry gratitude and wonder instead of fear or anger. Your focus will be on God and how He will help you solve your situation instead of on the problem itself. Discipline in FOCUS—concentrating only on a successful outcome—is imperative. Do this as BEST as you can, especially in the face of adversity or during times of despair. ALWAYS watch your states of mind, and never give in to adverse states for long. FORCE yourself to think of things other than thoughts which will keep you down. It is so important to find a harmonious and peaceful state of mind! Not just a neutral mind—there is no energy in that, no motion. To attract Divine guidance and excellent circumstances you must elevate your frequency. Neutral states of mind bring nothing. Do anything you can think of to elevate your state from anger or despair, then concentrate on raising it further to Peace and Gratitude.

"*It is in the Peace where you will find and attract answers.* Keep your mind focused upon the expectation of answers; that automatically puts you into a hopeful state. Impatience and worry are very low states of mind; avoid them like the plague! Even though things are not where you want them to be now, continue to focus on and ask for spiritual answers. It is a decision, a CHOICE, to do so. You WILL see results. Do your part, use your time wisely, and be expectant. Remember to think, 'How will God do this for me?' after you have put forth your intentions and have visualized what you need."

* * *

I like to compare this to how one feels as a child when it is Christmastime and there is a big package under the tree with your name on it. You know it is just for you, and that it must be something wonderful. Having this kind of expectation will help you get through the wait of things lining up for you in the material world. I know what it is like to wait for a very long time to manifest what you need. I also know what it is like to have what you need manifest instantly. In each case I could see, afterward, what I had done wrong, and what I had done right. Experience *is* the best teacher.

Chapter 40

Looking back, I can see that emotion DOES matter when manifesting what you need. It is the rocket fuel that launches your request into the God Stuff. When my car mysteriously broke down in the height of rush hour traffic in Denver (with two small children in the backseat) I appealed to God in this way: "Okay, Spirit, you told me that whenever I really needed you, you would be there. Well, I need you RIGHT NOW!" Spirit told me to open and close my car door, and the car started. It would not start when I got home. Later, it was determined that something in the computer was out and had to be replaced. The car should not have started, but Divine Energy got the job done.

My favorite story about God working immediately for someone in need, is the tale of my sister looking for her résumé. She had a very important interview in just forty-five minutes, and she was looking everywhere for her typed work history. She had searched the filing cabinets and her entire house, and the clock was ticking. Sue stood in the living room and yelled at the heavens, "God, I KNOW that You know where my résumé is, and I need it RIGHT NOW!" She and her husband heard a thunderous noise upstairs in the den. Racing up the stairs, they expected to see that a filing cabinet had fallen, but there on the floor, in the center of the tidy room, was one manila folder, labeled "I." In the folder was her résumé. Sue was very happy and her husband was absolutely incredulous. Sue has unshakable faith, and she knew God could find it. I later asked her what her résumé was doing in a folder with the letter "I" on it. "Oh," she said, "that stands for 'Important Papers.'"

I tested the powers of manifestation once in an exercise that I had read about in a book. It had said to carry a one hundred dollar bill around in your wallet to feel prosperous. I was so broke at the time that I did not have a hundred dollars. I got myself into the state of Peace by feeling grateful for all that I did have, and then pictured a one hundred dollar bill in my wallet. I prayed and told Spirit that I really wanted to see this work, so I could have the faith to keep trying this method. Two hours later there was a knock at my door. I opened it to see my ex-husband there, holding out a one hundred dollar bill to me! He said that he had just gotten a hunch that this would help and he wanted me to have it. Boy, was I impressed! *God works through people*, and you never know how or where or when He will present Himself to you.

Chapter 40

My husband and I used the Creation Equation to get us out of a very serious situation, and now we KNOW that it works. I have decided to include this story so that people who are at the end of their rope will know that things can improve, and fast. Being psychic does not guarantee that your life will go smoothly. Life is life, and that is the way it is. Life means change; it means good times and bad times. It is how you deal with these changes that matters. We had found ourselves in a real mess, and had little time to set things right. My husband had gone through the West Nile virus, which almost took his life, he was out of work, we had no insurance, we were being sued by credit card companies, and couldn't pay the mortgage. We had used all of our savings and had sold all of our stock just to make ends meet. The technical job market was dying in Colorado. "Grim" doesn't even come close to describing how bad things looked. Thank God for family and friends who helped support us in every way imaginable during that time. They made it bearable.

A friend of ours recommended that we view a video called "The Secret" to find out what we were doing wrong. We were good people, so why was all of this bad luck on our door step? It turned out that we were doing everything wrong, even after being lectured on the Creation Equation by Spirit. Sometimes the answer is right in front of your eyes and you can't see it. *The main thing we were doing incorrectly was focusing on all that was wrong in our lives.* Negativity creates more things to be negative about. After the success of the hundred dollar bill, I began to take the Law of Attraction very seriously. I began to do meditations devoted only to visualizing and feeling more prosperous. This helped, but it didn't take away the really serious problems, which by then were ready to crush us. Foreclosure steps were being taken. The anxiety and depression levels were monstrous for Joe and me, and we could not understand why our attempts at using the tools of manifestation weren't working. Joe added anger to his list of feelings of despair, worry, and helplessness.

Then one night in mediation, after praying deeply for guidance and to be shown what we were doing wrong, an angel came to me and said, "Follow me." She took me (in a vision/consciousness travel) to a river that had a very strong current. In the river were several huge trees with their trunks underwater. Holding onto one of these trees for dear life was a woman. I

Chapter 40

looked closer and saw that it was me. Suddenly, I was IN the water, not seeing it from a third-person perspective anymore, and I could feel myself holding onto the trunk of the large tree. The angel was floating above me in the air. "Let go!" she commanded. I hesitated, and she repeated the words very strongly, "LET GO!" I let go and immediately began to go backward with the very fast current. The angel was still above me in the air, and she called down to me. "Now then, are you hurt?" she asked.

"No," I shouted up to her, really zipping along with the flow of the river.

"Are you in danger?" the angel asked. Again, I replied no. "Are you hitting any boulders or logs?" she persisted.

I answered, "No," finally understanding what was going on. The current slowed to a leisurely pace, and I floated along for awhile in the peace. I washed ashore on a sandy river bank.

"Look up there," the angel said to me. I looked up and saw a beautiful log house among the trees. "You have to let go!" she told me, and then the vision vanished.

I understood it at once. We had to move. I had been adamant that I was not leaving my house and Colorado. My children were brought up in this house. I told myself that this house was my safety net. My husband had talked about moving, but I was praying like mad to keep this house in my safe little cul-de-sac. We had been praying for different things! The old saying "a house divided cannot stand" is so very true. Whose prayers were going to win? No one's! I understood that God was showing me my fears were unfounded, and that all would be well if I let go. So I did. Joe and I began praying and visualizing together. We tried to stop the negative thoughts, even though no improvement in our situation happened for weeks. Joe was working seven-day weeks for months on end, doing assembly work just so we could eat. We were very grateful for that job, but it was very hard on him.

We put the house up for sale in a market that was dying, and we only had two months before the auction for foreclosure would occur. One of the biggest and most crucial things in the steps of manifesting what you want is to *FEEL that you already have it*. For Joe that was really hard. He is a scientist, and the logical side of his brain kept saying, "But you don't have what you

Chapter 40

want; things are terrible!" When we practiced visualization together, I guided him in a meditation so that all he had to do was picture what I was saying. Then one day, after submitting over two hundred résumés online, he saw a job in another state that really got him excited. Now he could picture having that job. It made all the difference in the world, being able to believe for a few minutes that he actually could get a job he wanted at good pay. Within a few short weeks he began to get interviews and then, suddenly, it all happened at once. On his birthday we sold the house, he got an interview that led to a new job and a move, and he received a small inheritance from a person who had died the year before. We could pay for food and overdue bills and part of Joe's expenses out of state. All on the same day!

The relief was enormous, and we were incredulous at how using the tools of manifestation really worked. It seemed like a miracle. We beat the foreclosure by two weeks, a dear friend helped us out with the moving expenses, and Joe started his job in another state two weeks later. Our friends were as incredulous as we were, so we told them about using the Law of Attraction to create what you want. Adding the Divine Energy tangent was crucial, I think, for it made us open to the perfect solution, not just what we could think of. *God's ideas are always better than yours, for He can see everything that you cannot.* I was not open to moving out of state until Spirit reminded me that I was holding on in fear, and that God needed me to let go so He could help me.

When I coach people about the tools of manifestation I tell them our story, because it proves that it can work for them, too. I stress the need to FEEL the feelings you would have if you were to be successful in attaining your desires. The biggest feelings that I worked on in my visualizations were relief and gratitude. And let me tell you, that is exactly what I felt when it all came together. Spirit once told me not to use the words, "God, I really need this," because we humans associate the word "need" with being weak. Spirit said to use this phrase instead, "Father this is what I require" and then present these requirements to the Divine Energy. When you "require" something, it takes the personal worry-factor out of it. You are not so emotionally involved, and can concentrate on knowing that your Father will help you with it, instead of being involved and focused on NOT having it. You can pray in confidence for something you require.

Chapter 40

All of these little things help, because we are not used to creating what we desire consciously. We were not taught how to do this, so this new concept is hard for adults, who are used to begging God for things. *Begging prayers are not high in energy, and go nowhere.* Always pray in confidence, and visualize yourself having what you want already. Then wait with Divine Expectation and do not give in to frustration when your answer takes longer than you want it to. My Master teacher says to avoid depression like the plague, for it sabotages your efforts and you will have to start over.

I have been teaching this method to my children, and it certainly worked for my son, Tyler, who really wanted to go to a university in Pennsylvania for his freshman year. He had a one in a thousand chance to get accepted with special financing for this university. Four years ago, I helped him with a guided meditation, seeing himself already there, on campus. I told him to visualize his dad helping him move into one of the dorms and them laughing at all of the crap he had taken with him. I reminded him to visualize this every night before bed.

"Will you help me pray for this, Mom?" he asked me after a visualization session.

"No," I answered.

He was shocked. "Why not?"

"Because I already see you there. I really believe it," I explained.

My son graduated from that university in Pennsylvania this year.

THE EMOTION WAVE: THE STAMP OF GOD

A being of Light takes me into a human cell and reveals a grand secret

I have been very privileged to have seen many things through the Holy Spirit, and one of the most astonishing events in my life was to be shown the Stamp of God that resides in every single cell of the human body. One afternoon, in deep meditation, a Spirit Guide came to me and said, "Want to see something?" I always say yes to that question, for these are times of incredible exploration of God's universe. This particular day we explored more of the inner universe. I had been doing some chakra work, balancing the "wheels of light" that align in the human body. Each one of these chakras carries a special frequency of energy along the spine. Eastern religion, philosophy, and medicine have been aware of these centers for many centuries. Each chakra has a specific function, and they are crucial to our well-being, both emotionally and physically. On this day, my Guide told me that we were going to go into a cell in my body through consciousness travel. I was instructed to allow my consciousness to become Light, and was told that I would then be able, through thought, to become very, very tiny. I was not sure where to begin.

"Where do we start?" I asked my Guide.

"The Heart Chakra," she answered.

Chapter 41

"You mean the heart organ, don't you?" I inquired. After, all we were exploring the human cell.

"To me they are as one, but yes, the heart 'organ' will help orient you," she agreed.

I became very tiny by projecting my consciousness into the muscle of the heart, and then into a cell in the tissue. I experienced a wave of gladness and of approval, but I am not sure where that came from. I could perceive that my heart was healthy; the rhythm was good, the flow of blood was right, and the tissues were clean and energized. Suddenly, I was standing in a cell. And it was *huge*, like the size of a city, and I was a speck standing with my Guide inside of it. I looked up.

"WHAT IS THAT?!" I asked in awe. I was seeing something in "the sky" of the cell. It looked like the aurora borealis! Beautiful! A ribbon of different hues of light stretched all across the expanse of the cell.

"That is the Emotion Wave. You could call it 'the Stamp of God.' God is in each and every cell of your body. *He is literally inside of every human being all the time*, down to the smallest particle," my Guide explained.

"What is in there? Can we go inside of that?" I asked excitedly.

"Yes, of course," she smiled.

"How do we do that?"

"Like everything else, through thought," she instructed. "Just experience it."

Concentrating on the Emotion Wave brought it *to* me, and suddenly I was inside of it. I was aware that it was composed of seven bands of light and that I was in the first band. I felt a very strong sense of SURVIVAL there: the instinct that God gave us to be able to live in our physical world. I also felt tremendous love! CONTINUOUS LOVE, LOVE, LOVE! It was intoxicating.

Chapter 41

"I could stay in here!" I said to my Guide, feeling the tears well up inside of me.

"Go beyond the love," she said, urging me into the next band. I pushed myself through.

Wow! CURIOSITY! Great curiosity composed the second band of the Emotion Wave. It was a drive to know and to experience everything. Everything! The feeling was overwhelming, and I heard, as if from far away, my Guide say, "Go beyond." I dragged myself out of the band to enter the third one.

This was a place of contemplation and LOGIC. It was a space for thinking about what curiosity had discovered, a place for reflection and a collection of facts. A serious place. It felt enormous and was very still, but full. Again I heard, "Go" from my Guide, whom I had lost sight of when I entered the Emotion Wave.

The next band was full of emotion. It was a place of REACTION to what had been discovered by curiosity and contemplated by logic. How did I feel about what I had experienced? This was a place of many emotions and opinions. It was a powerful place, and was not very organized, I am afraid to say. It was not unpleasant, but was chaotic. In the distance somewhere, I heard the suggestion, "Go."

The fifth band was a place for planning, making decisions, and forming opinions on a level that was more rigid. It was organized. It was an area that looked at everything and placed it in a box, collecting more and more of these boxes and stacking them into patterns of certainty. It was safe, predictable, and constructive. It was civilized and ordered. There was forward movement, as long as the movement stayed within the boundary of expectation and STRUCTURE. This was the place that tried to make sense of all of the information gathered from the four previous bands. The questioning of the soul's existence was beginning here, and yet there was the need for certainty, because there were no answers to any of the soul's questions in this band. My Guide said, "Go," and I slipped easily into the next band's expression.

Chapter 41

DANGER! I recoiled in fear. This band was a place of great unease and a deep sense of personal danger. I felt ALONE there, and my stomach was turning. What was this? Panicking, I sought for the mind of my Guide somewhere next to me, asking for an explanation.

"This is the band that was tampered with. This is the band that is veiled for most of humanity on Earth. Look here and SEE this and remember this," she said to me.

It felt *tight*, and I could not breathe well. I felt constricted. The light was gone, and it appeared smoky, like a black fog had rolled in. I really wanted to get out of there, but was having trouble. "GO!" I heard my Guide yell. It was hard to get through the fog. The fear was making me nauseous, and I could not see a thing. I prayed, "God help me," and suddenly I was through it and into the next band.

Ahhhh! The seventh band was PEACE. It was beautiful in there, calm, serene, and full of light. I could breathe again, and I turned to see where I had just come from. There was the murky band. What in the world was such an awful band doing in the Emotion Wave? Why would the Stamp of God have that in it? As I looked back, I realized that my Guide had appeared and was standing next to me.

"What is that shadow covering? What is the sixth band?" I asked her.

"*Self-acceptance.* The band before the God-Realization band is self-acceptance, self-appreciation, self-approval, SELF-KNOWING. Before you reach the band of God you must 'know thyself,' see? It feels dangerous to people, which is why they turn away from introspection. This is a very small tour of the Emotion Wave, Losara. We will go more in depth later. This is excellent for now. Contemplate this."

I was suddenly back in my bedroom, sitting in the lotus position on my bed. I had a feeling of great euphoria that lasted for several days. I could not get the visions and words about the Emotion Wave out of my mind, and could hardly wait for the next installment of knowledge about its secrets. I finally received more information on the Emotion Wave *seven years* later!

Chapter 41

I had been contacted by a client who was going through a very black time in his life. Everything in his world was a mess, and he was in a very deep depression. In speaking with him, I suddenly asked him why he wanted to live. "It is not enough to fight for life because you are afraid to die," I told him. "Why do you want to live?" He had no answer. In my meditation that night I questioned my spiritual teacher. "What do I say to people who have no idea of why they should live? There are many other people who just go through the motions of living, and have no purpose or passion in life. What is causing their depression? What is it that causes a person to just fold up?" I asked him. Here is his response:

* * *

SPIRITUAL TEACHER:

"All of life is a matter of perspective, of focus. Mankind must go through all seven perspectives to reach God. It is the same as you have seen in the Emotion Wave of each cell. Man can focus through one, two, three, or four of these bands at a time. Each particular focal point exemplifies a range of maturity of soul.

"When a person is anchored in one or two of the bands, or perspectives, of the Emotion Wave, he has PURPOSE; or in other words, his viewpoint is fixed and unwavering, and he uses this focus to sustain him throughout a physical life span on Earth. When the soul begins to grow beyond levels in the band there is a danger point where one is not anchored. This point is where the MOST growth occurs, for he begins to question himself and his life, or life in general. The leap to the next band in the Emotion Wave signifies a deepening of maturity and understanding.

"Let us review the levels of perspective, or the bands in the Emotion Wave:

1) Survival: A person in this band is at his lowest viewpoint, the survival of self. It is a form of self-love based entirely on fear and *selfishness*.

2) Curiosity: A person in this band (who can also hold onto the first band perspective at the same time) usually has a zest for life, as

number two is immense curiosity, and he goes for life with more creativity and an impulse to *achieve*.

3) Logic: A person who focuses on this band (who can also retain aspects of numbers one and two) begins to feel a little introspective about life and forms attachments to family and friends that do not necessarily override the drive to achieve. This is the band of *thinking*.

4) Emotion: A person who focuses on the fourth band (who can also keep the perspectives of one through three within him) goes deeper into the weighing of experiences and *feelings*, and begins a process of comparison, or the awakening of the concept of cause and effect. These ones plan their lives, not living by the seat of their pants as ones in the first, second, and third bands do.

5) Seeking, through structure: A person in this band of focus broadens his view with love and asks "*Why?*" He has many questions about life, but doesn't know where to find the answers. Religion doesn't offer enough, but at least it is something. This person has an uneasiness that is in the back of his mind, but he cannot quite articulate it. The first four bands influence the life but are not as present as before.

6) Realization: A person who begins to go through the sixth band has a great *yearning* to understand LIFE. He hungers for answers to the incongruousness of existence. It can become all consuming, all important to the point of detachment from the anchor in the perspective of the number one (selfishness/survival) band. The sixth band can be a very unsettling focal point, for it is the band that was deliberately veiled by the Dark side. Because there are no answers here (the view of the seventh band is blocked by the veil of ignorance), it creates great frustration, fear, hopelessness, and despair.

Each person will react in several different ways when they enter the sixth band:

a) RETREAT: They go back into the safer, but dissatisfying, fifth band, either to religion, New Age entertainment, or atheism. All of these alternatives carry *arrogance* in them and are a dead end. These three options carry no open-ended "why?"

Chapter 41

to them, as all assume they have the answer to life and there is no more.

b) ABANDONMENT: These people give up, not moving forward or backward. This is especially dangerous because deep despair and depression can lead to disease or suicide. There are no answers to the *pain* they feel, and it is better NOT to feel, they conclude. The anchors in numbers one (survival), two (curiosity), three (logic), four (emotion), and five (seeking) are gone or tenuous at best.

c) DETERMINATION: The leap forward! This reaction in a person sets up a *decision* to find God no matter what it takes. He will endure all manner of roadblocks, feeling intuitively that there IS a reason for life. The viewpoints of one through five are not enough, nor do they carry as much importance as the deep desire to see and feel the seventh band: reunion with the Creator. Many trials and the ever-present veil of fear and danger (the sixth band) test his tenacity of Will. The sixth band is the decree of KNOW THYSELF. If a person is successful in this great quest, he will cross into the seventh band.

7) Illumination: A person who experiences the seventh band, even briefly, has 'seen God,' feeling at last, His true presence. All questions are answered here, and he is surprised at how LOVE is the answer, the REASON, for everything. Again and again, a person will try to dip into the all-knowing consciousness of God, learning then of the further bands to be experienced inside the seventh. It is coming *HOME*, and it is what all souls seek.

"When a person is leaping from one viewpoint (band) of maturity to the next, for a brief time his foot is suspended with no anchor. This is a precarious time. Love is ALWAYS the answer. Asking the Self WHY he wishes to continue to live will surely identify which of the bands of the Emotion Wave he is in, or which one he is in-between. No one can give another person a reason to live. They must feel it for themselves. This is why suicides happen: the mind and the heart of the person cannot latch onto a purpose or perspective for their life, or a person who is in the sixth band wearies of the struggle to know Self and tries to take the easy way out (death). They cross to the realm of Spirit for the answers. These ones are disappointed, for they do NOT advance and are stuck in the awareness level they departed from.

"Deep introspective thought and feeling is the only way to gain answers to the 'why?' questions. When a soul asks himself all of these to the best of his ability and comes to the conclusion that only God can answer him, he does one of two things: he finds religion, where others tell him what to believe, or he finds God through meditation and gets the answers himself.

"It is not for you to provide a reason for anyone to continue living, Losara. It is for you to be the example, hoping to awaken the true meaning for experiencing life: to return home and to share with your Beloved Creator all you have learned in His Wondrous Universe. He awaits ALL with open arms! Excellent question, Losara. Thank you for paying attention."

* * *

It is truly astonishing how beautiful and complex our Creator's universe is, right down to the tiny cells of our body. After this experience, I thought differently about God, realizing that He truly IS inside of us, and that the plan for our bodies included the way home. I could imagine that if a person had a problem in a mental or physical area the cause might be way down in that tiny, but important Emotion Wave. These waves could be influenced by the patterns of past-life opinions or present-day experiences. The presence of the blocking of the sixth band to Self-Awareness was especially intriguing to me, because I know, personally, the effort it takes to override it. I am forever grateful to the Holy Spirit for showing me this wondrous wave of Light inside the human cells. Just this dissertation from my Master teacher alone is enough to keep me thinking for years. And, of course, I have a million more questions!

THE GOAL

HOW DOES SHE DO THAT?

What happens when I contact Spirit

Often I hear the remark, "You are amazing!" from clients after a spiritual reading. I always say to them, "Holy Spirit is amazing, I just know how to listen." I cannot, and do not, take credit for the incredible words of wisdom that come out of my mouth during a trance channeling or go onto the paper through my pen during a dictation from Spirit. I am just along for the ride, hoping to glean some wisdom myself, and I feel incredibly privileged to be able to hear Spirit. In the first chapter of this book I tell my personal story of how this talent developed in my life. People often ask me if I can teach them how to do this. No, I can't. I am not a teacher of meditation and mediumship. I can suggest things that work for ME, but they may not work for you. There are other teachers of meditation out there, however, and if a person is really serious about taking up meditation (and is willing to have the discipline it takes to change habits that interfere with that process) they can learn. The *desire* for change and *the decision to take action* are the keys to mastering anything.

So how do I do this? I do not know. Obviously, the communication I am able to attain with Spirit is all related to thought and the ability to shut out the noise of the "real" world, focusing on the spiritual world. I have read of psychics explaining how they tune into other frequencies, like a radio does, to pick up the higher energies of Spirit. That sounds good, and is most likely true, but I do not consciously say, "Okay, Losara, let's raise the frequencies now and tune into station WGOD." I am, of course, being facetious here, but what I want to get across is that it is your *intent* in reaching for "spiritual abilities" that is most important. For example, one night I came into the room where my husband had just finished his lesson in meditation that he was studying, and Spirit gave me a message for him. As I walked past Joe, my Master Teacher said, "Tell him that even more important than technique is *devotion*." The goal is not channeling, the goal is *God*.

I often ask people if they remember God. He is the Father of All that Is, and we cannot recall anything about Him at all! Such is the veil of ignorance on Earth. We only "know" what others have told us. *The goal is to have your own personal experience of God.* Years ago, during a channeling session I was doing for a woman who had done many years of reading about metaphysics, Spirit corrected the notion she had that this was her last life before enlightenment. They then told her a small story to illustrate why she was not "done" yet.

* * *

HOLY SPIRIT:

"There once was a man who achieved the goal of reaching the Highest Lake in the world, and he came back and told everyone, 'The lake is cold.' The people were very excited about this information, and invited him to lecture on his discovery, and he eventually wrote a book about The Lake. The book was a success, and the people who read the book began to talk to others about The Lake. They would nod with knowing smiles and say, 'The Lake is cold.' Soon those students became 'authorities' on The Lake, and they wrote books and spread the word that The Lake was cold.

There were others who decided to visit this Lake for themselves, and they got very close to The Lake, but stopped short of going into The Lake. Close was good enough for them. They came back with tales of The Lake also, and became 'experts' on the subject. Then one fellow decided that he MUST see The Lake, because reading about it was not enough. The desire consumed him and filled his every thought. He climbed the mountain to The Lake, and was overjoyed to behold The Lake with his own eyes. He came closer and reached out a toe to touch The Lake. It WAS cold! But what else was it? He wanted to experience all of The Lake, for just knowing that is was cold was not enough.

Chapter 42

"Bravely, he ran and dived into The Lake. It took his breath away, it was so cold. But, it was also DEEP, and CLEAR, and WONDROUS. And . . . *there were other worlds in The Lake*! He stayed in The Lake a very long time. His joy was immense, and he had a great feeling of reverence for The Lake, for its secrets, and its immeasurable depth. He came back down the mountain and the people saw how different he was after spending time in The Lake. He was calm, confident, positive, disciplined, and appreciative. Folks wanted to know, what was it REALLY like in The Lake? The man smiled and simply replied, 'The Lake is cold.'"

* * *

This story shows that all of the studying and reading of metaphysical material in the world does not make up for actual experience in Spirit. There are some things that cannot be explained adequately by language. God is one of them. I often work with people who want to learn more about Spiritual Truth, and I make up a list of my favorite books for them to read. Most of them do not read them, though a few will read one or two of the titles on the list. Of those people, most will race through the books (or not finish the books at all) and not gain anything from these volumes of wisdom. That tells me they have no burning desire to climb to The Lake, or to touch it, or dive in. Strong desire and a steadfast work ethic in learning to meditate is vitally important in a person's search for spiritual knowledge. Deep introspection about the spiritual truths you are studying is an absolute must. The most important question to ask yourself is *why* you want to know the real Truth.

The "cool stories" (as my son calls them) in this book show how much God cares about us. They show how God knows what we are going through, and that He has solutions for us, *if we will but ask for His guidance* through the Holy Spirit. The stories show how we are all alike, and that we all go through the same trials and tribulations in life. I could print any of these stories onto pamphlets and pass the copies out to people on the street corner, because one size does fit all in the tapestry of life on Earth. They show how, as Spirit has told me countless times, "The only problem with you is YOU," and that we need to get out of our own way in order to hear, feel, and intuit the perfect solutions from God.

Chapter 42

INTENT IS ALL! The *reason* you are pursuing this quest for Truth will be the fuel to your success. Is your fuel watered down by half-hearted attempts? Is your fuel pump too clogged to fire the engine of your desire because you are rigid in your beliefs? Is the fuel hose severed because you cut the line to God long ago? Is the fuel that is getting to your engine too rich, causing it to sputter and die out because you want the big results now (visions and voices) and not the quiet, pure wisdom?

How do I do these things? I can tell you that my spiritual abilities have grown over the years because I REALLY want to know God personally, and I REALLY want others to experience what I have seen and felt. I want you to know that God IS real, and that He is *right here*, with you, all the time.

Made in the USA
Lexington, KY
13 June 2015